Adobe

# Dreamweaver CS5.5
## Designing and Developing for Mobile with jQuery, HTML5 and CSS3
## STUDIO TECHNIQUES

David Powers

Adobe

# Adobe Dreamweaver CS5.5 Studio Techniques:
## Designing and Developing for Mobile with jQuery, HTML5, and CSS3

**David Powers**

This Adobe Press book is published by Peachpit.
For information on Adobe Press books, contact:

**Peachpit**
1249 Eighth Street
Berkeley, CA 94710
510/524-2178
510/524-2221 (fax)

For the latest on Adobe Press books, go to www.adobepress.com
To report errors, please send a note to errata@peachpit.com
Peachpit is a division of Pearson Education.

Associate Editor: Valerie Witte
Production Editor: Cory Borman
Developmental Editor: Anne Marie Walker
Copyeditor: Anne Marie Walker
Proofreader: Patricia Pane
Composition: WolfsonDesign
Indexer: Joy Dean Lee
Cover Image: Alicia Buelow
Cover Design: Charlene Charles-Will

## Notice of Rights

## Notice of Liability

## Trademarks

ISBN-13:  978-0-321-77325-8
ISBN–10:  0-321-77325-X

9 8 7 6 5 4 3 2 1

Printed and bound in the United States of America

# Contents

## About the Author

David Powers started developing websites in 1994 while at the BBC (British Broadcasting Corporation). He'd just taken on the role of Editor, BBC Japanese TV, and needed a way of advertising the fledgling channel in Japan. The problem was that he had no advertising budget. So, he begged the IT department for a corner of server space and singlehandedly developed an 80-page bilingual website, which he regularly maintained for the next five years—on top of all his other duties.

After three decades as a radio and TV journalist, David left the BBC in 1999 to work independently. He created multilingual websites for several leading clients, including the Embassy of Japan in London and Oxford Analytica. In 2003, he decided to combine his professional writing and editing expertise with his passion for the web, and began writing books on web development. This is his fourteenth so far. Readers frequently comment on David's ability to explain complex technical subjects in a jargon-free style that's easy to understand. At the same time, he doesn't talk down to readers, thereby appealing equally to more experienced web developers.

David is an Adobe Community Professional and Adobe Certified Instructor for Dreamweaver. You'll often find him giving help and advice in the Dreamweaver forums and Adobe Developer Center—to which he has contributed many popular tutorials and training videos. He greatly enjoys traveling and taking photos—all the photos used in this book were taken by him.

David has also translated a number of musical plays from Japanese into English, and he likes nothing better than sushi with a glass or two of cold sake.

## Acknowledgments

Writing a book about new software is a solitary activity, grappling with a constantly moving target and pounding the keyboard to deliver the chapters on time. But none of it would be possible without an army of helpers. First, there's Scott Fegette, Senior Product Manager for Dreamweaver, who kept me informed of the engineering team's plans. Then there's Kin Blas, a Dreamweaver engineer actively involved in developing jQuery Mobile, who clarified points I found difficult to understand. My thanks go to them and to the rest of the Dreamweaver team for their help both directly and indirectly.

I've also had a strong backup team at Peachpit: Victor Gavenda, who accepted the concept of this book and liked it so much that he persuaded Adobe Press that it was high time one of my books was printed in color; Valerie Witte, my editor, who calmly accepted my frequent changes of mind about the structure of the book; Anne Marie Walker, my development editor, who picked up inconsistencies and helped me (mis)spell the American way; Tom Muck, my technical editor, who spotted problems with code and made suggestions to improve it; and Cory Borman, who oversaw the production process.

Many others have helped indirectly. At times, the Twitter stream felt like an annoying distraction, but it provided some invaluable leads, alerting me to changes in this fast-moving industry. It also provided some essential light relief, although I'm not sure I'm ready to watch another cat video just yet.

# Introduction

Don't be fooled. Although the .5 might give the impression that Dreamweaver CS5.5 is a point release, it's anything but. Dreamweaver engineers have packed a stunning amount of new features into this version. To mention just a few, there's code hinting for the popular jQuery JavaScript library, the ability to see what pages will look like at different screen resolutions without leaving the Document window, support for jQuery Mobile widgets, and integration of PhoneGap to build native apps for Android or iOS (the operating system used in the iPhone, iPad, and iPod touch).

The emphasis in Dreamweaver CS5.5 is firmly on mobile development and designing for multiple screens, but that's not all. There's improved support for HTML5 and CSS3, including tools to simplify the creation of rounded corners and drop shadows without images. Previous versions of Dreamweaver supported only a limited range of CSS selectors. Live view now supports them all. Oh yes, Dreamweaver CS5.5 supports web fonts, too.

There's a lot to absorb, and this book aims to guide you through all the new features with the help of three case studies. The first one centers on redesigning a website for display on desktops, tablets, and smartphones using HTML5, CSS3, and media queries. The second takes a cut-down version of the same site and builds a dedicated mobile version using jQuery Mobile, a sophisticated JavaScript and CSS framework designed to work consistently on all major mobile platforms. The final case study develops a simple app that stores information in a database, accesses a mobile phone's GPS sensor, and displays a map.

## Is This the Right Book for You?

The new features in Dreamweaver CS5.5 are aimed at web designers and developers who are already comfortable with HTML and CSS. It also helps to have at least a basic understanding of JavaScript and some jQuery experience. If the thought of diving into code sends shivers up your spine, this might not be the most appropriate book for you. Web development is becoming increasingly sophisticated, and the days of just copying and pasting snippets of code are rapidly drawing to a close.

Having said that, you don't need to be an expert. I firmly believe that if you understand why you're being told to do something a particular way, you're more likely to remember and be able to adapt it for your own projects. Each step is explained, as are new concepts, but I don't go back to basics, such as describing what a function or event handler is.

## Mac or Windows?

The differences between the Mac and Windows versions of Dreamweaver are so few as to be negligible. In the rare cases where there is a difference, I point it out and show a screen shot if necessary. The most important difference, as far as this book is concerned, lies in PhoneGap integration. Both Windows and Mac support Android, but the software necessary to build apps for iOS runs only on a Mac. The other difference, as always, lies in keyboard shortcuts. I provide both versions, Windows first, followed by Mac.

Using a multibutton mouse is now so common among Mac users that I refer only to right-click instead of giving Control-click as the alternative. On most Macs, the F keys now control hardware features, such as sound level and brightness. When I refer to F keys, you need to hold down the Fn key at the same time. Alternatively, open Keyboard in System Preferences and select the "Use all F1, F2, etc. keys as standard function key" check box.

Although I test on both operating systems, I had to choose one for taking screen shots. Most of them have been taken on Windows 7, but some have been taken on Mac OS X 10.6 where appropriate. However, this is a book about mobile development. So, many screen shots have also been taken on Android (HTC Desire and Samsung Galaxy Tab) and iOS (iPad and iPod touch). I also tested on a BlackBerry Torch and Windows Phone 7.

## Downloading the Case Study Files

This book doesn't come with a CD. However, you can download the files used in the case studies from my website at http://foundationphp.com/dwmobile. In most cases, all the necessary files are supplied. However, for licensing reasons, you need to obtain the Calluna Regular web font directly (the details are in Chapter 2). Also, the download files don't include the jQuery Mobile or PhoneGap libraries. Dreamweaver copies them directly to your site when you create a jQuery Mobile page (see Chapter 5) or define the Native Application Settings (see Chapter 7).

## Keeping Up to Date

The jQuery Mobile framework was feature complete at the time Adobe locked down the code for the release of Dreamweaver CS5.5. However, work continued on stabilizing and optimizing performance. Consequently, newer versions of the jQuery Mobile style sheet, external JavaScript files, and images are likely to be available by the time you read this. Adobe plans to release extensions to update the files in Dreamweaver. Chapter 5 also describes how to change the source folder for the files so that you can use your own customized versions.

Because jQuery Mobile is a new framework, it's likely to continue to develop. I'll try to keep abreast of its progress and will post updates that affect this book on my website at http://foundationphp.com/dwmobile.

Adobe is a jQuery Mobile project sponsor, and Dreamweaver engineers are playing an active role in its development. That holds the promise of even greater things to come.

SECTION I

# Dreamweaver CS5.5

# 1

# Dreamweaver Goes Mobile

*Change is inevitable in a progressive country.*
*Change is constant.*

—Benjamin Disraeli

## Dreamweaver Goes Mobile

**G**roundbreaking web technologies are like London buses. You wait seemingly forever for one to come, and then three come at the same time. Unlike buses, which take you to a fixed destination, the journey promised by HTML5, CSS3, and mobile is far less predictable. The road map is constantly evolving, and the timetables implemented by the major participants are rarely—if ever—coordinated. It sounds like a nightmare.

Just as all leading browsers finally offered web designers the prospect of stability through reasonably consistent support for CSS2.1, everything is about to change again. At the same time, it's an exciting challenge: creating websites and applications that take advantage of the new features offered by HTML5, CSS3, and related technologies. Only a couple of years ago, accessing the Internet on a mobile device was relatively uncommon. That's no longer the case.

In its key predictions for 2010 and beyond, Gartner, a leading research company, forecast that mobile phones would overtake desktop computers as the most common web access device worldwide by 2013 (www.gartner.com/it/page.jsp?id=1278413). Industry experts don't all agree on when it will happen, but there's little dispute that the explosive growth of mobile devices is making fundamental changes to the way people access the Internet.

The dramatic early growth of Apple iPads prompted Gartner to update its predictions the following year, estimating that by 2013, 80 percent of businesses will support a workforce using tablets. With regard to mobile phones, it predicted that enterprises will need to support a variety of mobile platforms rather than be able to standardize on one or two.

After years of designing for increasingly bigger desktop monitors, web designers now face the need to display content in a wide range of screen resolutions—from tiny mobile phones to tablets and laptops to large desktops. This forces web designers not only to think about the size of the screen, but also the size of files. Mobile networks tend to be slower than broadband connections, and many users must pay extra if they exceed their monthly data limit.

To help web designers rise to the new challenges, Adobe Dreamweaver CS5.5 incorporates a set of tools focused on HTML5, CSS3, and development for mobile devices. This book is your guide to using those tools.

This chapter provides a broad overview of the new features in Dreamweaver CS5.5 and discusses some of the main considerations you need to bear in mind when designing websites likely to be viewed on a variety of devices. The remaining chapters are project based:

▶ Chapters 2 and 3 adapt an existing website so that it works equally well on a desktop computer, tablet, or mobile phone. The starting point is a small website designed using XHTML 1.0 Strict. I'll show you how to convert it to HTML5 and add some sophisticated style flourishes with CSS3, before using *media queries* to optimize each page for display on different-sized devices.

▶ Chapter 4 explains how to make your site available to users even when they're not connected to the Internet by creating a *cache manifest*, a new feature in HTML5 that tells browsers which files to store locally.

▶ Chapters 5 and 6 focus on building a dedicated website for display on mobile phones and tablets using jQuery Mobile, a new JavaScript framework that is integrated into Dreamweaver CS5.5. As its name suggests, it's based on jQuery, the widely popular cross-browser JavaScript library.

**CLOSE-UP**

**Media Queries**

Introduced in CSS3, media queries are similar to the HTML media attribute in that they let you specify which devices your styles should be applied to. But they're much more powerful, because you can serve different styles depending on such factors as screen width. Media queries are supported by most modern browsers, including Internet Explorer 9, but you need to provide a basic set of styles for earlier browsers.

▶ Chapter 7 describes how to package a web application built with HTML, CSS, and JavaScript for deployment as a native app on Android or iOS using PhoneGap. PhoneGap is an open-source framework that allows you to author native apps without the need to learn Java or Objective-C. Dreamweaver CS5.5 automatically installs PhoneGap and simplifies the packaging process.

Before describing the new HTML5, CSS3, and mobile-related features in Dreamweaver CS5.5, I'll address what I suspect is a burning question for many of you.

## Assessing HTML5 and CSS3

Are HTML5 and CSS3 ready to use? The simple answer is yes—as long as you know what you're doing.

The editor of the HTML5 specification, Ian Hickson, provoked an uproar in 2008, when he estimated that it would take until 2022 for the World Wide Web Consortium (W3C) to adopt the specification as a proposed recommendation (http://blogs.techrepublic.com.com/programming-and-development/?p=718). This was widely misinterpreted as meaning that HTML5 wouldn't be ready for use before then. In fact, he was actually referring to the W3C's stringent requirements for approval. To qualify, the specification must pass tens of thousands of test cases, and at least two browsers must implement every feature completely. In February 2011, the W3C announced it was speeding up the process and set 2014 as the target for formally approving the HTML5 specification. But you don't need to wait until then. Many aspects of HTML5 are widely supported, even by the browser everyone loves to hate, Microsoft Internet Explorer (IE) as far back as IE 6.

**W3C**

### Using HTML5 Now

One of the fundamental principles underlying HTML5 is that it is backwards compatible. With only a small number of exceptions—such as <font> tags and frames—valid code written according to the HTML 4.01 or XHTML 1.0 specifications is also valid HTML5. Simply replace your existing DOCTYPE declaration with the shorter HTML5 one:

```
<!DOCTYPE HTML>
```

That's all there is to it! One of the reasons this DOCTYPE was chosen is that it's the shortest string that reliably prevents browsers from rendering pages in quirks mode.

Of course, HTML5 introduces many new tags and attributes, but there's no obligation to use them unless you need to—just as you probably never used every tag and attribute in HTML 4.01. You also need to be aware of the capabilities of the browsers your target audience is likely to use. This is a constantly changing scenario, so it's impossible to lay down hard-and-fast rules in a book. In addition to your own testing, a website like http://caniuse.com is more likely to provide up-to-date information on what you can use and what's best to avoid.

Much of the discussion about HTML5 has focused on the new *semantic elements*, such as <section>, <header>, <footer>, and <nav>. The idea behind the introduction of these tags is to give page markup greater meaning. Up to now, the only way of grouping related elements on a page has been with <div> tags. On its own, a <div> has no meaning, so it's common to indicate its role through an ID or class. Rather than using <div id="nav">, it's more logical (and less code) to use <nav>—as long as your target browser supports the new tag.

**Figure 1.1** shows the level of support for HTML5 semantic elements as reported by caniuse.com in April 2011. Light green shows full support; darker green shows partial support; and pink shows no support.

**TIP**

Dreamweaver CS5.5 uses uppercase for the DOCTYPE declaration, but it's equally valid to use lowercase or even a combination of uppercase and lowercase. According to the HTML5 specification, the DOCTYPE is case-insensitive.

**CLOSE-UP**

**Quirks Mode**

According to the CSS specification, the width and height of an element refer only to its content. Padding and borders are added outside. In the early days of CSS, IE misinterpreted this rule, but other browsers got it right. Microsoft eventually acknowledged the error of its ways, and IE 6 applied the rules correctly.

To prevent existing sites from breaking, browsers used the DOCTYPE to switch between standards and quirks modes. In standards mode, the browser renders width and height according to the specification. In quirks mode, it emulates IE's original, incorrect behavior. The only browser known to slip into quirks mode with the HTML5 DOCTYPE is Netscape 6, which has an estimated market share of less than 1 percent.

**NOTES**

Semantic means "related to meaning in language or logic." It's derived from the Greek word for "significant."

# New semantic elements - **Working Draft**

*HTML5 offers some new elements, primarily for semantic purposes. The elements include: section, article, aside, hgroup, header, footer, nav, figure, figcaption*

Global user stats[*]:

| | |
|---|---|
| Support: | 14.01% |
| Partial support: | 28.36% |
| Total: | 42.37% |

Resources: <u>Workaround for IE</u>  <u>Alternate workaround</u>  <u>Examples of usage</u>

| | IE | Firefox | Safari | Chrome | Opera | iOS Safari | Opera Mini | Opera Mobile | Android Browser |
|---|---|---|---|---|---|---|---|---|---|
| Two versions back | 7.0 | 3.5 | 3.2 | 8.0 | 10.5 | 3.2 | | | 2.1 |
| Previous version | 8.0 | 3.6 | 4.0 | 9.0 | 10.6 | 4.0-4.1 | | 10.0 | 2.2 |
| Current | 9.0 | 4.0 | 5.0 | 10.0 | 11.0 | 4.2-4.3 | 5.0 | 11.0 | 2.3 |
| Near future | | 5.0 | | 11.0 | 11.1 | | | | |
| Farther future | 10.0 | 6.0 | 6.0 | 12.0 | 11.5 | | | | |

**Note:** Partial support refers to missing the default styling. This is easily taken care of by using display:block for all these elements.

Feedback

Figure 1.1  Support for HTML5 elements depends on the browser version.

If you're in the fortunate position of being able to target only the most recent browsers, you can forge ahead immediately with the new semantic tags. However, most designers need to cater to IE 6–8, which still represent a significant proportion of the browser market and are likely to do so for some time.

## Supporting HTML5 Semantic Tags

Dealing with browsers listed in Figure 1.1 that offer only partial support for HTML5 semantic tags is easy. All that's needed is to add the following rule to your style sheet:

```
article, aside, hgroup, header, footer, figure,
figcaption, nav, section {
    display: block;
}
```

You can apply other styles to these elements in exactly the same way as you would to paragraphs or other HTML elements. For example, the following rule applies the same font family and size to both <p> and <article> elements:

```
article, p {
    font-family: Arial, Helvetica, sans-serif;
    font-size: 14px;
}
```

Unfortunately, IE 8 and earlier require an extra jolt of encouragement to recognize the new HTML5 tags. You need to use JavaScript to create a dummy element for each type of semantic tag you want to use. For example, if you want to use the <header>, <footer>, and <nav> tags, you need to add the following in the <head> of each page:

```
<script>
    document.createElement('header');
    document.createElement('footer');
    document.createElement('nav');
</script>
```

**TIP**

In HTML5, you no longer need to add type="text/javascript" in the opening <script> tag. JavaScript is the default.

Alternatively, you can load a tiny script from the Google content distribution network (CDN) by adding the following just before the closing </head> tag:

```
<!--[if lt IE 9]>
<script src="http://html5shiv.googlecode.com/svn/
➥ trunk/html5.js"></script>
<![endif]-->
```

This is a 2 KB file that contains a little bit of JavaScript wizardry devised by Remy Sharp that forces earlier versions of IE to recognize the new HTML5 tags and apply CSS to them. It creates dummy elements for all semantic tags, saving you the bother of using createElement() for each one. Although the file is small enough to host on your own site, the advantage of using Google's CDN is that the file might already be in the user's browser cache after visiting other sites, so it doesn't need to be downloaded again.

**TIP**

Remy Sharp and Bruce Lawson are authors of *Introducing HTML5* (New Riders, 2010), a practical guide to using HTML5 in websites today.

The predefined HTML5 CSS layouts in Dreamweaver CS5.5 (File > New > Blank Document) use Remy Sharp's script in combination with a style rule to display the semantic tags as block-level elements, ensuring *almost* universal support for them.

Therein lies the problem: It's not 100 percent foolproof. If JavaScript is disabled in the browser, IE leaves the HTML5 tags completely unstyled. This wouldn't be such a problem if the whole page was unstyled, but you end up with a horrendous mix of styled and unstyled elements.

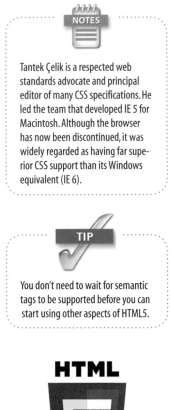

Tantek Çelik is a respected web standards advocate and principal editor of many CSS specifications. He led the team that developed IE 5 for Macintosh. Although the browser has now been discontinued, it was widely regarded as having far superior CSS support than its Windows equivalent (IE 6).

You don't need to wait for semantic tags to be supported before you can start using other aspects of HTML5.

**HTML**

**Figure 1.2** The HTML5 logo was officially adopted by the W3C in April 2011.

In *HTML5 Now* (New Riders, 2010), Tantek Çelik advocates a belt and suspenders (braces, if you're British) approach. He recommends wrapping HTML5 semantic tags in a `<div>` and assigning it a class named after the tag like this:

```
<div class="header">
    <header>
    <!-- header content goes here -->
    </header>
</div>
```

This is undoubtedly the safest way to implement HTML5 semantic tags in a website, but it duplicates markup needlessly. Although IE 9 and other modern browsers support the HTML5 tags, assistive technology for the disabled hasn't caught up yet. Websites tend to need to be redesigned on a regular basis, so there's a strong argument in favor of waiting for broader support for semantic tags.

### HTML and CSS as Living Standards

Ian Hickson is no stranger to controversy. Barely a day had passed after the W3C launched its proposed logo for HTML5 (**Figure 1.2**) in January 2011, when he declared that he was dropping the number 5 in favor of plain HTML. This threw many web designers into total confusion, but the decision made a lot of sense. However, to understand why, you need to know a little history.

#### *A breakaway group pulls HTML back from the brink*

In the late 1990s, the W3C decided that HTML should no longer be developed, and that the future of the web rested with XML (Extensible Markup Language). As the first step in the transition, HTML 4.01 was reformulated according to the stricter rules of XML and released as XHTML 1.0. Work then began on the XHTML 2.0 specification. The idea was to start from a clean slate, devising a "perfect" markup language without worrying about backwards compatibility.

Eventually, this led to the establishment in 2004 of a breakaway group called the Web Hypertext Application Technology Working Group (WHATWG), composed of individuals from Apple, the Mozilla Foundation (which creates the Firefox browser), and Opera Software. Disillusioned by the prospect of XHTML 2.0 breaking billions of existing web pages, they began work on revising the HTML standard to add new features without breaking existing pages. Two years later, the W3C acknowledged the need to develop HTML incrementally and revived the HTML Working Group, which also included Microsoft. Work on XHTML 2.0 was finally abandoned in 2009.

The HTML5 specification is unusual in that it has been developed simultaneously by both the W3C and the WHATWG, with Ian Hickson as the editor of both versions. His decision to drop the number from HTML5 is intended to reflect the fact that the web is constantly evolving. In fact, the WHATWG's online version at http://whatwg.org/html is now officially called a "living standard" (**Figure 1.3**).

## HTML

Living Standard — Last Updated 30 March 2011

You can take part in this work. Join the working group's discussion list.
**Web designers!** We have a FAQ, a forum, and a help mailing list for you!

**Multiple-page version:**
http://whatwg.org/html

**Figure 1.3** The WHATWG version of the HTML specification is a constantly evolving "living standard."

Meanwhile, the version of the W3C website at http://dev.w3.org/html5/spec/Overview.html still uses the number (**Figure 1.4**). Like the WHATWG version, the editor's draft is updated on an almost daily basis. But the W3C version makes it clear that some features in the WHATWG version have been omitted because "they are considered part of future revisions of HTML, not HTML5." In other words, the W3C version is a snapshot of HTML at a particular stage of development. Any new features will be part of a different specification.

**TIP**

For a humorous, musical interpretation of what a "living standard" means, visit http://www.brucelawson.co.uk/2011/living-standard.

**Figure 1.4** The W3C version of the specification is a snapshot of HTML at a particular stage of development.

### Innovation from outside formal standards

You might be asking if any of this matters. The decision to call the WHATWG version a living standard simply reflects the reality that web designers have been working with for years. Formal web standards play a useful role as a common framework; but some of the most useful developments come from innovation outside the W3C specifications.

The <canvas> element, which allows you to draw dynamic shapes and images onscreen, was originally a nonstandard element introduced by Apple in its Safari browser. Firefox and Opera liked what they saw and adopted it, leading to its inclusion in HTML5. Similarly, the innerHTML property and XMLHttpRequest object were IE proprietary innovations, but they proved so useful that all other browsers decided to support them. The innerHTML property has been formally adopted as part of HTML5, and XMLHttpRequest has a W3C specification all its own (www.w3.org/TR/XMLHttpRequest).

### Early adopters drive web standards

Until all the hype about HTML5, people rarely talked about using a particular version of HTML, XHTML, or CSS. It didn't matter whether position: fixed was part of CSS1, CSS2, or CSS2.1. All everyone cared about was which browsers supported it and what happened in browsers that didn't.

**Rebels that Became Standards**

The innerHTML property is a convenient JavaScript shortcut that allows you to read or write the content of an HTML element on the fly. It's much easier to use than the cumbersome node manipulation methods laid down in the W3C Document Object Model (DOM).

The XMLHttpRequest object enables the browser to communicate with the web server in the background, for example, to query a database. When it receives the server's response, the data can be used to update part of the web page without needing to reload (Ajax). Although IE's method of creating the object was proprietary, the agreed standard works cross-browser.

The CSS2.1 specification still hadn't reached formal approval by the beginning of 2011, but that hasn't stopped designers from using those parts of it that have reliable cross-browser support. The same should be true for both HTML5 and CSS3. Browser support will come in stages. Fortunately, you can use many features to enhance the user experience in modern browsers without causing problems in earlier ones. For example, HTML5 defines new input type attributes, such as date and number, for forms. Browsers that don't recognize these values simply display a standard text input field. By using the new type attributes now, your forms will automatically display the specialized input fields as soon as browsers support them.

### Using vendor-specific prefixes for CSS

You can also use many CSS3 properties with vendor-specific prefixes that ensure they won't affect other browsers if their implementation is buggy. To create rounded corners with the border-radius property, you need to use three style declarations like this:

```
-moz-border-radius: 8px;
-webkit-border-radius: 8px;
border-radius: 8px;
```

The -moz- and -webkit- prefixes indicate properties that will be used only by Mozilla (Firefox) or WebKit (Safari and Google Chrome) browsers. By placing the version without a prefix last, the normal rules of the cascade ensure that browsers will implement the standard property as soon as the bugs are ironed out. This involves writing more code, but is far better than resorting to hacks, which were the bane of every web designer's life until quite recently.

Browsers that don't recognize the vendor-specific prefixes or standard CSS3 properties simply ignore them. So, you can use them without worrying.

### Doesn't HTML5 Encourage Poor Markup?

Web standards enthusiasts recoiled in horror when they realized that HTML5 doesn't insist on enclosing the value of attributes in quotes or on using closing tags for

**TIP**

The small amount of extra work needed to add the vendor-specific prefixes to create rounded corners and drop shadows with CSS3 is more than made up for by the time saved in not having to create the same effects with graphics. Your pages load more quickly, too, because there are no images for the browser to fetch.

### Goodbye to XHTML

Web standards advocates embraced XHTML with enthusiasm, attracted by its insistence on strict adherence to rules. However, the fatal flaw in XHTML is that most web servers don't serve it with the correct MIME type (application/xhtml+xml), and if they do, the smallest error, such as a missing closing tag or quotation mark, results in the page failing to display.

Saying goodbye to XHTML doesn't mean saying goodbye to the stricter coding standards it encouraged. You can continue to use all the rules of XHTML in HTML5, and your pages will validate. However, if you choose an HTML5 DOCTYPE in Dreamweaver, you must bid farewell to unnecessary markup, such as a forward slash before the closing angle bracket of an <img> tag. There is no way to force Dreamweaver to use XHTML syntax with an HTML5 DOCTYPE. If you have doubts about the wisdom of following the new standard, take a look at http://wiki.whatwg.org/wiki/FAQ. The WHATWG gives detailed explanations of its decisions and makes it clear that it doesn't legitimize tag soup.

paragraphs and list items. This seemed like a massive step backwards from the strict rules imposed by XHTML 1.0. However, it has been done for a very practical reason: to avoid breaking the web. Countless millions of existing web pages use poor markup, yet browsers manage to display them.

The looser rules adopted by HTML5 are not intended as a signal to adopt bad practices. Clean, well-formed markup is easy to maintain and is likely to be handled more efficiently by browsers. Just because HTML5 allows you to omit the closing </p> tag of a paragraph doesn't mean you *should*.

When you select an HTML5 DOCTYPE, Dreamweaver CS5.5 encloses all attribute values in quotes and always uses closing tags. Converting XHTML pages to HTML5 in Dreamweaver CS5.5 is simple. Just choose File > Convert > HTML5.

## Using HTML5 and CSS3 with Dreamweaver CS5.5

Adobe took the initial steps to support HTML5 and CSS3 with the release of the 11.0.3 updater for Dreamweaver CS5 in August 2010. The updater added code hints for HTML5 tags and attributes, as well as widely supported CSS3 properties. The other main feature was the introduction of the Multiscreen Preview panel, which made it possible to visualize the effect of media queries in screens of three different resolutions.

Dreamweaver CS5.5 builds on those features by improving the method of applying CSS3 properties, such as border-radius, box-shadow, and text-shadow, and streamlining the way it handles media queries. In addition, it has integrated support for the jQuery Mobile and PhoneGap frameworks to speed up the development of dedicated mobile websites and the deployment of native applications on Android or iOS. Code hints for jQuery have also been added.

These features are covered in detail in later chapters, but the next few pages offer a brief description of each one.

## Authoring HTML5

Dreamweaver CS5.5 has full support for all the new tags and attributes in HTML5. But if you're expecting to add semantic elements, such as <header>, <nav>, and <footer>, through the Insert panel/bar, you'll be disappointed. To add a semantic element to a page, you need to type it manually in Code view. Alternatively, highlight an existing element in Design view, right-click, and choose Wrap Tag from the context menu. This brings up code hints for all tags, including those added in HTML5 (**Figure 1.5**).

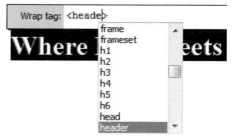

**Figure 1.5** Wrapping an existing element in a <header> tag.

The Property inspector treats the new HTML5 tags as text. This allows you to assign an ID or class to an element, but it doesn't give you access to any of the new HTML5 attributes. Instead, you need to edit HTML5 tags manually in Code view or use the Tag Inspector panel (Window > Tag Inspector, or F9/Option+Shift+F9).

The Tag Inspector's role is very similar to that of the Property inspector. The difference is that the Tag Inspector provides access to every attribute that can be applied to the selected element, whereas the Property inspector concentrates on those most widely used. The Tag Inspector panel also plays host to Dreamweaver's JavaScript behaviors, so you need to make sure the Attributes button is selected at the top left (**Figure 1.6**). The two icons immediately below toggle the display between attributes sorted by category and an alphabetical list. Figure 1.6 shows the options available for an <input> tag. By selecting the type attribute, you can convert a text input field to one of the many new form fields. The Tag Inspector also lets you set other new attributes for form elements, such as min, max, placeholder, and required.

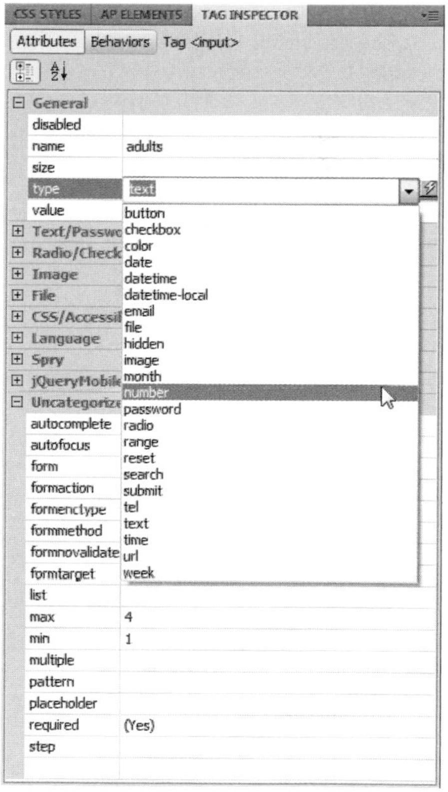

## CSS3 Support Takes Off

Unlike previous versions, CSS3 is not a single specification, but has been divided into modules to make it easier to roll them out as soon as they're ready. Dreamweaver is following a similar rollout policy, adding support for those parts of CSS3 that have already been implemented by the most recent versions of browsers, as well as those expected to become available in the not-too-distant future.

**Figure 1.6** The Tag Inspector provides complete access to HTML5 attributes.

Technically speaking, text-shadow was originally part of the CSS2 specification. Lack of browser support resulted in it being removed from CSS2.1. Ironically, once it had been dropped, browsers began to support it.

CLOSE-UP

**Naming Confusion**

If you're new to Dreamweaver, you're likely to be confused by two aspects of the user interface (UI) with almost identical names. The Property inspector is the large panel located beneath the Document window in the default Designer workspace layout. The Properties pane is the bottom section of the CSS Styles panel. What's doubly confusing is that the tab at the top left of the Property inspector is labeled Properties. So, it's not unreasonable to think it should be called the Properties panel, but it has always been known as the Property inspector, and that's its official name.

The main role of the Property inspector is to provide quick access to HTML attributes. It's context-sensitive, and its contents depend on what's currently selected in the Document window. On the other hand, the Properties pane of the CSS Styles panel displays the CSS properties defined in the selected style rule.

## Creating rounded corners and drop shadows

The border-radius, box-shadow, and text-shadow properties are among the first CSS3 properties with widespread support in modern browsers, answering designers' prayers for a way to create rounded corners and drop shadows without the need for images. Dreamweaver CS5.5 makes it straightforward to apply and adjust these properties through the CSS Styles panel and Live view.

To apply one of the properties, use the following steps:

1. Click the Live View button.

2. In the CSS Styles panel, select the rule affecting the element you want to style, or create a new style rule.

3. In the Properties pane, click Add Property and select the property from the list that appears. Alternatively, choose the property in Category view.

4. Click the icon that consists of a plus sign and a triangle ⁺◢ next to the property.

5. Fill in the values in the subpanel that appears (**Figure 1.7**). Live view automatically refreshes each time you make a change, allowing you to adjust the effect visually rather than relying on the numerical values.

**Figure 1.7** Applying rounded corners visually in the CSS Styles panel and Live view.

### Using embedded fonts

For years, web designers have been frustrated by the narrow range of "web safe" fonts at their disposal, because browsers use the fonts installed on the visitor's computer. CSS2 sought to solve this problem through @font-face, but browser support was lacking, so it was dropped. However, @font-face now has widespread browser support and is part of CSS3.

Unfortunately, the situation is complicated by licensing issues and the font formats supported by different browsers. Chapter 2 discusses these problems and potential solutions. The good news is that Dreamweaver CS5.5 supports @font-face in Live view (**Figure 1.8**), making it easier to visualize how your page will look in a browser.

> **TIP**
>
> Live view currently supports the W3C border-radius and text-shadow properties, but not box-shadow. To apply a drop shadow on an element, you must choose -webkit-box-shadow from the Categories view of the Properties pane.

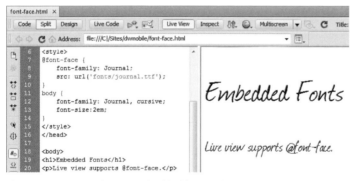

**Figure 1.8** Live view displays embedded fonts as they will appear in a browser.

### Expanded support for CSS3 selectors

Previous versions of Dreamweaver had support for only a limited range of CSS selectors. A notable omission was support for attribute selectors, such as input[type=submit] (to select submit buttons). These have been part of CSS ever since 1998, but have been of limited use because of IE 6's lack of support. However, IE 7 caught up with all other browsers by adding support not only for CSS2.1 attribute selectors, but also three new ones from CSS3. Dreamweaver CS5.5 now supports all attribute selectors, which are listed in **Table 1.1**.

**TABLE 1.1** CSS Attribute Selectors

| SELECTOR | DESCRIPTION | EXAMPLE |
|----------|-------------|---------|
| e[attr] | Matches an e element with the attr attribute regardless of the attribute's value. | img[title] |
| e[attr=val] | Matches an e element with the attr attribute whose value is exactly equal to val. | input[type=submit] |
| e[attr~=val] | Matches an e element with the attr attribute whose value is a space-separated list of words; one of which is exactly val. | p[class~=aside] |
| e[attr\|=val] | Matches an e element with the attr attribute whose value is exactly val or val followed by a hyphen. Used mainly to match language codes and subcodes. | span[lang\|=fr] |
| e[attr^=val] | Matches an e element with the attr attribute whose value begins with val. | a[href^=http] |
| e[attr$=val] | Matches an e element with the attr attribute whose value ends with val. | a[href$=.pdf] |
| e[attr*=val] | Matches an e element with the attr attribute whose value contains the substring val. | div[class*=wide] |

**TIP**

Peter-Paul Koch has published a useful set of CSS compatibility charts at www.quirksmode.org/css/contents.html. According to his tests, all selectors in Table 1.2 are supported by IE 9, Firefox 3.5, Safari 4, Chrome 4, and later versions. Opera 10 also supports them but has bugs with :nth-child() and :nth-of-type(). According to my own tests, these bugs were fixed in Opera 11.

CSS3 gives designers a much finer degree of control over the selection of elements. With the exception of IE, browsers have been quick to adopt the new selectors, many of which will be familiar to you if you use jQuery. IE 9 has done a lot of catching up, so Dreamweaver CS5.5 now supports all the structural pseudo-classes listed in **Table 1.2**.

The :nth-child() and related pseudo-classes all take an argument that indicates the position of the element you want to select. The possible values are the following:

▶ **The keywords odd or even.** To select every even-numbered matching element, use :nth-child(even).

▶ **A single number counting from 1.** Using :nth-child(5) picks the fifth matching element.

▶ **The formula an+b or an-b.** The letters a and b represent numbers, and n is the literal character. This divides the child elements into groups, each composed of the number specified by a; and within that group, it selects the element specified by b. For example, tr:nth-child (5n+2) selects the second, seventh, twelfth, and so on rows of a table. If b is negative, it counts back from the end of the group. For example, `tr:nth-child(5n-2)` selects the third, eighth, thirteenth, and so on rows.

TABLE 1.2  CSS3 Structural Pseudo-classes

| SELECTOR | DESCRIPTION |
| --- | --- |
| `:root` | Selects the root of the document. In HTML, this is always the `<html>` element. |
| `:nth-child()` | Selects elements based on their position in relation to their siblings within the document tree. See main text for a description of how the position is calculated. |
| `:nth-last-child()` | Same as `:nth-child()` but counting backwards. |
| `:nth-of-type()` | Selects elements of the same type in relation to their siblings within the document tree. For example, `img:nth-of-type(odd)` selects alternate images that are children of the same parent element. |
| `:nth-last-of-type()` | Same as `:nth-of-type()` but counting backwards. |
| `:first-child` | Selects an element that is the first child of some other element. |
| `:last-child` | Selects an element that is the last child of some other element. |
| `:first-of-type` | Selects an element that is the first of its type in the list of children of its parent element. |
| `:last-of-type` | Selects an element that is the last of its type in the list of children of its parent element. |
| `:only-child` | Selects an element that is the only child of its parent element. |
| `:only-of-type` | Selects an element that has no siblings of the same type. For example, `img:only-of-type` selects an image only if its parent element contains no other images. |
| `:empty` | Selects elements that contain no other elements or text. For example, `div:empty` matches `<div></div>` but not `<div>Hi!</div>`. |

Lack of support in IE 8 and earlier reduces the usefulness of the selectors listed in Table 1.2 unless you are targeting only the most recent browsers. However, it's useful to know they're supported by Dreamweaver CS5.5.

A rather obscure change is the addition of support for the CSS3 syntax for pseudo-elements. In CSS2.1, these were preceded by a single colon. In CSS3, they're preceded by a double colon, as shown in **Table 1.3**.

**TIP**

In her book *Stunning CSS3* (New Riders, 2010), Zoe Mickley Gillenwater suggests a simple way of dealing with the formula for `nth-child()`. Treat it as $a \times n \pm b$. Start n at 0 and increment it by 1 each time. So, $5 \times 0 + 2 = 2$, $5 \times 1 + 2 = 7$, and so on.

TABLE 1.3 CSS Pseudo-elements

| CSS2.1 | CSS3 | MEANING |
|---|---|---|
| :first-line | ::first-line | Applies styles to the first line of an element. |
| :first-letter | ::first-letter | Applies styles to the first letter of an element. |
| :before | ::before | Adds generated content before the element. |
| :after | ::after | Adds generated content after the element. |

Browser support for the double-colon syntax is limited. Also, the requirement for backwards compatibility means that the single-colon versions should continue indefinitely.

### Support for other CSS3 properties

To get an idea of which new properties are supported by Dreamweaver CS5.5, click the leftmost button at the bottom of the Properties pane in the CSS Styles panel to switch to Category view (**Figure 1.9**).

Eight new categories have been added, namely:

▶ **User Interface.** The only property currently widely supported is box-sizing, which emulates the old quirks mode box model when its value is set to border-box. This forces the browser to include padding and borders in the width and height of an element rather than adding them outside. IE 8 and Opera support box-sizing without a vendor prefix. Use -moz-box-sizing for Firefox and -webkit-box-sizing for Safari and Chrome.

▶ **Multi-column Layout.** Properties that allow you to display text in newspaper-style columns. These properties are currently supported only by Firefox, Safari, and Chrome using vendor-specific prefixes.

▶ **Line Layout.** Properties designed to give greater control over the alignment of text and other elements. The W3C ranks them as "low priority."

▶ **Animations, Transforms, Transitions.** Properties that rotate and animate objects in 2D and 3D. These properties are increasingly supported by recent browsers.

▶ **Mozilla.** Vendor-specific (-moz) properties used by Firefox.

**NOTES**

The ::before and ::after pseudo-elements and their single-colon equivalents work only in Live view.

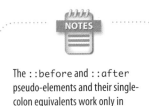

**Figure 1.9** Seven new categories have been added to the Properties pane of the CSS Styles panel.

- ▶ **Microsoft.** Vendor-specific (-ms) properties used by IE.
- ▶ **Webkit.** Vendor-specific (-webkit) properties used by Safari and Chrome.
- ▶ **Opera.** Vendor-specific (-o) properties used by Opera.

### Support for CSS3 color values and opacity

The CSS3 Color module specifies several new ways to handle colors in addition to hexadecimal and RGB (red, green, blue) values. It allows you to use HSL (hue, saturation, lightness) and to set the color's opacity (or transparency, depending on your point of view).

There are two basic ways of controlling opacity:

- ▶ Specify the color using either rgba() or hsla().
- ▶ Set the opacity property on the element.

The degree of opacity is always expressed as a number between 0 (transparent) and 1 (opaque). With rgba() and hsla(), it's the fourth value in a comma-separated list of RGB or HSL values. The opacity property takes it as its sole value.

The color picker in previous versions of Dreamweaver supported only hexadecimal notation, but it now supports all formats. To switch to a different color format, click the right-facing arrow at the top right of the color picker, and choose the Color Format submenu (**Figure 1.10**) before using the eyedropper tool to select the color.

**TIP**

Live view is powered by the WebKit engine, so the only vendor-specific properties it renders are those pre-fixed with -webkit.

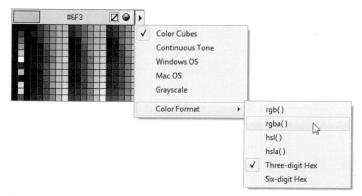

**Figure 1.10** Dreamweaver CS5.5 supports all CSS3 color formats.

**Opacity in CSS**

The opacity property affects not only the element it's applied to, but also all of the element's children. To demonstrate the difference between opacity and rgba(), opacity.html in the ch01 folder contains two <div> elements styled using the following rules:

```
#opacity_test {
    background-color: #F90;
    opacity: 0.5;
}
#rgba_test {
    background-color:
    ↪ rgba(255, 153, 0, 0.5);
}
```

As **Figure 1.11** shows, the 50% opacity value is applied in the top <div> not only to the background color, but also to the text inside. In the bottom <div>, the opacity is applied only to the background color without affecting the text.

Opacity has been applied to this div.

**The background color of this div has been set using rgba().**

Figure 1.11 The opacity property affects the entire element.

Dreamweaver CS5.5 supports rgba(), hsla(), and opacity only in Live view. Design view renders all colors fully opaque.

When you choose rgba() or hsla(), Dreamweaver automatically sets the fourth value to 1 (opaque). You need to edit the value manually in the CSS Styles panel or in the style sheet.

The new color formats and the opacity property are supported by most modern browsers, including IE 9. They don't work in IE 8 or earlier.

You set the opacity property like any other CSS property in the CSS Styles panel or in a style sheet.

### Designing for Multiple Screen Resolutions

The Multiscreen Preview panel allows you to see what your pages look like at three different screen resolutions (**Figure 1.12**). Links within the panel are navigable. If you click a link to another page, all three subpanels are updated simultaneously. You can also configure the subpanels to display other viewport sizes.

The panel was added to Dreamweaver CS5 by the 11.0.3 updater, but its functionality has been improved by making it easier to define CSS media queries for different devices and attach them automatically to pages. Chapter 3 describes this feature and the use of media queries in detail.

The other major change is the ability to set the size of the Document window viewport to match different screen resolutions. To switch sizes, click the down arrow to the right of the Multiscreen button in the Document toolbar at the top of the Document window (**Figure 1.13**).

The viewport sizes at the top of the list are predefined, but you can edit the available range by choosing Edit Sizes at the bottom. This opens the Dreamweaver Preferences panel where you can edit the width, height, and description of the preset sizes, as well as add new definitions and delete existing ones.

The values displayed in the lower half of the list depend on the media queries applied to the current page.

**Figure 1.12** The Multiscreen Preview panel shows the same page at three different screen resolutions.

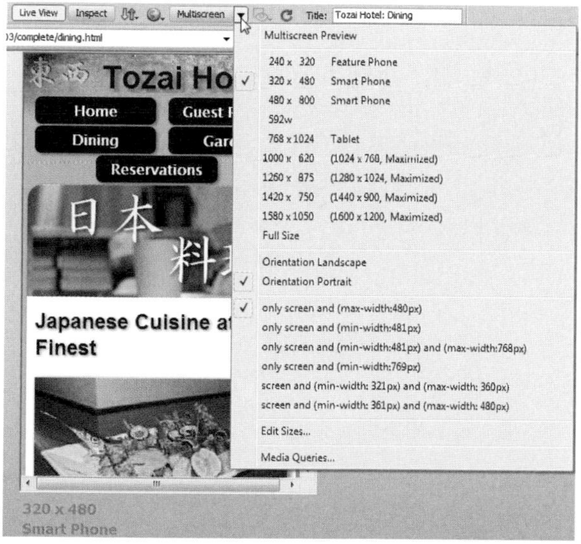

**Figure 1.13** You can change the size of the Document window viewport to match target devices.

jQueryMobile: page
# Page One
jQueryMobile: listview
- Page Two
- Page Three
- Page Four

**Page Footer**

# Page Two
Content

**Page Footer**

# Page Three
Content

**Page Footer**

# Page Four
Content

**Page Footer**

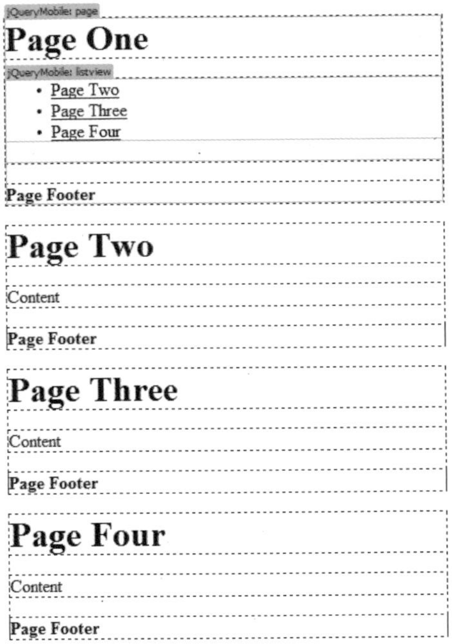

**Figure 1.14**  A Mobile Starter page contains placeholders for a basic four-page mobile site or application.

## Building Dedicated Mobile Sites with jQuery Mobile

Using media queries to change the look of a website in different devices gives you great flexibility, but it's not always the optimal solution. Very long pages can be difficult to read on a small screen. Also, image-heavy sites are slow to download on a mobile device. In many cases, it's best to create a custom-built site for mobile users.

The jQuery Mobile framework is ideal for doing this, and it has been developed with the active participation of Dreamweaver engineers. It's designed to work on all mainstream mobile operating systems and browsers, including all versions of Android and iOS, BlackBerry OS version 5 and later, Windows Phone 7, and Symbian S60 version 5 (used mainly by Nokia, Sony Ericsson, and DoCoMo).

Dreamweaver CS5.5 speeds up the development of dedicated mobile sites by integrating the jQuery Mobile framework and widgets.

To create a skeleton mobile site with jQuery Mobile:

1. Choose File > New to open the New Document dialog box.

2. Choose Page from Sample on the left of the dialog box.

3. Select Mobile Starters from the Sample Folder list. This offers a choice of loading the jQuery Mobile library from a CDN, using local versions of the files, or using jQuery Mobile with PhoneGap.

4. Choose one of the options and click Create to insert the basic structure of a jQuery Mobile site/application.

   A single page containing four `<div>` elements is displayed as independent pages when viewed in a browser or mobile device. Each "page" consists of nested `<div>` elements with placeholder text (**Figure 1.14**).

The Mobile Starter page automatically links to the jQuery Mobile JavaScript files and basic style sheet; each element is marked up with the code to build the individual pages, attach the touch-responsive JavaScript events, and style the content. In just a few minutes, you can convert the starter page to look like **Figure 1.15** on a smartphone.

The jQuery Mobile framework also features widgets to add extra pages and page elements, such as layout grids, collapsible panels, and form fields. You can insert them from the Insert panel (**Figure 1.16**) or by choosing Insert > jQuery Mobile.

Chapters 5 and 6 describe in detail how to use these features in Dreamweaver CS5.5.

### Code Hints for jQuery Core

As well as integrating jQuery Mobile into Dreamweaver, Adobe has added code hints for jQuery Core. The code hints are built into the program, so they're also available in external JavaScript files. As soon as you type a single or double quotation mark after $( to create a jQuery selector, Dreamweaver inserts the closing quote and displays a list of HTML tags to choose from. If you type a period, you're presented with a list of classes defined in your style sheet; if you type a hash or pound sign (#), the list displays all declared IDs (**Figure 1.17**).

**Figure 1.15** Just replace the placeholder text for a basic mobile website.

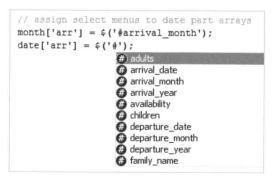

**Figure 1.16** A new category in the Insert panel is dedicated to jQuery Mobile widgets.

**Figure 1.17** Code hints speed up the creation of jQuery selectors by presenting a list of available IDs.

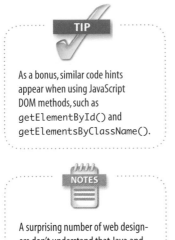

**TIP**

As a bonus, similar code hints appear when using JavaScript DOM methods, such as `getElementById()` and `getElementsByClassName()`.

**NOTES**

A surprising number of web designers don't understand that Java and JavaScript are completely unrelated languages. JavaScript was originally called LiveScript, but the name was changed by Netscape in what many regard as a misguided marketing ploy. Confusion has remained ever since. But you probably didn't need me to tell you that.

**NOTES**

The Windows version of Dreamweaver CS5.5 does not support packaging native apps for iPhone, iPod touch, and iPad, because it requires the iOS SDK (software development kit), which runs only on Mac OS X.

When you type a period after the closing parenthesis, Dreamweaver presents you with a list of jQuery methods, complete with hints for the arguments they expect. The code hints are smart enough to continue working even if you insert a new line for readability when chaining jQuery methods.

### Packaging Native Apps for Android and iOS with PhoneGap

The explosive growth of the smartphone and tablet market has been accompanied—or perhaps driven—by the phenomenal growth of applications specifically designed for them. However, a major barrier to creating native apps for mobile devices is the need to learn new languages and technologies. To develop native apps for the iPhone, iPod touch, and iPad, you need to use Objective-C. Android apps run on Java (not to be confused with JavaScript).

Fortunately, the open source PhoneGap framework (www.phonegap.com) allows web developers to build apps using technologies they already know—or are at least familiar with—HTML, CSS, and JavaScript. The framework converts the web files into code that runs as a native app on the mobile operating system of your choice. Dreamweaver CS5.5 not only automates the installation of the Android software development kit, but it also makes packaging apps with PhoneGap and testing them simplicity itself: Just enter a few details in a couple of dialog boxes, and you're done.

You can compile and test Android apps (**Figure 1.18**) in both Windows and Mac OS X. The Mac version of Dreamweaver CS5.5 also uses PhoneGap to compile and test apps for the iPhone (**Figure 1.19**) and iPad. This feature is covered in detail in Chapter 7.

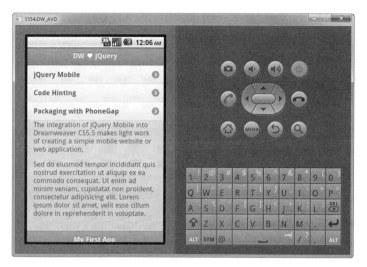

**Figure 1.18** Testing in the Android simulator after packaging the app with Dreamweaver's integrated version of PhoneGap.

**Figure 1.19** Testing in the iPhone simulator on Mac OS X.

## Developing for Multiple Devices

The rapid spread of mobile devices presents web designers and developers with challenges and opportunities. The main challenges lie in the different operating systems and the bewildering range of screen resolutions. However, we're fortunate that this coincides with a period when mainstream vendors are taking web standards seriously. Unlike desktop computers, mobile devices tend to be replaced relatively frequently—at least in industrialized countries—where a mobile phone is typically replaced at the end of a two-year contract. Although designs for desktops still need to accommodate earlier versions of IE, you can start using some aspects of HTML5 and CSS3 to provide an enhanced experience for other modern browsers and mobile devices.

This chapter provided an overall view of Dreamweaver CS5.5's new features designed to speed up the development process. The remaining chapters explore those features in greater detail, beginning with enhancing an existing website with HTML5 and CSS3.

**SECTION II**

# HTML5 and CSS3

# CHAPTER

# Progressive Enhancement with HTML5 and CSS3

*When we treat them as if they were what they should
be, we improve them as far as they can be improved.*

—Goethe

# Progressive Enhancement with HTML5 and CSS3

**B**ack in the 1990s, it was common for the front page of a website to inform visitors that it was "best viewed" in a particular browser. Designers often gave up trying to reconcile incompatible differences between Internet Explorer (IE) and Netscape. If you weren't using the recommended browser, that was just your hard luck. When IE eventually emerged as the victor in the browser wars, many designers breathed a sigh of relief and designed exclusively for IE. But if you weren't using IE—and many weren't—it was still your hard luck. A more enlightened approach known as graceful degradation emerged with the web standards movement in the first decade of the new century. If a feature couldn't be supported by a particular browser—usually Netscape 4—a fallback solution prevented the design from breaking completely.

In more recent times, leading designers have turned this idea on its head, arguing that you shouldn't need to wait for the majority of browsers to implement a feature before using it. They advocate progressive enhancement—building a website that works satisfactorily in all current browsers and then adding features to improve the experience for visitors using more advanced browsers. Visitors using earlier browsers get a satisfactory experience; when they upgrade, they automatically see the improved features.

In this chapter, you'll learn how to apply progressive enhancement to a website for a fictitious hotel. In the next chapter, I'll show you how to adapt it for display in mobile phones and tablets through the use of media queries.

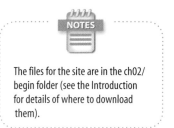

The files for the site are in the ch02/ begin folder (see the Introduction for details of where to download them).

## Improving an Existing Site

The Tozai Hotel site has been designed using an XHTML 1.0 Strict DOCTYPE. The main pages look identical in all current browsers. **Figure 2.1** shows index.html in IE 6.

**Figure 2.1** The basic design looks satisfactory in IE 6.

There's just one minor exception. The styles for the inquiry form in reservations.html include the following rules:

```
select + label, input + label {
    padding-left: 10px;
}
input[type=submit] {
    margin-left: 135px;
}
```

The first rule uses the *adjacent sibling selector* to add 10 pixels of padding to the left of `<label>` tags that immediately follow a `<select>` or `<input>` element. The second rule uses an attribute selector (see Table 1.1) to add a 135-pixel margin to the left of the submit button. The result is a neatly aligned form in all modern browsers (**Figure 2.2**).

### Adjacent Sibling Selector

Sometimes it's convenient to apply a style rule to an element only if it immediately follows another element at the same level of the document hierarchy (a sibling). For example, you might want to apply a different style to each first paragraph that follows a heading. The adjacent sibling selector, which consists of two selectors separated by a plus sign (+), is designed precisely for this purpose. The selector on the left of the plus sign identifies the element that must precede the element that matches the selector on the right. In other words, h1 + p tells the browser to apply the rule only to `<p>` elements that immediately follow an `<h1>` heading. If any other element comes between them, the rule doesn't apply.

Using selectors to target elements based on their relationship to their immediate siblings avoids the need to pepper your code with classes. The downside is that changes to the page structure might destroy the relationship, resulting in the style rule no longer being applied. The CSS3 Selectors module refers to the adjacent sibling selector as the *adjacent sibling combinator*, but it's simply a change of name. The syntax and functionality remain unchanged.

**Stay with Us**

| | |
|---|---|
| Title: | Specify if other: |
| First name: | |
| Family name: | |
| Arrival: | Jan 1 2011 |
| Departure: | Jan 1 2011 |
| Guests |
| Adults: | Children: |
| | Check Availability & Rates |

**Figure 2.2** In modern browsers, the form elements are neatly aligned.

IE didn't support adjacent sibling or attribute selectors until IE 7. As a result, the form is not so neatly aligned in IE 6 (**Figure 2.3**). Also, the word Guests appears in a different color, because it's the `<legend>` element of a `<fieldset>` surrounding the input fields for adults and children. These minor differences don't affect the usability of the form and can be ignored for a browser with a small and declining market share.

**Stay with Us**

Title: ☐ Specify if other: ☐

First name: ☐

Family name: ☐

Arrival: Jan ▼ 1 ▼ 2011 ▼

Departure: Jan ▼ 1 ▼ 2011 ▼

Guests

Adults: ☐     Children: ☐

[ Check Availability & Rates ]

**Figure 2.3** IE 6 doesn't recognize all the CSS styles, which results in a less pleasing but still usable layout.

In this chapter, you'll make the following enhancements to the site:

▶ Convert from XHTML 1.0 to HTML5

▶ Add accessibility attributes to key elements

▶ Use an embedded font for headings

▶ Enhance the design with CSS rounded corners and drop shadows

▶ Add HTML5 form elements and attributes

▶ Use jQuery to improve the date pickers

▶ Validate the finished pages

### Converting to HTML5

As mentioned in Chapter 1, all that's needed to convert a page to HTML5 is to replace the existing DOCTYPE declaration with the case-insensitive new one:

```
<!DOCTYPE HTML>
```

Because the pages in the Tozai Hotel site were created with an XHTML 1.0 Strict DOCTYPE, tags that don't have a corresponding closing tag, such as <img> and <link>, have a forward slash before the closing angle bracket like this:

```
<link href="styles/tozai.css" rel="stylesheet"
➥ type="text/css" />
```

**TIP**

Determining how far to go in supporting a particular browser is a decision that you should make only on a case-by-case basis. If your website's server statistics show that IE 6 still has a significant market share, you might need to take a different approach. Even if you make the radical decision to drop all support for IE 6, you should ensure that the site remains functional.

**CLOSE-UP**

### Picking the Right Tag

HTML contains many underused tags and attributes. Finding the right one for a specific situation isn't always easy, but it's likely to make your pages more meaningful. The first time a keyword is introduced in a page, consider wrapping it in `<dfn>` tags, which represent the defining instance of a term. You can use CSS to display the tag in bold, and use `<b>` tags for subsequent references to the keyword.

For a foreign language expression, use the `lang` attribute to indicate which language is being used, for example:

`<i lang="fr">Bonjour le monde!</i>`

This not only preserves the typographic convention, but also provides useful information to search engines and screen readers.

To ease the transition between XHTML 1.0 and HTML5, the closing slash is permitted, but it's no longer required. It was added to XHTML solely to conform to the rules of XML. Dreamweaver CS5.5 makes it easy to switch the DOCTYPE and strip out unnecessary code by choosing File > Convert > HTML5.

Another change you need to make when converting to HTML5 concerns the use of bold text and italics. For many years, it was considered best practice to use `<strong>` instead of `<b>` for bold text and `<em>` instead of `<i>` for italics. The idea was to handle all presentational aspects of a web page through CSS. The `<b>` and `<i>` tags were considered presentational, whereas `<strong>` and `<em>` were said to be related to the document's structure.

Although well intentioned, this practice frequently made little sense and simply replaced `<b>` and `<i>` with longer equivalents. In addition, it resulted in screen readers for the blind giving unnecessary emphasis to words styled in bold or italics. HTML5 has redefined the meanings of these tags to clarify their use, as summarized in **Table 2.1**.

**TABLE 2.1** HTML5 Tags for Bold, Italics, and Emphasis

| TAG | MEANING |
| --- | --- |
| `<b>` | A span of text stylistically offset from the surrounding text in bold type without conveying extra importance, for example, keywords in a document or product names in a review. |
| `<i>` | A span of text that needs to be offset from the surrounding text in italics, such as a technical term, foreign language expression, thought, or ship's name. |
| `<strong>` | Indicates strong importance, for example, `<strong>Warning!</strong>`. The level of importance can be increased by nesting `<strong>` tags like this: `<strong><strong>Very severe warning!</strong></strong>`. |
| `<em>` | Indicates that the word(s) should be emphasized if spoken aloud. Like `<strong>`, the level of emphasis can be increased by nesting `<em>` tags. |

By default, Dreamweaver uses `<strong>` and `<em>` for bold and italic type. If you're using an HTML5 DOCTYPE, you should change this setting in the Preferences panel.

To convert a page to HTML5 and change how bold text and italics are handled:

1. Open index.html in the Document window, and choose File > Convert > HTML5. This changes the DOCTYPE and strips out all closing slashes.

2. Open the Preferences panel by choosing Edit > Preferences (Dreamweaver > Preferences on a Mac).

3. Select the General category from the list on the left of the panel, and deselect the check box labeled Use `<strong>` and `<em>` in place of `<b>` and `<i>`.

4. Click OK to close the Preferences panel.

5. With index.html still in the Document window, switch to Split view by clicking the Split button in the Document toolbar or choosing View > Code and Design.

6. In Design view, double-click *Tozai* in the first paragraph to select the whole word. In Code view, the highlighted word is wrapped in `<em>` tags. *Tozai* is a foreign word, so it needs to be offset without giving it emphasis. The `<em>` tags need to be replaced with `<i>` tags.

7. Make sure the Property inspector is in HTML mode with the `<> HTML` button selected, and click the `I` button to remove the italics and the `<em>` tags.

8. Click the `I` button again. This restores the italics, but this time the word is wrapped in `<i>` tags (**Figure 2.4**).

The best way to understand how features work is to use them. Copy the files from ch02/begin to a new folder, and follow the steps in each section.

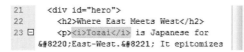

**Figure 2.4** The `<i>` tags offset the foreign word without giving it emphasis.

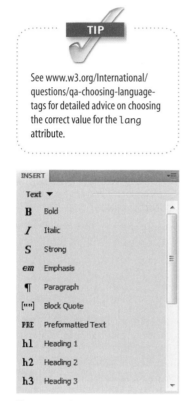

See www.w3.org/International/
questions/qa-choosing-language-
tags for detailed advice on choosing
the correct value for the lang
attribute.

**Figure 2.5** The `<strong>` and `<em>` tags can be inserted through the Insert panel.

The **B** and *I* buttons in the Property inspector can be used to remove `<strong>`, `<em>`, `<b>`, and `<i>` tags that you don't want regardless of the Preferences setting. However, make sure the `<> HTML` button is selected on the left of the Property inspector. If the `CSS` button is selected instead, you'll be prompted to create a style rule. An alternative way to remove unwanted tags is to select the element in the Tag selector at the bottom of the Document window, right-click, and choose Remove Tag.

9. With the word and its surrounding `<i>` tags still selected, open the Tag Inspector panel, expand the Language category, and click in the field next to the lang attribute. Choose ja from the list of values to indicate the language used is Japanese.

   Alternatively, position the insertion point just before the closing bracket of the opening `<i>` tag, and press Enter/Return. Select lang from the code hints list, and then select ja.

10. Repeat steps 6–9 with the other foreign words (*sashimi* and *sushi* in the second paragraph).

11. Convert dining.html, garden.html, reservations.html, and rooms.html to HTML5, and change the `<em>` tags to `<i>` tags in dining.html.

12. Choose File > Save All.

### Using `<strong>` and `<em>` tags

Resetting the Dreamweaver preferences to use `<b>` and `<i>` doesn't prevent you from using `<strong>` and `<em>` where appropriate. Instead of using the **B** and *I* buttons in the Property inspector in HTML mode, use the Text category of the Insert panel, which has separate options for each tag (**Figure 2.5**).

Alternatively, select the text in Design view, right-click, and choose Wrap Tag from the context menu. Then type either **strong** or **em**.

### Improving Accessibility with ARIA Roles

Until IE 8 and earlier disappear from the scene, using HTML5 semantic tags, such as `<header>` and `<nav>`, will remain problematic unless you wrap them in `<div>` tags (see "Supporting HTML5 Semantic Tags" in Chapter 1). An alternative worth considering is to mark up your pages with universally supported HTML elements, such as `<div>` and `<ul>`, and to indicate their meaning by adding the WAI-ARIA role attribute.

The role attribute has been adopted by HTML5, and it's understood by many screen readers. So, it provides a useful transition until such time as the new semantic tags are fully supported. The attribute has a large number of possible values (for a full list, see www.w3.org/TR/wai-aria/roles#role_definitions). **Table 2.2** lists the equivalent role attributes for the main HTML5 semantic elements. Where multiple values are shown, the primary one is listed first.

TABLE 2.2  WAI-ARIA Roles for HTML5 Semantic Elements

| HTML5 ELEMENT | WAI-ARIA ROLE |
| --- | --- |
| `<article>` | `article` |
| `<aside>` | `note`, `complementary`, `search` |
| `<footer>` | `contentinfo` |
| `<header>` | `banner` (see note) |
| `<nav>` | `navigation` |
| `<section>` | `region`, `contentinfo`, `main`, `search` |

Unfortunately, code hints in Dreamweaver CS5.5 don't support the role attribute. You need to edit the code manually. However, rather than accessing individual tags to add ARIA roles, it's more efficient to use Dreamweaver's Find and Replace dialog box.

1. Press Ctrl+F/Command+F or choose Edit > Find and Replace to open the dialog box. It doesn't matter whether you have any documents open.

2. Select Folder from the "Find in" list, and click the 📁 icon on the right of the text field to select the folder that contains your working copies of the Tozai Hotel site files.

3. Select Specific Tag from the Search list, and set the field on the right to "div."

4. If necessary, click the plus button to display the next option, and set it to With Attribute. Set the values of the three options to "id", "=", and "header" respectively.

5. If other search options are visible, click the minus button to remove them from the dialog box.

6. Set Action to Set Attribute.

7. Type **role** in the next field, and **banner** in the To field.

8. Check that the settings in the Find and Replace dialog box look like **Figure 2.6**, and click Replace All.

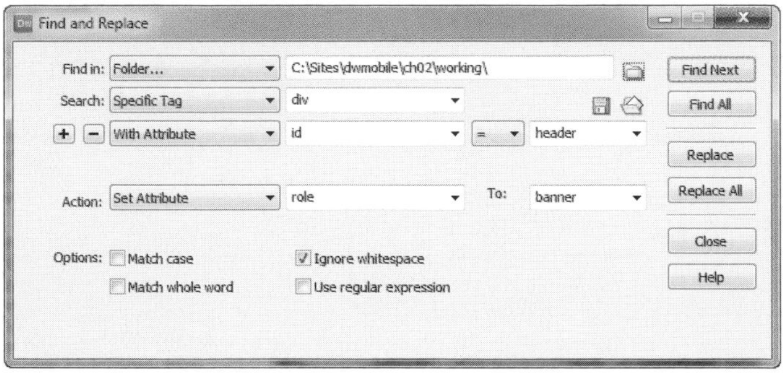

**Figure 2.6** Using Find and Replace is a quick way to add the `role` attribute to multiple pages.

9. If the files aren't currently open, Dreamweaver warns you that the operation can't be undone. Click Yes to confirm you want to proceed.

10. Dreamweaver displays the results in the Search tab of the Results panel (**Figure 2.7**). It should confirm that five items were affected.

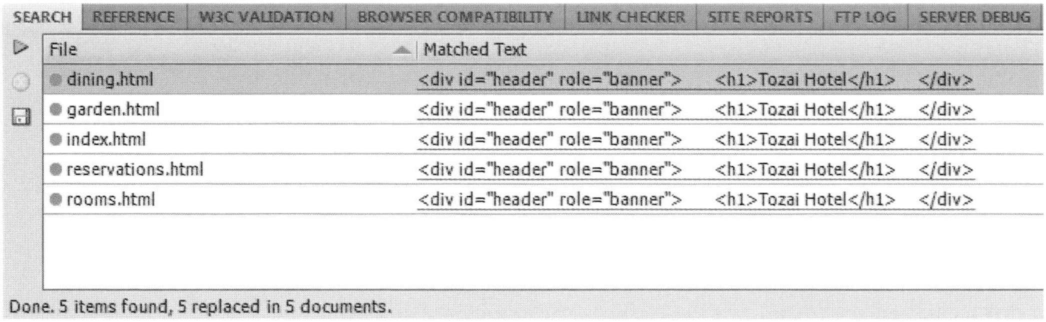

| File | Matched Text | | |
| --- | --- | --- | --- |
| dining.html | \<div id="header" role="banner"\> | \<h1\>Tozai Hotel\</h1\> | \</div\> |
| garden.html | \<div id="header" role="banner"\> | \<h1\>Tozai Hotel\</h1\> | \</div\> |
| index.html | \<div id="header" role="banner"\> | \<h1\>Tozai Hotel\</h1\> | \</div\> |
| reservations.html | \<div id="header" role="banner"\> | \<h1\>Tozai Hotel\</h1\> | \</div\> |
| rooms.html | \<div id="header" role="banner"\> | \<h1\>Tozai Hotel\</h1\> | \</div\> |

SEARCH | REFERENCE | W3C VALIDATION | BROWSER COMPATIBILITY | LINK CHECKER | SITE REPORTS | FTP LOG | SERVER DEBUG

Done. 5 items found, 5 replaced in 5 documents.

**Figure 2.7** The Results panel displays the affected tags.

11. Click the right-facing green arrow at the top left of the Results panel to reopen the Find and Replace dialog box.

**12.** The main content in index.html is in a `<div>` with the ID `hero`. In rooms.html, it's in a `<div>` with the class `content-wide`. In both pages, the main content stretches the full width of the page.

In the other three pages, the main content is in a `<div>` with the class `content-medium`. These pages also have a sidebar, which is a `<div>` with the class `aside`.

Add the `role` attribute to these sections using the settings in **Table 2.3**.

**TABLE 2.3** Find and Replace Settings for ARIA Roles

| SPECIFIC TAG | WITH ATTRIBUTE | TO |
|---|---|---|
| ul | id = nav | navigation |
| div | id = hero | main |
| div | class = content-wide | main |
| div | class = content-medium | main |
| div | class = aside | complementary |
| div | id = footer | contentinfo |

**13.** After making the changes, close the Results panel by right-clicking the gray area to the right of the tabs and choosing Close Tab Group. Alternatively, collapse it by pressing F7.

### Embedding a Font with @font-face

Greater font choices in web pages have been a long time coming. Believe it or not, but IE has supported embedded fonts since the release of IE 4 in 1997, and `@font-face` was part of the original CSS2 proposals in 1998. But a combination of technical and licensing problems prevented widespread use of embedded fonts. Now they're truly back on the agenda.

The W3C has published a proposed new standard called Web Open Font Format (WOFF). It has received the backing of many font foundries and is supported in Firefox 3.6, IE 9, and Chrome 5. It's not available in Safari 5 but is expected to be supported in later releases.

WOFF is relatively new but has enjoyed a rapid rate of adoption, leading to the prospect of a standard, unified format for embedded fonts. That still leaves the problem of earlier browsers. Prior to IE 9, IE used a proprietary format called Embedded Open Type (EOT). Opera and Safari currently support TrueType (TTF) and OpenType (OTF).

One solution is to use an online font library service, such as Typekit (http://typekit.com). Instead of storing the font files on your web server, they're downloaded from the font library's content distribution network. The download script detects the correct format to serve the browser, and the library handles all licensing issues on your behalf. A disadvantage—at least in the case of Typekit—is that it doesn't work if JavaScript is disabled in the browser. Some free options are available, but you normally have to pay, and the pricing model varies from company to company.

**TIP**

Using embedded fonts is a complex subject. For detailed coverage, see *Stunning CSS3* by Zoe Mickley Gillenwater (New Riders, 2010).

**NOTES**

At the time of this writing, Calluna Regular is free for unlimited use on websites. Please check the price and license terms applicable at the time of downloading.

Another solution is to use WOFF only and specify several web-safe fonts as backup. You should always specify fallback fonts anyway in case the embedded fonts can't be downloaded. However, for the most reliable cross-browser support, it's best to offer the font files in multiple formats and let the browser choose.

To demonstrate the use of @font-face in Dreamweaver CS5.5, I have chosen a free font called Calluna Regular, which was created by the Dutch font designer Jos Buivenga. The following instructions describe how to obtain the font and embed it with @font-face:

1. Go to www.fontspring.com/fonts/exljbris/calluna, scroll down to Calluna Regular, and click Add to Cart.

2. Go to the checkout. If you haven't used fontspring.com before, you will be asked to create an account.

3. Click the download link, and save the ZIP file to your local hard disk when prompted.

4. Unzip the contents of the file to a new folder. It should contain a folder called web fonts, plus a copy of the license and a file called Calluna-Regular.otf. This last file is for desktop use. It should not be used in your website.

One of the conditions of the web font license is that you must put a link to www.exljbris.nl on your site. Alternatively, you can add a notice to your style sheet crediting the creator of the font.

5.  Inside the web fonts folder is another called calluna_regular_macroman, which contains the following files:

```
Calluna-regular-webfont.eot
Calluna-regular-webfont.svg
Calluna-regular-webfont.ttf
Calluna-regular-webfont.woff
```

These files contain the Calluna Regular font in the various formats needed to support all browsers.

6.  Create a folder called fonts in your working copy of the Tozai Hotel site, and copy the four files from the calluna_regular_macroman folder into the new folder.

7.  Insert the following @font-face rule at the top of styles/tozai.css:

```
@charset "utf-8";
@font-face {
    /* A font by Jos Buivenga (exljbris) ->
        www.exljbris.com */
    font-family: 'CallunaRegular';
    src: url('../fonts/Calluna-Regular-
        ➥ webfont.eot') format('eot');
    src: url('../fonts/Calluna-Regular-
        ➥ webfont.eot?iefix') format('eot'),
        url('../fonts/Calluna-Regular-
        ➥ webfont.woff') format('woff'),
        url('../fonts/Calluna-Regular-
        ➥ webfont.ttf')  format('truetype'),
        url('../fonts/Calluna-Regular-
        ➥ webfont.svg#webfontrsodunSr')
        ➥ format('svg');
}
body {
```

This adds the credit to the font designer, as required by the license, declares CallunaRegular as a font-family property, and then tells the browser where to find the

**NOTES**

Efforts to perfect the `@font-face` syntax to work in a reliable cross-browser way have gone through several iterations. The version shown here is widely acknowledged to be the most reliable—at least at the time of this writing.

font files. For an explanation of the syntax, see www.fontspring.com/blog/further-hardening-of-the-bulletproof-syntax.

The value after the hash sign for the `.svg` file comes from the stylesheet.css file in the calluna_regular_macroman folder. It might be different in the version that you download, so check the value.

8. Now that `CallunaRegular` has been defined with `@font-face`, you can use it in `font-family` property declarations like any other font. Add the following style rule to tozai.css immediately after the `@font-face` declaration:

```
h1, h2, h3 {
    font-family: CallunaRegular, "Palatino
 ↪ Linotype", "Book Antiqua", Palatino,
 ↪ serif;
}
```

9. Save tozai.css, and open one of the HTML pages in the Document window. Activate Live view to see how the font in the headings changes from a heavy sans-serif (**Figure 2.8**) to a more delicate serif (**Figure 2.9**).

**Figure 2.8** Design view displays the headings using the computer's installed font.

**Figure 2.9** Live view uses the embedded font defined by the `@font-face` rule.

## Adding a Drop Shadow to Text

The text-shadow property adds a drop shadow to text without the need for graphics. It's not supported by IE, but IE simply ignores it and renders the text as normal.

The text-shadow property usually takes a space-separated list of four values:

▶ The horizontal distance of the shadow from the text

▶ The vertical distance from the text

▶ The amount of blur

▶ The color of the shadow

The first three values can be expressed in pixels, ems, or any other measurement valid in CSS. The first two values can be positive or negative: Positive values position the shadow to the right and down; negative values move it to the left and up. The third value cannot be negative, although it can be 0, or omitted.

To simplify the application of text-shadow, Dreamweaver CS5.5 provides a subpanel of the CSS Styles panel, which works in conjunction with Live view.

To add a drop shadow to the headings:

1. With one of the Tozai Hotel pages open in the Document window, click anywhere in the text of the <h1> heading, and open the CSS Styles panel. If it's not already selected, click the Current button at the top left of the panel to display the properties for #header h1 (**Figure 2.10**).

2. Activate Live view.

3. Click the Add Property link at the bottom of the Properties pane in the CSS Styles panel, and select text-shadow from the list.

4. Click the ✚ icon displayed to the right of the property name to open the subpanel where you set the text-shadow values.

**NOTES**

The text-shadow property accepts an optional fourth measurement to define how far the shadow spreads in all directions. This is rarely used and is not supported by the Dreamweaver subpanel.

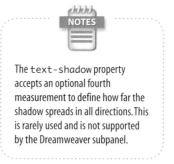

**Figure 2.10** The Properties pane of the CSS Styles panel shows the styles for the main heading.

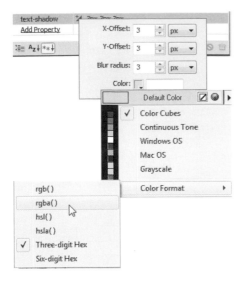

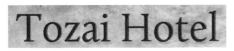

**Figure 2.11** Change the color format for the drop shadow to rgba().

**Figure 2.12** Using opaque black produces an overpowering drop shadow.

**Figure 2.13** Reducing the opacity of the drop shadow results in a subtler effect.

> **TIP**
>
> The Color Picker panel always displays the opacity value as 1, even if you have changed it. When the panel closes, Dreamweaver preserves your original opacity setting but rounds the number to one decimal place. For example, 0.25 is rounded up to 0.3.

5. Set X-Offset, Y-Offset, and Blur radius to **3px** each. You won't see any change in Live view until you set the value for Color.

6. Click the color box at the bottom of the subpanel to open the color picker. Then click the right-facing arrow at the top right of the color picker, and choose Color Format > rgba() (**Figure 2.11**).

7. Use the eyedropper tool to select black, and click away from the color picker to close it. Live view displays a drop shadow on the main heading, but the effect of the opaque black shadow is rather overpowering (**Figure 2.12**).

8. In the Properties pane of the CSS Styles panel, click the field that displays the `text-shadow` setting to edit it, and change the final `rgba()` value from 1 (opaque) to **0.25** (25 percent opacity) like this:

   `3px 3px 3px rgba(0,0,0,0.25)`

9. Press Enter/Return to save the change. Live view updates the drop shadow, which now looks subtler (**Figure 2.13**).

10. If you're not happy with the drop shadow, you can adjust the settings by clicking the ⚒ icon to reopen the subpanel. Live view automatically updates with each change. There's no need to close the subpanel to see the effect. If you decide to change the color, Dreamweaver remembers your choice of color format.

11. With Live view still active, click the heading of the page's main content or of a sidebar to select the properties for the h2, h3 style rule in the Properties pane of the CSS Styles panel.

12. Repeat steps 4–9 to add the `text-shadow` property, setting X-Offset and Y-Offset to **2px**, and Blur radius to **3px** (**Figure 2.14**).

| Properties for "h2, h3" | |
|---|---|
| color | ■ #003 |
| font-size | 26px |
| margin-top | 0px |
| text-shadow | 📐 2px 2px 3px rgba(0,0,0,0.25) |
| Add Property | |

Figure 2.14 The drop shadow offset for the other headings is smaller.

### Adding Shadows to Page Elements

The property that adds a drop shadow to elements other than text is box-shadow. It works almost identically to text-shadow, but the shadow can be inset instead of extending beyond the element. The Dreamweaver box-shadow subpanel also allows you to define how far the shadow spreads in all directions.

**Figure 2.15** demonstrates how box-shadow works. The examples in the top row display the shadow outside the element. Using negative offset values in the example on the right casts the shadow to the left and up. The examples in the middle row use the same offsets and blur radius, but the inset keyword puts the shadow inside the element.

```
box-shadow:
8px 8px 5px #666;
```

```
box-shadow:
-8px -8px 5px #666;
```

```
box-shadow:
inset 8px 8px 5px #666;
```

```
box-shadow:
inset -8px -8px 5px #666;
```

```
box-shadow:
8px 8px 5px 6px #666;
```

```
box-shadow:
8px 8px 5px 12px #666;
```

Figure 2.15 Examples of box-shadow effects.

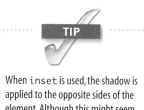

**TIP**

When inset is used, the shadow is applied to the opposite sides of the element. Although this might seem counterintuitive, positive values cast the shadow to the right and down, so it needs to be applied to the left and top sides to remain inside the element. It might help to think of positive values putting the light source at the top left of the page.

The examples in the bottom row add a value for spread, which affects all four directions after the horizontal and vertical offsets have been applied. In the example on the

TIP

You can examine the code in the examples shown in Figures 2.15 and 2.16 in box-shadow.html and multiple_box-shadow.html in the ch02/examples folder.

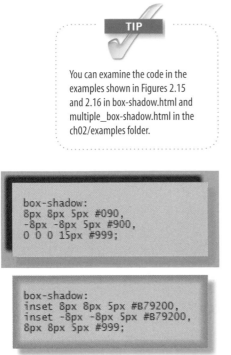

```
box-shadow:
8px 8px 5px #090,
-8px -8px 5px #900,
0 0 0 15px #999;
```

```
box-shadow:
inset 8px 8px 5px #B79200,
inset -8px -8px 5px #B79200,
8px 8px 5px #999;
```

**Figure 2.16** Multiple shadows can be applied as a comma-separated list.

**Figure 2.17** Selecting one of the classes used for images in the CSS Styles panel.

left, the spread (6px) is smaller than the horizontal and vertical offsets (8px). As a result, the spread to the left and top remains hidden behind the element. The spread in the example on the right is greater than the offsets, so a small part of the shadow appears to the left and top, but the main shadow extends to the right and down.

You're not limited to a single shadow. You can apply complex shadow effects by listing a comma-separated list of shadow values as shown in **Figure 2.16**. The top example applies red and green shadows on opposite sides, followed by a gray shadow with no offsets or blur but a 15-pixel spread. The shadows are stacked with each successive one displayed behind its predecessors. The bottom example applies two inset shadows, followed by an external drop shadow.

Using the box-shadow subpanel is very similar to adding text-shadow, but it involves several extra steps, because browser support for box-shadow hasn't reached the same level of stability.

To add drop shadows on page elements:

1.  Open one of the following pages in the Tozai Hotel site—dining.html, garden.html, or rooms.html—and deactivate Live view, if necessary.

2.  In the CSS Styles panel, click the All button at the top left of the panel, and select .floatright in the All Rules pane (**Figure 2.17**).

    Selecting a rule in the All Rules pane before creating a new style rule tells Dreamweaver to insert the new rule immediately after the selected one. This helps keep your style sheet logically organized and easier to maintain.

3.  Click the New Style Rule icon 🗟 at the bottom right of the CSS Styles panel to open the New CSS Rule dialog box.

**4.** Use the following settings:

> ▶ **Selector Type:** Compound
>
> ▶ **Selector Name:** .floatleft, .floatright
>
> ▶ **Rule Definition:** tozai.css

This creates a group selector for the floatleft and floatright classes. All images in the site, apart from background images, use one of these classes. So, this new style rule will affect all inline images.

**5.** Click OK to open the CSS Rule Definition dialog box.

**6.** The box-shadow property is not supported by the CSS Rule Definition dialog box, so click OK to close it and create an empty style rule.

**7.** Check that the new style rule is selected in the All Rules pane, and click the  icon at the bottom left of the CSS Styles panel to switch the Properties pane to Category view.

**8.** Activate Live view, and make sure you can see one of the inline images in the Document window.

**9.** In the Properties pane of the CSS Styles panel, expand the Webkit category, and locate -webkit-box-shadow.

**10.** Click the 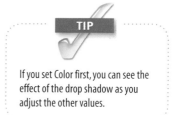 icon next to the property name, and use the following settings:

> ▶ **Inset:** Deselected
>
> ▶ **X-Offset:** 3px
>
> ▶ **Y-Offset:** 3px
>
> ▶ **Blur radius:** 5px
>
> ▶ **Spread:** Leave blank
>
> ▶ **Color:** #999

**NOTES**

Dreamweaver supports comma-separated values for box-shadow in Live view, but you need to code them manually. The subpanel of the CSS Styles panel supports only single shadows.

**TIP**

You need to be in Category view because Dreamweaver CS5.5 needs a vendor-specific version of box-shadow to display the effect in Live view.

**TIP**

If you set Color first, you can see the effect of the drop shadow as you adjust the other values.

11. Click away from the subpanel to close it. The inline images should now have a subtle drop shadow that makes them stand out from the page (**Figure 2.18**).

**Figure 2.18** The box-shadow property adds a subtle drop shadow.

12. The vendor-specific property has done the trick in Dreamweaver, Safari, and Chrome, but it won't work in IE 9 or Firefox. You need to expand the style rule to work cross-browser.

Select the .floatleft, .floatright rule in the All Rules pane, right-click, and choose Go to Code. This opens tozai.css in Split view with the insertion point inside the style definition. Edit the rule to look like this:

```
.floatleft, .floatright {
    -webkit-box-shadow: 3px 3px 5px #999;
    -moz-box-shadow: 3px 3px 5px #999;
    box-shadow: 3px 3px 5px #999;
}
```

NOTES

Opera and IE 9 recognize the standard box-shadow property. Earlier versions of IE ignore the entire style rule.

The values for each property are the same, so the quick way is to copy and paste the -webkit-box-shadow declaration twice, and then edit the property name. Make sure the standard property (without prefix) comes last.

If you would like further practice applying drop shadows, add them to the navigation menu by selecting the #nav li a rule and amending it like this:

```
#nav li a {
    display: block;
    width: 160px;
    padding: 10px;
    text-align: center;
    text-decoration: none;
    color: #FFF;
    background-color: #003;
    -webkit-box-shadow: 2px 2px 3px #999;
    -moz-box-shadow: 2px 2px 3px #999;
    box-shadow: 2px 2px 3px #999;
}
```

Also add a drop shadow to the main content and sidebar containers by selecting the .content-wide, .content-medium, .aside rule and amending it like this:

```
.content-wide, .content-medium, .aside {
    background-color: #fff;
    padding: 20px;
    margin: 20px;
    font-size: 14px;
    -webkit-box-shadow: 3px 3px 5px 2px #999;
    -moz-box-shadow: 3px 3px 5px 2px #999;
    box-shadow: 3px 3px 5px 2px #999;
}
```

## Adding Rounded Corners

The CSS3 border-radius property creates rounded corners in seconds—no more fiddling about with images and nested elements. In spite of its name, the element doesn't need a border to use border-radius. A really cool feature is that it clips background images, so they share the same rounded edge.

### Vendor-specific Properties and the Cascade

The CSS *cascade* controls the way style rules are applied to individual elements, adding together values inherited from higher up the document's structure. When there's a conflict between two style rules of equal importance (specificity), the cascade gives precedence to one lower down in the style sheet. Browsers recognize only their own vendor-specific properties, so you can list them in any order.

You should always list the standard property last. This ensures that the cascade gives precedence to the standard version as soon as a browser supports it. For example, Google Chrome has supported box-shadow in version 9, but earlier versions rely on the -webkit prefix. At the time of this writing, all versions of Safari require the -webkit prefix. Listing box-shadow last ensures that the cascade overrides -webkit-box-shadow and -moz-box-shadow in compliant browsers.

Although you can control each corner individually, there are some inconsistencies between browsers; however, applying the same value to each corner is widely supported.

To apply equally rounded corners to a page element:

1. Open dining.html, garden.html, or reservations.html in the Tozai Hotel site, and activate Live view.

2. Open the CSS Styles panel with the All button at the top left selected.

3. If necessary, click the ⁺⁺↓ icon at the bottom of the panel (it's the third from the left) to display only set properties in the Properties pane.

4. Select the .content-wide, .content-medium, .aside rule in the All Rules pane, and click the Add Property link in the Properties pane.

5. Choose border-radius from the list of properties.

6. Click the ⁺◢ icon next to the property name.

7. Make sure the "Same for all" check box is selected, and set Top Left to 18px. Live view should immediately refresh to display the rounded corners (**Figure 2.19**).

**Figure 2.19** The border-radius property creates rounded corners in seconds.

8. Click away from the subpanel to close it.

9. Although Dreamweaver supports the standard border-radius property, it's wise to use the vendor-specific prefixes as well, so right-click the style rule in the All Rules pane, and choose Go to Code.

**10.** Amend the style rule like this:

```
.content-wide, .content-medium, .aside {
    background-color: #fff;
    padding: 20px;
    margin: 20px;
    font-size: 14px;
    -webkit-box-shadow: 3px 3px 5px 2px #999;
    -moz-box-shadow: 3px 3px 5px 2px #999;
    box-shadow: 3px 3px 5px 2px #999;
    -webkit-border-radius: 18px;
    -moz-border-radius: 18px;
    border-radius: 18px;
}
```

Add rounded corners to the navigation menu by amending the #nav li a rule like this:

```
#nav li a {
    display: block;
    width: 160px;
    padding: 10px;
    text-align: center;
    text-decoration: none;
    color: #FFF;
    background-color: #003;
    -webkit-box-shadow: 2px 2px 3px #999;
    -moz-box-shadow: 2px 2px 3px #999;
    box-shadow: 2px 2px 3px #999;
    -webkit-border-radius: 8px;
    -moz-border-radius: 8px;
    border-radius: 8px;
}
```

Also add rounded corners to the main content of index. html by amending the #hero rule like this:

```
#hero {
    background-color: #FFF;
    background-image: url(../images/exterior.jpg);
    background-repeat: no-repeat;
    background-position: 340px center;
    width: 896px;
    padding: 20px;
    margin: 20px;
    border: #003 solid 2px;
    height: 404px;
    min-height: 404px;
    -webkit-border-radius: 15px;
    -moz-border-radius: 15px;
    border-radius: 15px;
}
```

### Improving Forms with HTML5 Features

HTML5 heralds a quiet revolution in the way you create online forms. What's revolutionary is that HTML5 offers a wide range of new input elements, such as date pickers and number steppers. In addition, when browsers implement all the new features, they will automatically validate user input before submitting the form. No need for JavaScript validation anymore.

The reason it's quiet is because the overwhelming majority of new features use the <input> tag. By default, browsers display a single-line text input field if the type attribute is missing or if they don't recognize the attribute's value. This means you can use the new features now. Existing browsers display them as ordinary text fields. **Table 2.4** describes the new <input> type attributes defined by HTML5.

**TIP**

Client-side validation in the browser is mainly a convenience to the user, avoiding the need for a round-trip to the server if there are any errors. Your form-processing script on the web server should still validate user input, because it's all too easy for spam bots and attackers to evade client-side validation.

TABLE 2.4 New Type Attributes for <input> Elements

| Type | Description |
| --- | --- |
| color | Color picker |
| email | Single-line text field for email address or list of addresses |
| number | Single-line text field or number stepper |
| range | Slider control for numeric value (exact value unimportant) |
| search | Search field |
| tel | Single-line text field for phone number |
| url | Single-line text field for URL |
| datetime | Date and time picker with time zone set to UTC |
| date | Date picker |
| month | Date picker for year and month only |
| week | Date picker for year and week number only |
| time | Time picker |
| datetime-local | Date and time picker for local time zone |

Another new type of form input is a <datalist> element, which associates a list of options with a text input field. It's very similar to a <select> menu but is more versatile, as described in the following section.

TIP

At the time of this writing, Opera is the only desktop browser that supports <datalist>, but it's widely supported on smartphones and tablets.

### Creating an editable drop-down menu

A <select> menu provides users with a list of options to choose from. It works fine when there's a fixed range of options, but there's often a need to supply a text field for users to enter a different value. The <datalist> element avoids this problem by displaying a preset list of options but allowing the user to enter a custom option. **Figure 2.20** shows how it works. The <datalist> offers the preset options of Mr., Mrs., and Ms. but allows the user to type in another value, such as Dr.

**Figure 2.20** The <datalist> element creates an editable <select> menu.

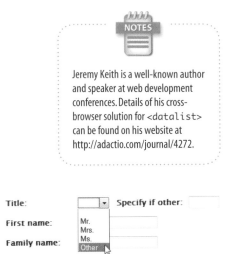

Jeremy Keith is a well-known author and speaker at web development conferences. Details of his cross-browser solution for <datalist> can be found on his website at http://adactio.com/journal/4272.

Figure 2.21 Normally, a separate text input field is needed for user input.

Thanks to some clever experimentation by Jeremy Keith, it's possible to incorporate a <datalist> into a form so that it works seamlessly in browsers that support it and provides an elegant fallback for browsers that don't.

The form in reservations.html in the Tozai Hotel site contains a <select> menu for the user's title with the options Mr., Mrs., Ms., and Other. Next to the menu is a text input field for users to type a value if they choose Other (**Figure 2.21**).

The code for the two form elements looks like this:

```
<label for="title">Title: </label>
    <select name="title" id="title">
        <option> </option>
        <option>Mr.</option>
        <option>Mrs.</option>
        <option>Ms.</option>
        <option>Other</option>
    </select>
<label for="other">Specify if other:</label>
<input name="other" class="narrowField" id="other">
```

Notice that the <option> elements don't contain a value attribute. When you omit this attribute, the browser automatically submits the value between the opening and closing tags of the selected item.

You need to edit the code manually, but Dreamweaver CS5.5 helps with code hints for <datalist>. The following instructions explain the process:

1. On a new line between the first <label> element and the opening <select> tag, create the opening <datalist> tag and give it an ID like this:

```
<datalist id="titlelist">
```

The ID associates the <datalist> with the text input field.

2. Delete the ID from the opening <select> tag. Only the *name* attribute is required.

3. Set an explicit value attribute for the Mr. option:

```
<option value="Mr.">Mr.</option>
```

4. Do the same for the Mrs. and Ms. options but *not* for Other.

5. Replace the <label> tags around "Specify with other" with <span> tags.

6. Change the *name* and *id* attributes of the <input> element to match the name of the <select> element (title).

7. Add list="titlelist" to the <input> tag. This identifies the <datalist> options as belonging to this field.

The finished code looks like this (with the changes highlighted):

```
<label for="title">Title: </label>
    <datalist id="titlelist">
        <select name="title">
            <option> </option>
            <option value="Mr.">Mr.</option>
            <option value="Mrs.">Mrs.</option>
            <option value="Ms.">Ms.</option>
            <option>Other</option>
        </select>
        <span>If other, please specify:</span>
    </datalist>
<input name="title" class="narrowField"
➥ id="title" list="titlelist">
```

On its own, a <datalist> consists only of the <option> elements. It's linked to an <input> element through the list attribute, which is set to the <datalist> ID. According to the HTML5 specification, the <datalist> must be hidden by the browser. What's clever about Jeremy Keith's solution is that it borrows the <option> elements of the <select>

Figure 2.22 The Tag Inspector panel provides access to HTML5 form attributes.

menu for the `<datalist>`. If a browser recognizes the `<datalist>` element, it hides the `<select>` menu but uses its `<option>` tags. The `<datalist>` ignores `<option>` elements that don't have an explicit value attribute. Browsers that don't recognize `<datalist>` ignore the tag and display the `<select>` menu instead. Everyone's happy!

In step 5, you replaced the `<label>` tags with `<span>` tags, so the adjacent sibling style rule needs to be amended like this to maintain the padding in browsers that don't yet support `<datalist>`:

```
select + label, input + label, select + span {
        padding-left: 10px;
}
```

To fix a problem with WebKit browsers, you also need to add the following style rule to the style sheet:

```
datalist {
    display: inline-block;
}
```

### Using HTML5 attributes with form elements

In addition to the new values for the type attribute, HTML5 introduces new attributes, such as autofocus and placeholder to improve usability, and required to aid validation. To add or change any of these attributes, use the code hints in Code view, or select the `<input>` element in Design view and use the Tag Inspector panel. **Figure 2.22** shows changes made to the Adult `<input>` tag, setting type to number, min to 1, and max to 4, and turning on the required attribute.

In browsers that support the number type, the input field is displayed as a number stepper (**Figure 2.23**). If the min and max attributes are set, the number stepper limits values to that range. Opera allows you to type in a number directly but displays an alert when you submit the form with an out-of-range value (**Figure 2.24**).

TIP

For an in-depth discussion of HTML5 form elements and attributes, see *Introducing HTML5* by Bruce Lawson and Remy Sharp (New Riders, 2010).

**Adults:** 2

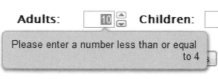

**Figure 2.23** HTML5-compliant browsers display number input fields as number steppers.

**Figure 2.24** Opera automatically displays an error message for out-of-range values.

### Choosing a foolproof date picker

Inputting dates is a minefield. Europeans write dates in the order date, month, year. Chinese and Japanese reverse the order: year, month, date. Americans use the format month, date, year. Even if you can force users to input dates in a particular order, there's always a danger of choosing an invalid date, such as September 31. HTML5 seeks to solve this problem with the date type. Opera has pioneered the way by automatically displaying a date picker when you click in a date field (**Figure 2.25**).

Chrome 9 offers a different solution—a date field that acts like a number stepper. However, users are in for a shock if you don't also set the min attribute to a recent date. **Figure 2.26** shows what happens when the user first clicks the stepper arrow. To get to today's date, you would need to click more than 730,000 times!

You can avoid this problem by setting a min value using the yyyy-mm-dd format. For example, the following code starts the date stepper at February 7, 2011:

```
<input name="date" type="date" min="2011-02-07">
```

That's still not much use if you want users to enter their date of birth. Until there's reliable cross-browser support for the date type, you need an alternative solution. One that I experimented with for this book was using <select> elements for the year and month, combined with a text input field for the date. I then used jQuery to hide the year and month menus, and displayed a jQuery UI Datepicker widget (http://jqueryui.com/demos/datepicker) when the focus was in the date field. A browser with JavaScript enabled would use the widget. Otherwise, the user would fill in separate fields for each date part.

**Figure 2.25** Opera's date picker is automatic—no coding is required.

**Figure 2.26** Chrome's date stepper goes back in the mists of time.

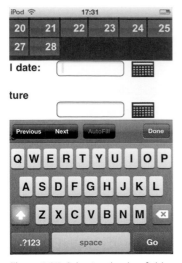

**Figure 2.27** Selecting the date field brings up both the widget and the mobile keyboard.

**TIP**

The script is also in custom_datepicker.js in ch02/complete/js. If you want to use it in your own pages, give the `<select>` menus the same IDs as those used in reservations.html.

It worked beautifully—until I tested it on several mobile devices. **Figure 2.27** shows what happened on an iPod touch. Triggering the widget also popped up the mobile keyboard, cluttering the screen and making it very difficult to use.

To prevent the mobile keyboard from appearing, I used jQuery to make the date field read-only. However, tests on a BlackBerry Torch revealed that the widget didn't always render correctly. With browser sniffing, I was able to restrict making the field read-only on iOS and Android, but that meant that BlackBerry users still had to dismiss the mobile keyboard to access the widget.

In the end, I decided that the most reliable cross-browser solution was to create three `<select>` menus, one each for the month, date, and year. When JavaScript is disabled, the values default to January 1, 2011. However, if JavaScript is enabled in the browser, a jQuery script initializes the arrival and departure dates to today and tomorrow, respectively. The script automatically resets the number of days in the date `<select>` menu to match the month, taking leap year into account when the month is February. It also prevents the user from setting dates in the past or setting a departure date that isn't at least one day after arrival.

It's a long script, so I have broken it into sections to explain how it works. Add the following code just before the closing `</body>` tag in reservations.html.

```
<script type="text/javascript" src="js/
➥ jquery-1.5.min.js"></script>
<script>
$(function() {
    // initialize variable for date parts
    var dateParts;

    // create object for select menus
    // set all parts of a specific date
    // return Date object for next day
    // limit year to current and following years
    // adjust date options according to month
```

```
    // return number of days in selected month
    // change handler for select menus
    // run the script
});
</script>
```

This includes the jQuery core library into the page, and creates a <script> block with a jQuery document-ready handler, which runs automatically as soon as the page loads. Apart from declaring a single variable, the document-ready handler doesn't yet do anything. The series of comments outlines the structure of the script. Each of the following sections needs to be added under the appropriate comment.

The first section is a function that creates a JavaScript object with properties that store a reference to each of the <select> menus in the page using jQuery selectors. It looks like this:

```
// create object for select menus
function initMenus() {
    var menus = {};
    menus.arr_month = $('#arrival_month');
    menus.arr_date = $('#arrival_date');
    menus.arr_year = $('#arrival_year');
    menus.dep_month = $('#departure_month');
    menus.dep_date = $('#departure_date');
    menus.dep_year = $('#departure_year');
    return menus;
}
```

This function is used to store an object in dateParts, which is passed as an argument to subsequent functions. Each property name consists of arr_ or dep_ followed by the date part. This naming convention is designed so that the same functions can be used to set the arrival and departure dates.

**TIP**

Creating an object to reference the <select> menus avoids using global variables within the functions that adjust the date parts.

The next part of the script is a function that sets all parts of a specific date. It looks like this:

```
// set all parts of a specific date
function setValues(dateParts, menu, theDate) {
    // advance date by one day for departure menu
    if (menu == 'dep') {
        theDate = getNextDay(theDate);
    }
    // get the individual date parts
    var m = theDate.getMonth() + 1,
        d = theDate.getDate(),
        y = theDate.getFullYear(),
        today = new Date();
    // adjust options for date and year menus
    populateDate(dateParts, menu, m, y);
    populateYear(dateParts, menu,
    ➥ today.getFullYear());
    // set the values for each select menu
    dateParts[menu + '_month'].val(m);
    dateParts[menu + '_date'].val(d);
    dateParts[menu + '_year'].val(y);
}
```

The `setValues()` function takes three arguments:

▶ The `dateParts` object containing references to the `<select>` menus

▶ A string (`'arr'` or `'dep'`) identifying whether to set the arrival or departure date

▶ A JavaScript `Date` object representing the date to be set

When the page first loads, the arrival date is set to the current date, and the departure is set to the following day. So, if the value of menu is `'dep'`, the `Date` object in `theDate` is advanced by one day by a function called `getNextDay()`, which is defined shortly.

**CLOSE-UP**

**JavaScript Dates**

JavaScript stores dates and times as the number of milliseconds before or after midnight UTC (Coordinated Universal Time) on January 1, 1970. The valid range is plus or minus 100 million days (273,785 years) from this date.

If no arguments are passed to the `Date` constructor, an object representing the current date and time (to the nearest millisecond) is created. Alternatively, you can create a `Date` object for a specific date and time using any of the following:

▶ An integer representing the number of milliseconds since January 1, 1970

▶ A date string, such as `'05 May 2011'`

▶ A comma-separated list of integers, representing date parts in the order year, month, date, hour, minutes, seconds, milliseconds

Care needs to be taken when using a date string, because the syntax can be difficult to get right. When using a comma-separated list of date parts, the last four values are optional. JavaScript counts months from zero, so 4 represents May, not April.

See https://developer.mozilla.org/en/JavaScript/Reference/Global_Objects/Date.

The function then uses standard JavaScript Date methods to assign the date part values to local variables. JavaScript counts months from zero, so 1 is added to the value assigned to m.

To prevent incorrect dates from being selected, the function calls two other functions, populateDate() and populateYear(), to adjust the values displayed by the date and year <select> menus. These functions are described later.

Finally, setValues() uses the jQuery val() method to set the values of the <select> menus, using square bracket notation to access the appropriate properties of the date-Parts object. For example, if 'arr' is passed as the second argument to setValues(), the last three lines of the function equate to this:

```
dateParts['arr_month'].val(m);
dateParts['arr_date'].val(d);
dateParts['arr_year'].val(y);
```

This is the equivalent of using the following dot notation to access the object's properties:

```
dateParts.arr_month.val(m);
dateParts.arr_date.val(d);
dateParts.arr_year.val(y);
```

The getNextDay() function is defined next. It takes a Date object as its sole argument, and returns a new Date object for the following day by adding the number of milliseconds in 24 hours to the current value. The code looks like this:

```
// return Date object for next day
function getNextDay(date) {
    return new Date(date.getTime() +
    ➥ (1000*60*60*24));
}
```

**TIP**

Using square bracket notation to access object properties makes it possible to build the property name from a combination of a variable and a string literal. You can't build property names dynamically with dot notation.

The next two functions adjust the values in the year and date <select> menus, taking into account the number of days in a month and whether it's a leap year. The code looks like this:

```
// limit year to current and following years
function populateYear(dateParts, menu, yr) {
    dateParts[menu + '_year'].html('<option>' + yr
    ↪ + '</option>' +
    '<option>' + (yr + 1) + '</option>');
}
```

```
// adjust date options according to month
function populateDate(dateParts, menu, mon, yr) {
    var len = getNumDays(mon, yr);
    var html = '';
    for (var i = 1; i <= len; i+=1) {
        html += '<option>' + i + '</option>';
    }
    dateParts[menu + '_date'].html(html);
}
```

Both functions use the jQuery html() method to generate a new set of <option> elements to replace the existing ones. The populateYear() function limits the years displayed to the current and following years. The populateDate() function takes both the year and month among its arguments, because February has 28 or 29 days depending on whether it's a leap year. The calculation regarding the number of days to display is carried out by getNumDays(), which is defined next.

```
// return number of days in selected month
function getNumDays(mon, yr) {
    var num_days = 31;
    if (mon == 4 || mon == 6 || mon == 9 ||
    ↪ mon == 11) {
        num_days = 30;
    } else if (mon == 2) {
        // if leap year, Feb has 29 days
```

```
        if (yr % 400 == 0 ||
          ➥(yr % 4 == 0 && yr % 100 != 0)) {
            num_days = 29;
        } else {
            num_days = 28;
        }
    }
    return num_days;
}
```

The getNumDays() function takes two arguments: a month and a year. Most months have 31 days, so that's set as the default value of the local variable num_days. If the month is April, June, September, or November, the value of num_days is changed to 30. The else if clause checks if the month is February and calculates the correct number of days.

The nested conditional statement uses modulo division to calculate whether it's a leap year. Leap years occur every four years on years wholly divisible by 4. The exception is that years divisible by 100 are not leap years unless they are also divisible by 400.

The main part of this script is the change handler function bound to all six <select> menus. It looks like this:

```
// change handler for select menus
function resetDates(e) {
    // find out whether arrival or departure
    // was changed, and get its value
    var dateParts = e.data.dateParts,
        menu = e.data.menu,
        m = dateParts[menu + '_month'].val(),
        d = dateParts[menu + '_date'].val(),
        y = dateParts[menu + '_year'].val(),
        num_days = getNumDays(m, y),
        today = new Date(),
        selected, arrival, departure;
    // make sure date menu displays
    // correct number of days
    populateDate(dateParts, menu, m, y);
    // if the month contains fewer days than
```

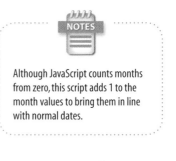

**CLOSE-UP**

**Modulo Division**

Modulo division uses the percentage sign (%) as its operator and produces the remainder left over after a division. If a number is wholly divisible by another, the remainder is zero. For example, 2000 is wholly divisible by 400, so 2000 % 400 produces 0 as its result.

Modulo division by 2 is frequently used to find whether a number is odd or even. If the result is 0, the number is even.

```
                        // currently selected value, reset date
                        // menu to last day of month
                        d = (d <= num_days) ? d : num_days;
                        dateParts[menu + '_date'].val(d);
                        // create Date objects for selected dates
                        selected = new Date(y, m-1, d);
                        arrival = new Date(dateParts.arr_year.val(),
                                    dateParts.arr_month.val()-1,
                                    dateParts.arr_date.val());
                        departure = new Date(dateParts.dep_year.val(),
                                      dateParts.dep_month.val()-1,
                                      dateParts.dep_date.val());
                        // if changes were made to arrival date
                        if (menu == 'arr') {
                            // if the arrival earlier than today,
                            // reset to today's date
                            if (selected < today) {
                                setValues(dateParts, 'arr', today);
                                setValues(dateParts, 'dep', today);
                            }
                            if (departure <= selected) {
                                // set departure date to following day
                                setValues(dateParts, 'dep', arrival);
                            }
                        } else {
                            // if selected departure is today or
                            // earlier, reset both dates to default
                            if (selected <= today) {
                                setValues(dateParts, 'arr', today);
                                setValues(dateParts, 'dep', today);
                            } else if (selected <= arrival) {
                                // if selected departure date is same
                                // as arrival date or earlier, reset
                                // departure to one day after arrival
                                setValues(dateParts, 'dep', arrival);
                            }
                        }
                    }
```

The resetDates() function is bound to each <select> menu using the jQuery change() method. The function takes as its only argument the event object triggered by a change in the value of the <select> menu to which the function is bound. To allow you to pass other values to an event-handler function, jQuery creates a data property on the event object. You'll see how to pass these values shortly, but you retrieve them from the data property through dot notation like this:

```
var dateParts = e.data.dateParts,
    menu = e.data.menu, // more definitions
```

This gives you access to the dateParts object and the string identifying whether the value that has changed belongs to the arrival or departure date. With this information, the resetDates() function gets the current values for each part of the affected date and calculates the correct number of days in the month. The populateDate() function resets the <option> tags for the date menu. But before you can set the value of the date part, you need to find out if the current value exceeds the number of days in the month. For example, if the original date is January 31 and you change the month to September, you end up with an invalid date. So, the following line uses the ternary operator to reset d to num_days if the month is shorter:

```
d = (d <= num_days) ? d : num_days;
```

If d is less than or equal to num_days, its original value is preserved.

The jQuery val() method then sets the date menu to the correct value, and three Date objects are created. The first of these Date objects, selected, represents the complete value of the date that has just been changed. The other two Date objects represent the arrival and departure dates, respectively. The rest of the function consists of a series of conditional statements that prevent the arrival date from being earlier than the current date, and ensuring that the departure date is at least one day after the arrival date.

**Ternary Operator**

The ternary operator is a shorthand way of assigning a value using a simple if/else condition. The condition is placed between the assignment operator (an equal sign) and a question mark. If the condition equates to true, the value between the question mark and a colon is assigned. If the condition is false, the value after the colon is assigned.

The line of code that uses the ternary operator in resetDates() can be rewritten like this:

```
if (d <= num_days) {
    d = d;
} else {
    d = num_days;
}
```

Finally, add the code to run the script:

```
// run the script
dateParts = initMenus();
// set initial menu values to today and tomorrow
setValues(dateParts, 'arr', new Date());
setValues(dateParts, 'dep', new Date());

// bind the resetDates function as the onchange
//event handler to each select menu
$('#arrival_date, #arrival_month, #arrival_year')
    .change({dateParts: dateParts, menu: 'arr'},
    ↪ resetDates);
$('#departure_date, #departure_month,
↪ #departure_year')
    .change({dateParts: dateParts, menu: 'dep'},
    ↪ resetDates);
});
```

This initializes the menus and sets the arrival and departure dates to today and tomorrow, respectively. The resetDates() function is then bound to each select menu as its onchange event handler. The first argument to the jQuery change() method is an object literal containing the values to be passed to the resetDates() function. In both cases, the dateParts object is assigned to a property of the same name. The menu property for the arrival date menus is set to 'arr', and for the departure date, it's set to 'dep'. As you saw earlier, you access these values in resetDates() through the data property of the event object.

Prior to version 1.4.3, the jQuery change() method does not support passing an object literal as an argument. If you're using an earlier version of jQuery, you must use the bind() method like this:

```
$('#arrival_date, #arrival_month, #arrival_year')
    .bind('change', {dateParts: dateParts, menu:
    ↪ 'arr'}, resetDates);
$('#departure_date, #departure_month,
↪ #departure_year')
    .bind('change', {dateParts: dateParts, menu:
    ↪ 'dep'}, resetDates);
```

Even with all the comments, the script is a lightweight 5 KB. Contrast that with the jQuery UI Datepicker widget, which is approximately 115 KB and consists of 16 files. For desktop use, the widget is excellent. But for a site likely to be accessed on mobile devices, the smaller the file size, the better.

### Validating the Adapted Pages

Dreamweaver CS5.5 restores the option to validate your pages within the Document window. However, instead of relying on its own validating tool, Dreamweaver now uploads your files to the W3C validator.

To validate a page:

1. In the Document window, open one of the pages you have edited.

2. Make sure you're connected to the Internet, and choose File > Validate > Validate Current Document (W3C).

    Dreamweaver displays an alert telling you that it will send the document to the W3C validation service. If you don't want to see this every time you validate a document, select the "Don't show this dialog again" check box.

3. Dreamweaver connects to the W3C and displays the results in the W3C Validation tab of the Results panel (**Figure 2.28**).

**NOTES**

Adobe removed the internal validator from Dreamweaver CS5 because it occasionally produced inaccurate results. Because HTML5 is still evolving, it was decided to entrust validation to the most reliable source, the W3C. You must be online to validate pages.

**TIP**

Server-side code, such as PHP or ColdFusion, needs to be parsed by a web server before it can be submitted to the validator. Specify a testing server in the Site Setup dialog box, make sure the server is running, and activate Live view. Then choose File > Validate > Validate Live Document (W3C). Validate only complete pages, not individual include files.

| SEARCH | REFERENCE | W3C VALIDATION | BROWSER COMPATIBILITY | LINK CHECKER |
|---|---|---|---|---|

| File/URL | Line | Description |
|---|---|---|
| ch02\working\dining.html | | No errors or warnings found. [HTML5] |

Current document validation complete [ 0 Errors, 0 Warnings, 0 Hidden ]

**Figure 2.28** Confirmation that the edited page is valid HTML5.

4. To test other pages, open the page first in the Document window. You can then click the right-facing triangle at the top left of the Results panel, and choose Validate Current Document (W3C).

5. Test reservations.html. As **Figure 2.29** shows, it fails validation because HTML5 doesn't permit an empty value for the `action` attribute in the opening `<form>` tag.

**Figure 2.29** HTML5 doesn't allow the form `action` attribute to be empty.

| SEARCH | REFERENCE | W3C VALIDATION | BROWSER COMPATIBILITY | LINK CHECKER | SITE REPORTS | FTP LOG | SERVER |
|---|---|---|---|---|---|---|---|
| File/URL | | Line | Description | | | | |
| ch02\working\reservatio... | | 23 | Bad value  for attribute action on element form: Must be non-empty. [HTML5] | | | | |

6. Double-click the error report or right-click and choose Go to Line from the context menu. This takes you to the line that needs to be edited.

7. Delete `action=""`, save the page, and revalidate it. This time it passes without errors.

## Sacrificing a Uniform Look

HTML5 and CSS3 often speed up development and result in less code and use of decorative images. Smaller page downloads are particularly important for sites that will be viewed on mobile devices. Using CSS3 for rounded corners and drop shadows means sacrificing those effects in earlier browsers. But as long as you provide an acceptable basic design for them, it's a sacrifice worth making. Attempting to make websites look identical in every browser makes little sense when increasing numbers of people browse the web on a variety of devices—a desktop in the office, a smartphone while commuting, and a tablet at home.

To see what the Tozai Hotel website looks like after its transformation with HTML5 and CSS3, view ch02/complete in a variety of desktop browsers. The next chapter takes the transformation further with the help of CSS media queries to prepare the site for viewing on mobile devices using different screen resolutions.

**NOTES**

The `action` attribute tells the browser where to submit the form for processing. If it's missing, the browser simply reloads the page. A common technique with a server-side language, such as PHP, is to use what's known as a self-processing form. The processing script is wrapped in a conditional statement in a code block above the DOCTYPE declaration, and it runs when the page reloads. Processing the contents of forms is beyond the scope of this book. To learn about processing forms with PHP, see my book *Dreamweaver CS5 with PHP: Training from the Source* (Adobe Press, 2010).

**NOTES**

The files in ch02/complete do not include the Calluna Regular font. You should download the font files directly to obtain a personal license to use them.

# CHAPTER

# 3

# Adapting Pages for Mobile with Media Queries

*The great source of pleasure is variety. Uniformity
must tire at last, though it be uniformity of excellence.*
—Samuel Johnson

# Adapting Pages for Mobile with Media Queries

The need for dedicated style sheets for mobile devices was recognized as far back as 1997, when the HTML and CSS specifications included handheld among the permitted values for the media attribute. However, the specifications describe handheld devices as "small screen, monochrome, [and] limited bandwidth." Apart from screen size, modern smartphones and tablets frequently have capabilities that rival and even surpass desktops. Fortunately, the W3C had the foresight to establish rules for the way browsers should handle the media attribute, paving the way for future extensions. The result is the CSS3 Media Queries module, which allows you to specify rules for different devices through simple queries about the device's features, such as screen width, device width, color depth, and orientation.

The W3C began work on media queries in 2001, and the specification has reached a high level of maturity and stability. According to http://caniuse.com, all modern browsers, including Internet Explorer (IE) 9, support media queries (**Figure 3.1**). Perhaps most important of all, media queries are well supported by iOS and Android. As a result, they're ideal for delivering different styles to smartphones and tablets. The problem, as usual, is lack of support by IE 6–8, but you can overcome this with a little planning.

In this chapter, you'll learn how to use media queries to adapt the styles for the Tozai Hotel website from Chapter 2 for display on smartphones and tablets. Although Dreamweaver provides the tools that assist in the process of designing for devices with different screen resolutions, the success of designing a site with media queries relies principally on your knowledge of CSS.

| CSS3 Media Queries - Candidate Recommendation | | | | | | | | Global user stats*: | | |
|---|---|---|---|---|---|---|---|---|---|---|
| Method of applying styles based on media information. Includes things like page and device dimensions | | | | | | | | Support: | | 49.41% |
| | | | | | | | | Partial support: | | 0.07% |
| | | | | | | | | Total: | | 49.48% |
| Resources: IE demo page with information   Demo page for page width | | | | | | | | | | |
| | IE | Firefox | Safari | Chrome | Opera | iOS Safari | Opera Mini | Opera Mobile | Android Browser | |
| Two versions back | 6.0 | 3.0 | 3.2 | 7.0 | 10.5 | 3.2 | | | 2.1 | |
| Previous version | 7.0 | 3.5 | 4.0 | 8.0 | 10.6 | 4.0-4.1 | | | 2.2 | |
| Current | 8.0 | 3.6 | 5.0 | 9.0 | 11.0 | 4.2 | 5.0 | 10.0 | 2.3 | |
| Near Future (early 2011) | | 4.0 | | 10.0 | 11.1 | | | | | |
| Future (mid/late 2011) | 9.0 | 5.0 | 6.0 | 11.0 | | | | | | |

**Note:** Incomplete support by older webkit browsers refers to only acknowledging different media rules on page reload     Feedback

**Figure 3.1** Browser support for media queries.

The range of screen sizes on mobile devices is bewildering, so your designs need to be flexible. Some devices automatically reflow the layout when you switch from portrait to landscape orientation and vice versa. Others preserve the layout and scale the display. This involves testing the design on as many mobile devices as possible, and inevitably leads to some compromises. Don't expect the redesign to be a five-minute job. It's a lot of work, but the result can be very satisfying.

Let's first take a look at how media queries work.

## Understanding Media Queries

The media attribute lets you specify which types of devices should use your style rules. For example, the screen media type is intended primarily for color computer screens, whereas print is intended for printers.

Media queries allow you not only to specify the media type, but also to set conditions, such as minimum or maximum screen width. Therefore, you can optimize your sites for different devices, sending one set of style rules to desktop computers and other rules to mobile phones and tablets. You set the conditions using one or more of the *media features*

NOTES

For a full list of media types and their intended uses, see www.w3.org/TR/CSS21/media.html#media-types.

listed in **Table 3.1** to describe the characteristics of the target devices.

TABLE 3.1 Media Features for Setting Conditions in Media Queries

| FEATURE | VALUE | MIN/MAX | DESCRIPTION |
| --- | --- | --- | --- |
| width | Length | Yes | Width of display area |
| height | Length | Yes | Height of display area |
| device-width | Length | Yes | Width of rendering area |
| device-height | Length | Yes | Height of rendering area |
| orientation | portrait or landscape | No | Orientation of device |
| aspect-ratio | Ratio | Yes | Ratio of width to height |
| device-aspect-ratio | Ratio | Yes | Ratio of device-width to device-height |
| color | Integer | Yes | Number of bits per color component (if not color, the value is 0) |
| color-index | Integer | Yes | Number of entries in output device's color lookup table |
| monochrome | Integer | Yes | Number of bits per pixel in the monochrome frame buffer (if not monochrome, the value is 0) |
| resolution | Resolution | Yes | Density of pixels of output device |
| scan | progressive or interlace | No | Scanning process used by TV devices |
| grid | 0 or 1 | No | If set to 1, this specifies that the device is grid-based, such as a teletype terminal or a phone display with only one fixed font (all other devices are 0) |

You can prefix most media features by min- or max- to indicate minimum or maximum values. For example, in addition to width, you can use min-width and max-width to specify a condition. The Min/Max column in Table 3.1 indicates which media features you can prefix this way.

You specify the value for a media feature after a colon in the same way you do for a CSS property. Each condition is wrapped in parentheses and added to the media declaration using the keyword and.

For example, the following media query targets visual displays with a minimum width of 361 pixels:

```
media="screen and (min-width: 361px)"
```

To restrict the targeted devices to displays in the range of 361–768 pixels, add a second condition like this:

```
media="screen and (min-width: 361px) and
➥ (max-width: 768px)"
```

Some media features, such as color, grid, and monochrome, can be used as conditions without specifying a value. For example, the following targets all color visual displays:

```
media="screen and (color)"
```

### Hiding Styles from Earlier Browsers

Browsers that don't recognize media queries expect a comma-separated list of media types, and the specifications say they should truncate each value immediately before the first nonalphanumeric character that isn't a hyphen. So, with all the examples in the preceding section, IE 6 and other noncompliant browsers should simply see this:

```
media="screen"
```

As a result, style rules intended for a particular type of device should also be displayed by noncompliant browsers. If you don't want this to happen, precede the media type with the keyword only like this:

```
media="only screen and (min-width:361px) and
➥ (max-width:768px)"
```

Browsers that don't recognize media queries should truncate the value just before the first space like this:

```
media="only"
```

In the Value column of Table 3.1, length refers to a number followed immediately by a unit of measure valid in CSS, such as *em* or *px*. Ratios are expressed as two integers separated by a forward slash, for example 16/9. The forward slash can optionally be surrounded by spaces. So, 16 / 9 is equally valid. Resolution is expressed as an integer immediately followed by *dpi* (dots per inch) or *dpcm* (dots per centimeter).

The full media queries specification is at www.w3.org/TR/css3-mediaqueries. It's quite short and easy to understand. It also contains many examples.

**IE Conditional Comments**

IE conditional comments are extremely useful for hiding from other browsers code that you want to be seen only by IE. For example, you can wrap a link to an external style sheet in an IE conditional comment to serve a special set of styles to specific versions of IE. Although IE conditional comments use proprietary Microsoft code, they're wrapped in standard HTML comment tags, so your code remains valid and other browsers ignore them.

The basic structure of an IE conditional comment looks like this:

```
<!--[if condition]>
Content seen only by IE
<![endif]-->
```

The *condition* is built using an optional comparison operator followed by IE and an optional version number. The main comparison operators are

▶ `lt` (less than)

▶ `lte` (less than or equal to)

▶ `gt` (greater than)

▶ `gte` (greater than or equal to)

For example, the following IE conditional comment applies to IE 8 and earlier:

```
<!--[if lte IE 8]>
Content seen by IE 6–8
<![endif]-->
```

All other browsers—including IE 9—ignore the content inside the conditional comment.

There is no only media type, so the style rules are completely ignored by earlier browsers.

Unfortunately, IE 6–8 failed to implement the specification correctly. If you have access to any of these versions of IE, try the following experiment to see what happens when they encounter a media query.

1. Open dining.html from your work folder in the previous chapter (or use the file in the ch02/complete folder) and switch to Code view or Split view.

2. In the `<link>` tag that attaches the style sheet, add a media query like this (on line 6):

```
<link href="styles/tozai.css" rel="stylesheet"
➥ type="text/css" media="screen and
➥ (min-width:768px)">
```

3. Save dining.html and view it in one of the browsers listed in Figure 3.1 as supporting media queries. As long as the viewport is at least 768 pixels wide, the page remains fully styled. **Figure 3.2** shows what it looks like in Chrome.

4. Now view the same page in IE 6, IE 7, or IE 8. Although browsers that don't recognize media queries should truncate the `media` attribute to `media="screen"` and apply the styles, the page is completely unstyled. **Figure 3.3** shows the page in IE 7.

To ensure that your pages are styled in IE 6–8, you need to create a basic style sheet that is processed by all browsers and use media queries to override the styles for tablets and mobile phones. Alternatively, use an *IE conditional comment* to add a special style sheet for IE 6–8. Sometimes, a combination of both approaches is needed, as you'll see later in this chapter.

**Figure 3.2** The page displays as expected in a browser that recognizes media queries.

**Figure 3.3** Prior to IE 9, media queries result in IE completely ignoring the style sheet.

## Using Conditions with @media and @import

You can also make CSS @import and @media rules conditional using the same media query syntax. For example, the following @import rule loads the styles in phone.css only if the display is no wider than 360 pixels:

```
@import url("phone.css") screen and (max-width:
➡ 360px);
```

To hide the same @import rule from browsers that don't recognize media queries, add the only keyword like this:

```
@import url("phone.css") only screen and
➥ (max-width:360px);
```

Inside a style sheet, you can use an @media rule to set conditions for the use of certain style rules like this:

```
@media only screen and (max-width:360px) {
    #header h1 {
        font-size:36px;
    }
}
```

The style rule inside this @media block is applied only to displays no wider than 360 pixels.

### Specifying Width and Height

Dealing with width and height on mobile devices is like stepping into a minefield. First of all, the media queries specification draws a distinction between width and device-width, and similarly between height and device-height. According to the specification:

▶ width and height are the dimensions of the viewport, including any scrollbars.

▶ device-width and device-height are the dimensions of the screen.

In the case of desktop computers, this is an important difference, because not everyone runs a browser full screen. When it comes to mobile devices, the distinction is less clear. Mobile browsers fill the available screen, so it's not unreasonable to expect width and device-width to have the same meaning. Unfortunately, it's not so simple.

Apple has created its own definition of the viewport on the iPhone and iPod touch. Instead of regarding the viewport as the visible area of the 320 × 480-pixel screen, Apple sets it to a default width of 980 pixels. Consequently, if you use width, min-width, or max-width in media queries, the iPhone and iPod touch apply styles intended for a desktop version rather than those optimized for a mobile phone. The result is impossible to read without rescaling (**Figure 3.4**).

Using the device-width media features doesn't really improve the situation. The iPhone and iPod touch still treat the viewport as 980 pixels wide. As a result, fluid layouts become unacceptably stretched horizontally (**Figure 3.5**).

Fortunately, Apple has provided a simple solution: a new <meta> tag to control the viewport. Many other mobile phone manufacturers have adopted the viewport <meta> tag; those that haven't simply ignore it.

### Using the viewport <meta> tag

To ensure that styles are applied correctly through media queries, use the width, min-width, and max-width media features rather than those related to device-width, and add the following code in the <head> of your web pages:

```
<meta name="viewport" content="width=
➥ device-width">
```

This constrains the viewport in compliant mobile devices to the physical width of the screen (**Figure 3.6**).

**Figure 3.4** An iPod touch displays the desktop version instead of the styles optimized for a mobile phone.

**Figure 3.5** Using a device-width media query still treats the viewport as 980 pixels wide.

**Figure 3.6** The viewport <meta> tag ensures that the styles are applied correctly.

The content attribute in the viewport <meta> tag accepts a comma-delimited list of properties. **Table 3.2** lists the properties currently supported.

TABLE 3.2  Properties Supported by the Viewport <meta> Tag

| PROPERTY | ACCEPTED VALUES | DESCRIPTION |
|---|---|---|
| width | Integer or device-width | This sets the width of the mobile viewport to the specified number of pixels or to the width of the device. When specifying an actual width, the valid range is 200–10000. |
| height | Integer or device-height | On iOS, this sets the width of the viewport in landscape orientation to the specified number of pixels or to the height of the device. The valid range is 223–10000. |
| initial-scale | Number with decimal fraction | This sets the initial scaling factor of the display. The range is determined by the minimum-scale and maximum-scale properties. |
| minimum-scale | Number with decimal fraction | The valid range is any number above zero to 10.0. The default is 0.25. |
| maximum-scale | Number with decimal fraction | The valid range is any number above zero to 10.0. The default is 1.6. |
| user-scalable | yes or no | This determines whether the user can zoom the display in and out. The default is yes. |

**TIP**

For a detailed explanation of the viewport *<meta>* tag, see http://developer.apple.com/library/safari/#documentation/AppleApplications/Reference/SafariWebContent/UsingtheViewport/UsingtheViewport.html.

The following <meta> tag sets the viewport to 768 pixels and turns off the user's ability to zoom in and out:

```
<meta name="viewport" content="width=768,
➥ user-scalable=no">
```

What might come as a surprise is that the iPhone, iPod touch, and iPad use device-height to set the width of the viewport in landscape orientation. This is different from most other devices.

### Width and orientation

A simple way to check the width of a display is to add the following JavaScript to a web page:

```
<script>
alert(screen.width);
</script>
```

When you load the page in a mobile device, the script displays an alert with the screen width in pixels. On an iPhone, iPod touch, or iPad, it doesn't matter whether you're holding the device in portrait or landscape orientation; the result is always the same: Width is always reported as the width in portrait orientation. By contrast, Android and BlackBerry devices take orientation into account when reporting width. This affects the way media queries are interpreted:

▶ On iOS, media queries based on width-related media features are always applied on the basis of the width in portrait orientation. When the user switches to landscape orientation, the display is scaled up to fit the screen.

▶ Android and BlackBerry (and probably other) devices consider width to be the horizontal axis of the current orientation.

Another complication is that the media queries specification states that "user agents are expected, but not required, to re-evaluate and re-layout the page . . . if the device is tilted from landscape to portrait mode." In my experiments, the Samsung Galaxy Tab is particularly bad at responding to changes in orientation, but the HTC Desire smartphone responds immediately. Because both are running Android 2.2, the difference is device-specific, not related to the operating system.

This poses design problems, because the Galaxy Tab's 400 × 683 screen is more suited to a phone layout in portrait orientation. But the physical dimensions (4.8 × 7.4 inches or 11.8 × 18.7 centimeters) demand a tablet layout in landscape orientation. The HTC Desire's 320 × 533 screen also requires different portrait and landscape layouts. But in landscape orientation, it's considerably smaller than a tablet. Instead of just "one size fits all" for phones and tablets, you need to tailor some rules for a wide range of sizes.

## Adapting the Tozai Hotel Site

To display a website successfully on a range of devices, you need to create separate styles for at least these categories:

► **Mobile phones.** There's a wide range of screen sizes, but 320 pixels seems to be the most common among modern smartphones. However, the BlackBerry Torch screen is 360 pixels wide, and the Samsung Galaxy Tab is only 400 pixels wide in portrait orientation.

► **Tablets.** Again, there's a great deal of variety, but the iPad's 768-pixel width is probably a good choice for the maximum limit. This set of rules applies to all devices wider than a mobile phone but no wider than 768 pixels.

► **Desktops.** These rules apply to any device wider than 768 pixels.

### Organizing the Style Rules

Opinions differ on how to organize rules for use with media queries. The three main approaches available include:

► **Full style sheet for each type of target device.** Link to each one with a media query. The advantage is that each set of rules is independent from the rest. The disadvantage is that if you make a change that should be applied globally, such as background color or font size, you need to make the same changes to each style sheet.

► **Common style sheet plus specific overrides.** Locate all basic rules in a common style sheet, and then use media queries to attach separate style sheets to override only those rules that need to be different for specific types of device. This approach is more efficient, but it requires a strong understanding of the cascade.

**NOTES**

Categorizing style rules for each group of devices—phones, tablets, and desktops—is merely a convenience. As long as the browser recognizes media queries, the rules are applied according to the width of the viewport, not the type of device.

▶ **Single style sheet with @media rules.** Locate all rules in a single style sheet and use media queries in @media rules to target different devices. This reduces the number of server requests, but it results in mobile phones needlessly downloading the styles aimed exclusively at tablets and desktops. It also results in a long style sheet, which can be hard to maintain.

My preferred approach is a combination of the last two. I create a basic style sheet that is served to all browsers regardless of whether they recognize media queries. The rules for tablets and mobile phones are located in separate style sheets, but I also use @media rules within those files to handle special cases, such as phones that are wider than average but too small to be considered tablets. This keeps the style sheets relatively short and simple to maintain. Switching between style sheets is also easy thanks to Dreamweaver's Related Files toolbar.

An important consideration when planning to use media queries is how to handle images. Inline images—in other words, those embedded in the HTML with <img> tags—cannot be controlled by media queries. They are automatically downloaded by all devices, even if you create a style rule setting the display property to none. So, it's important for inline images to be an integral part of the content, not just used for decoration.

One way to control the size of inline images on different size screens is to remove the height attribute from the HTML <img> tag and to use CSS to override the width. It's a relatively crude, yet effective method.

Purely decorative images should be served as background images. Because background images are part of CSS, you can use media queries to serve optimized versions for different screen widths. However, printers ignore background images. So, if you expect your pages to be printed, use <img> tags for important images.

**CLOSE-UP**

### The display Property

The CSS display property tells the browser how to treat an element within the flow of a document. When its value is set to none, the element is removed completely from the page, and subsequent elements move up to fill the empty space. However, don't be fooled into thinking that setting display to none prevents the element from being downloaded. The element is still there; it's just not displayed.

This behavior has important implications for background images, which often need to be created in a range of sizes to match the target screen width. To prevent devices from downloading images they don't need, you should specify the appropriate background images for each type of device within style rules controlled by a media query.

**TIP**

In an ideal world, you should be able to serve inline images optimized for each type of device. A Boston-based design agency, Filament Group, has developed a technique called context-aware image sizing, which serves the smallest-size image by default and dynamically replaces it with a larger image, depending on the screen size. For details, see http://filamentgroup.com/lab/responsive_images_experimenting_with_context_aware_image_sizing.

The following style sheets adapt the Tozai Hotel site for display on multiple devices:

▶ **tozai.css.** This is the existing style sheet, which is served to all browsers, ensuring that the site remains styled even in browsers that don't recognize media queries. Most styles remain unchanged, but background images are moved to other style sheets to prevent mobile devices from downloading unnecessary images.

▶ **phone.css.** Most styles in this style sheet are targeted at screens with a maximum width of 320 pixels. However, alternate styles for screens up to 400 pixels are wrapped in `@media` rules.

▶ **tablet.css.** This style sheet contains rules for screen widths in the range of 401–768 pixels. Alternate styles for screens narrower than 680 pixels are wrapped in `@media` rules.

▶ **desktop.css.** This style sheet contains the background image styles from tozai.css, plus any rules designed to deal with bugs in IE 6–8. A media query serves this file to screens wider than 769 pixels. However, the style sheet also needs to be served to IE 6–8 through an IE conditional comment.

To attach these style sheets with media queries, you'll use Dreamweaver CS5.5 to create a site-wide media queries file.

### Creating a Site-wide Media Queries File

The 11.0.3 updater for Dreamweaver CS5 provided the ability to attach up to three style sheets to a page with media queries. In Dreamweaver CS5.5, this functionality has been considerably enhanced:

▶ You can add more than three media queries.

▶ You can add media queries to the current document or to a site-wide media queries file.

▶ An option to insert the viewport `<meta>` tag is available.

---

**CLOSE-UP**

### @import

You can attach an external style sheet in two ways: with the HTML `<link>` tag or with a CSS `@import` rule. As the name suggests, an `@import` rule imports the styles from another location. For example, the following line imports the styles from tablet.css:

```
@import url("tablet.css");
```

Because they're part of CSS, `@import` rules can be used only inside a `<style>` block or an external style sheet. They *must* come before other style rules in the same file or `<style>` block. Otherwise, the import fails. Consequently, imported styles are higher up the cascade and can be overridden by subsequent rules.

Browsers treat the style rules exactly the same regardless of whether `<link>` or `@import` is used to attach style sheets. In the past, `@import` was used mainly to hide style rules from Netscape 4 because it supported only `<link>`. However, all current browsers, including IE 6–8, support `@import` rules.

The role of the site-wide media queries file is to import styles from other style sheets using a series of @import rules and media queries. This avoids the need to link to each style sheet with media queries in every page. You just link to the site-wide media queries file, and it imports the relevant style rules. If you find the concept difficult to grasp, it should become clear once you have used it.

There are four ways to open the Media Queries dialog box:

▶ Click the Multiscreen button in the Document toolbar to open the Multiscreen Preview panel, and then click the Media Queries button at the top right of the panel.

▶ Choose Modify > Media Queries.

▶ Right-click in the CSS Styles panel, and choose Media Queries from the context menu.

▶ Click the ⚏ icon at the top right of the CSS Styles panel to open the panel menu, and then choose Media Queries.

### Using the Media Queries dialog box

The following instructions describe how to prepare the Tozai Hotel site for use with media queries:

1. Open index.html from the work files from the previous chapter. Alternatively, copy ch02/complete to a working folder and open index.html.

2. Detach the tozai.css style sheet from the page. You can do this by deleting the <link> tag on line 6 in Code view.

   Alternatively, open the CSS Styles panel, click the All button at the top left, and select tozai.css in the All Rules pane. Then click the 🗑 icon at the bottom right of the panel (**Figure 3.7**), or right-click and choose Delete from the context menu.

3. The page is now completely unstyled, but the styles will be restored by linking a site-wide media query file to it. Choose Modify > Media Queries or use one of the other methods outlined earlier to open the Media Queries dialog box (**Figure 3.8**).

NOTES

For licensing reasons, the ch02/complete folder does not contain the Calluna Regular font files. See "Embedding a Font with @font-face" in Chapter 2 for details on how to obtain them.

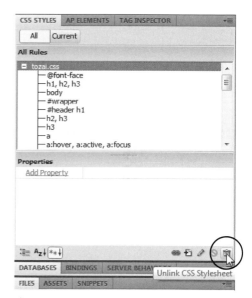

**Figure 3.7** Click the trash can icon to unlink the style sheet.

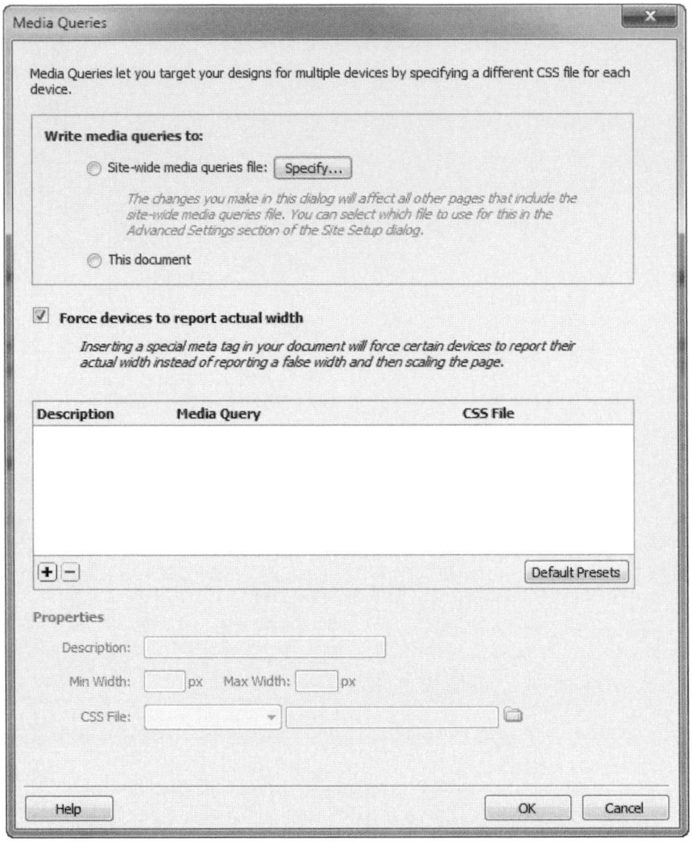

**Figure 3.8** The Media Queries dialog box has options to create site-wide media queries or media queries for only the current document.

4. In the section at the top of the dialog box, select the "Site-wide media queries file" radio button, and click the Specify button.

5. In the Specify Site-wide Media Query File dialog box, choose "Create new file" from the CSS File menu, and click the ⌷ icon next to the text field.

6. Navigate to the styles folder in your work files, type **tozai_mq.css** in the "File name" field, and click Save. This returns you to the Specify Site-wide Media Query File dialog box, which should now look like **Figure 3.9**.

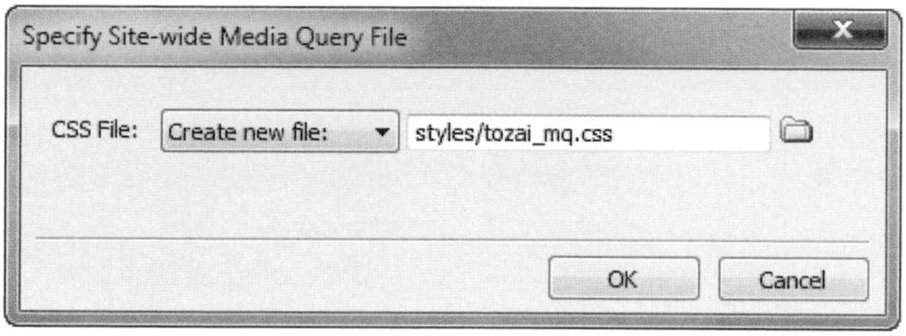

**Figure 3.9** Creating a new site-wide media query file.

7. Click OK to close the Specify Site-wide Media Query File dialog box. Although nothing appears to happen, tozai_mq.css is now listed as the file that media queries will be written to (**Figure 3.10**).

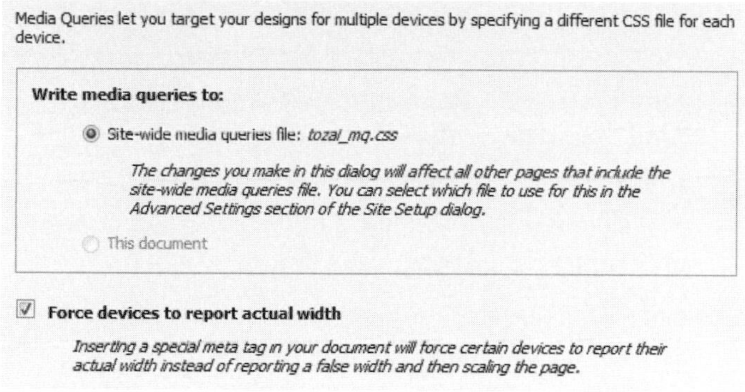

**Figure 3.10** Setting up a site-wide media queries file disables the option to write media queries to the current document.

8. As Figure 3.10 shows, the "Force devices to report actual width" check box is selected by default. This automatically inserts the viewport <meta> tag into each page attached to the site-wide media queries file and sets the width value to device-width. This is what you want, so leave the check box selected.

9. The bottom half of the Media Queries dialog box is where you specify which style sheets to attach with media queries. You can do this manually by clicking the ⊞ icon and filling in the fields at the bottom of the dialog box.

   However, it's much quicker to click the Default Presets button, which populates the area at the bottom of the dialog box with suggested values for mobile phones, tablets, and desktops (**Figure 3.11**).

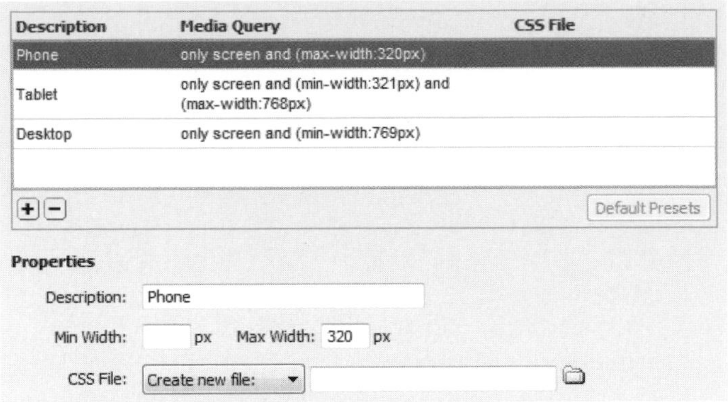

**Figure 3.11** The default presets speed up the creation of media queries.

| Description | Media Query | CSS File |
|---|---|---|
| Phone | only screen and (max-width:320px) | |
| Tablet | only screen and (min-width:321px) and (max-width:768px) | |
| Desktop | only screen and (min-width:769px) | |

⊕ ⊖      Default Presets

**Properties**

Description: Phone

Min Width: ☐ px    Max Width: 320 px

CSS File: Create new file: ▼ ☐ 📁

**NOTES**

When you navigate to the styles folder, don't worry if tozai_mq.css or the new CSS files you create aren't listed. Dreamweaver creates the new files when you finally close the Media Queries dialog box.

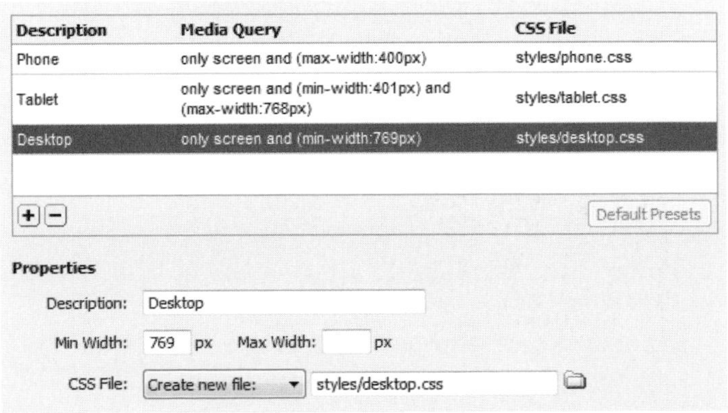

10. The Properties section at the bottom of the dialog box lets you change the description and the min- and max-width settings, as well as specify the CSS file to use.

    With Phone selected, change the value in the Max Width field from 320 to **400**.

11. Click the 📁 icon next to the CSS File field, and create a new CSS file called **phone.css** in the styles folder in the same way as you created tozai_mq.css in step 6.

12. Select Tablet, and change Min Width from 321 to **401**. Then create a new CSS file called **tablet.css**.

13. Select Desktop. Leave Min Width and Max Width at their default values, and create a new CSS file called **desktop.css**.

    The values at the bottom of the dialog box should now look like **Figure 3.12**.

**Figure 3.12** The default presets have now been edited.

| Description | Media Query | CSS File |
|---|---|---|
| Phone | only screen and (max-width:400px) | styles/phone.css |
| Tablet | only screen and (min-width:401px) and (max-width:768px) | styles/tablet.css |
| Desktop | only screen and (min-width:769px) | styles/desktop.css |

⊕ ⊖      Default Presets

**Properties**

Description: Desktop

Min Width: 769 px    Max Width: ☐ px

CSS File: Create new file: ▼ styles/desktop.css 📁

**14.** Click OK to close the Media Queries dialog box.

**15.** Select tozai_mq.css in the Related Files toolbar. It should contain the following code:

```
/* Phone */
@import url("phone.css") only screen and
➥ (max-width:400px);
/* Tablet */
@import url("tablet.css") only screen and
➥ (min-width:401px) and (max-width:768px);
/* Desktop */
@import url("desktop.css") only screen and
➥ (min-width:769px);
```

At the moment, the imported style sheets are empty. But browsers that recognize media queries will import the rules in phone.css only if they detect a screen no wider than 400 pixels. Similarly, the rules in tablet.css will be imported only if the screen width is in the range of 401–768 pixels, and those in desktop.css only if the screen is wider than 769 pixels.

**TIP**

The CSS comments in the media queries file are derived from the Description fields in the Media Queries dialog box.

**16.** The page is still unstyled. You need to import the original style sheet, tozai.css, *without* a media query. Because the style sheets controlled by media queries use the cascade to override the basic styles, tozai.css must be imported first. Add it to the top of tozai_mq.css like this:

```
/* Basic styles */
@import url("tozai.css");
/* Phone */
@import url("phone.css") only screen and
➥ (max-width:400px);
```

**17.** Click in Design view. The original styles are restored.

**18.** Choose File > Save All Related Files to save the changes to index.html and the new style sheets.

**19.** Inspect the changes that have been made to the <head> of the page in Code view:

```
<head>
<meta charset="utf-8">
<meta name="viewport" content="width=
➥ device-width">
<title>Tozai Hotel: Home</title>
<link href="styles/tozai_mq.css"
➥ rel="stylesheet" type="text/css">
</head>
```

The viewport <meta> tag forces mobile devices to use the actual screen width rather than a notional viewport when implementing media queries. An ordinary <link> attaches the site-wide media queries file to the page. This ensures that tozai_mq.css is accessed by all browsers, allowing IE 6–8 to read the styles in tozai.css but not in any of the other style sheets that use media queries. You'll add a link to desktop.css in an IE conditional comment later.

### *Attaching the site-wide media queries file to other pages*

After you have created a site-wide media queries file, Dreamweaver remembers the details, simplifying the process of adding the viewport <meta> tag and attaching the file to other pages.

**1.** Open dining.html in the Document window, and detach tozai.css in the same way as in step 2 of the preceding section.

**2.** Choose Modify > Media Queries or one of the other methods of opening the Media Queries dialog box.

**3.** Select the "Site-wide media queries file" radio button, and click OK.

**4.** Repeat steps 1–3 in garden.html, reservations.html, and rooms.html.

**5.** Choose File > Save All.

**NOTES**

If you modify any settings in the bottom half of the Media Queries dialog box, the site-wide media queries file is updated and the changes are applied to all pages attached to it. You can have only one site-wide media queries file in each site. If you want to attach alternative media queries files to different parts of a site, you need to do so manually.

## Hiding the Desktop Background Images from Mobile Devices

The style rules for mobile phones omit most background images, and tablets often use smaller versions. So, it's necessary to move the background image styles rules to desktop.css to prevent them from being downloaded by devices that won't display them.

It's also a good idea to hide the embedded fonts from mobile phones. They increase the amount of data that needs to be downloaded and add very little to the site when viewed on a small screen.

1. With one of the Tozai Hotel site's pages open in the Document window, click tozai.css in the Related Files toolbar to open the style sheet in Split view.

2. Select the @font-face rule at the top of tozai.css (**Figure 3.13**), and cut it to your clipboard.

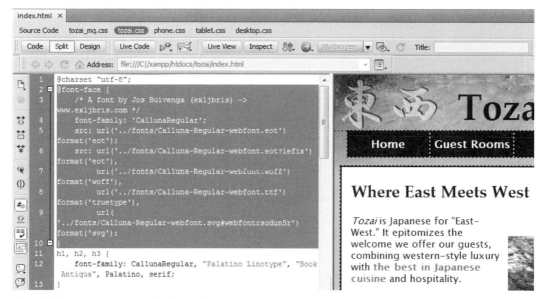

**Figure 3.13** Preparing to move the @font-face rule.

3. Switch to desktop.css by selecting it in the Related Files toolbar, and paste the @font-face rule into the style sheet.

4. Switch back to tozai.css, and scroll down to the #wrapper style rule (around lines 12–20), which looks like this:

```
#wrapper {
    width: 980px;
    margin: 0 auto;
    background-image: url(../images/
    ➤ basin_bg.jpg);
    background-repeat: no-repeat;
    background-color: #B4C4BA;
    border-left: #594431 solid 1px;
    border-right: #594431 solid 1px;
}
```

**TIP**

As you switch from tozai.css to desktop.css after cutting the background-image property, you'll see the background image disappear from the top of the page in Design view. When you have created the new rule in desktop.css, click in Design view to refresh it. The background image is restored. Keeping an eye on Design view is a good way to check the effect of your edits.

5. Select the line that defines the background-image property (highlighted in the preceding step), and cut it to your clipboard. It's only the image that you want to hide from mobile phones and tablets, so leave the other background properties untouched.

6. Switch to desktop.css, create a style block for #wrapper, and paste the background-image property inside:

```
#wrapper {
    background-image:url(../images/
    ➤ basin_bg.jpg);
}
```

7. Repeat steps 4–6 for the background-image property in the #hero style rule using #hero as the ID selector in desktop.css.

8. The background image in the #dining style rule is used in all layouts, so leave it untouched.

9. Locate the #sake style rule in tozai.css. It should now be around lines 161–166 and looks like this:

```
#sake {
    background-image:url(../images/sake.jpg);
    background-repeat:no-repeat;
    background-position:bottom;
    padding-bottom:140px;
}
```

This displays a background image at the bottom of the sidebar in dining.html (**Figure 3.14**).

The design for tablets moves the sidebar below the main content and displays a different background image next to the sidebar text (**Figure 3.15**).

Because the tablet layout is completely different and no background image is used for mobile phones, cut the entire #sake rule from tozai.css and paste it in desktop.css.

Figure 3.15 In the tablet layout, the background image and its position are different.

**Figure 3.14** In the desktop layout, the background image is at the bottom of the sidebar.

10. There's one more background image—in the #blossom style rule. It's purely decorative, but it's only 8 KB. The same image is used in all layouts, so leave the #blossom style rule as it is.

11. Choose File > Save All Related Files to save your changes.

**12.** The contents of desktop.css should now look like this:

```
@charset "utf-8";
@font-face {
    /* A font by Jos Buivenga (exljbris) ->
    ↪ www.exljbris.com */
    font-family: 'CallunaRegular';
    src: url('../fonts/Calluna-Regular-webfont
    ↪ .eot') format('eot');
    src: url('../fonts/Calluna-Regular-webfont
    ↪ .eot?iefix') format('eot'),
        url('../fonts/Calluna-Regular-webfont
        ↪ .woff') format('woff'),
        url('../fonts/Calluna-Regular-webfont
        ↪ .ttf')  format('truetype'),
        url('../fonts/Calluna-Regular-webfont
        ↪ .svg#webfontrsodunSr') format('svg');
}
#wrapper {
    background-image:url(../images/basin_bg
    ↪ .jpg);
}
#hero {
    background-image: url(../images/exterior
    ↪ .jpg);
}
#sake {
    background-image:url(../images/sake.jpg);
    background-repeat:no-repeat;
    background-position:bottom;
    padding-bottom:140px;
}
```

**13.** Activate Live view. With a full-size screen, you should see all background images.

**14.** Click the down arrow to the right of the Multiscreen button in the Document toolbar and choose Tablet from the list of screen sizes. Alternatively, click the window size in the status bar at the bottom right of the Document window, and choose Tablet (**Figure 3.16**). The background images, apart from chef.jpg and blossom.jpg, are hidden.

**Figure 3.16** Changing the size of the Document window viewport confirms that the background images are hidden from tablets.

15. Choose 320 × 480 Smart Phone from the list of screen sizes and verify that the background images are still not displayed.

### Serving desktop.css to IE 6–8

Although the media queries file hides desktop.css from devices with screens less than 769 pixels wide, IE 6–8 can't see it either. So, you need to attach desktop.css to each page in the normal way and wrap the <link> in an IE conditional comment. The Dreamweaver Snippets panel doesn't have a conditional comment that covers all three versions of IE, but it takes only a few moments to adapt an existing snippet.

1. Exit Live view, if necessary, and choose Format > CSS Styles > Attach Style Sheet.

2. Click the Browse button, select desktop.css in the styles folder, and click OK (Choose on a Mac).

**NOTES**

As with most features, Dreamweaver offers several different ways to attach an external style sheet. I have listed only one for brevity.

**Figure 3.17** The Snippets panel contains commonly used IE conditional comments.

> **TIP**
>
> Even though you no longer have a snippet for less than IE 8, the Less Than or Equal to IE 7 Conditional Comment snippet serves exactly the same purpose.

3. Select the Link radio button (it's the default), and click OK.

4. Open Split view. You should see the new `<link>` immediately before the closing `</head>` tag:

```
<link href="styles/tozai_mq.css"
➥ rel="stylesheet" type="text/css">
<link href="styles/desktop.css"
➥ rel="stylesheet" type="text/css">
</head>
```

5. Open the Snippets panel by choosing Window > Snippets. On Windows, you can also press Shift+F9, but there is no keyboard shortcut on a Mac.

6. Expand the Comments folder in the Snippets panel, and select If Less Than IE 8 Conditional Comment (**Figure 3.17**).

7. Click the ✎ icon at the bottom right of the panel to open the snippet for editing.

8. Amend the text in the Name field to **Less Than or Equal to IE 8 Conditional Comment**.

9. (Optional) Update the Description field to indicate that the browser version is less than **or equal to** Internet Explorer 8.

10. Amend the code in the "Insert before" block like this:

```
<!--[if lte IE 8]>
```

The settings in the Snippet dialog box should look like **Figure 3.18**.

11. Click OK to save the changes.

12. In Code view, select the `<link>` to desktop.css. Make sure the entire tag is selected.

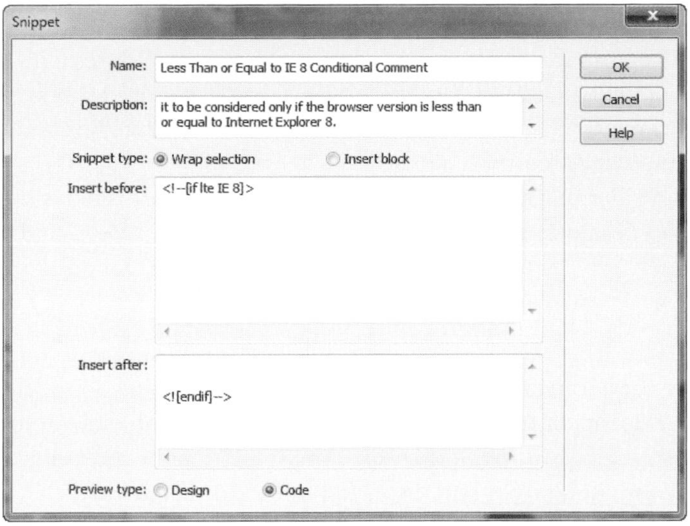

**Figure 3.18** Editing the snippet.

13. The edited snippet should still be selected in the Snippets panel. If not, select it before clicking the Insert button at the bottom left of the panel.

    The `<link>` should now be wrapped in an IE conditional comment like this:

    ```
    <!--[if lte IE 8]>
    <link href="styles/desktop.css"
    ➥ rel="stylesheet" type="text/css">
    <![endif]-->
    ```

14. Copy and paste the IE conditional comment and `<link>` into the other pages in the same location. Then save all files.

It's a nuisance having to attach desktop.css twice like this, but it's essential to prevent files from being downloaded unnecessarily by mobile devices. Although desktop.css is attached twice, browsers download it only once. Those browsers that recognize media queries import desktop.css through the site-wide media queries file. Only IE 6–8 use the `<link>` you just wrapped in a conditional comment.

**NOTES**

Because IE conditional comments are wrapped in standard HTML comment tags, they are grayed out in Code view, and any content is ignored by Design view and Live view.

## Creating the Styles for Tablets

The wide range of screen sizes in tablet devices poses considerable problems for designing a suitable layout. In portrait orientation, some tablets are barely wider than the average smartphone. But in landscape orientation, they all offer considerably more space. My strategy is to adapt the desktop design to fit the 768-pixel width of an iPad screen and then add supplementary @media rules to adjust the display for narrower screens.

In the Tozai Hotel site, dining.html, garden.html, and reservations.html all consist of a main content section with a sidebar on the right (**Figure 3.19**). To adapt the layout to increasingly narrower screens, the sidebar is moved below the main content and displayed full width (**Figure 3.20**).

**Figure 3.19** Several pages in the desktop version consist of main content and a sidebar.

**Figure 3.20** The sidebar is moved down and displayed full width in the tablet layout.

In my experiments, I found that the iPad handled embedded fonts without difficulty, but the Samsung Galaxy Tab and HTC Desire failed to render them correctly. So, I decided to use an @media rule to limit the use of embedded fonts to screens at least 700 pixels wide. This is far from ideal, but media queries handle only the media features listed in Table 3.1. They can't identify individual devices or the level of support they offer for fonts.

*Creating the basic rules for tablets*

The following instructions describe the style rules aimed at tablets and explain their purpose. To avoid lengthy descriptions, I show only the finished CSS code as seen in Split view. Choose your own preferred method of generating the rules.

TIP

To refresh Live view after you edit the style rules, click inside the Document window or press F5. There is no need to save the style sheet between each change, although it's a good idea to save your changes periodically.

1. Open index.html in the Document window, and click the down arrow to the right of the Multiscreen button to display the list of screen sizes. Choose 768 × 1024 Tablet, and activate Live view. This enables you to follow the effect of the changes as you progress.

2. Copy the @font-face rule from desktop.css to tablet.css:

```
@font-face {
/* A font by Jos Buivenga (exljbris) ->
    www.exljbris.com */
font-family: 'CallunaRegular';
src: url('../fonts/Calluna-Regular-webfont
    ➥ .eot') format('eot');
src: url('../fonts/Calluna-Regular-webfont
    ➥ .eot?iefix') format('eot'),
    url('../fonts/calluna-regular-webfont
    ➥ .woff') format('woff'),
    url('../fonts/calluna-regular-webfont
    ➥ .ttf') format('truetype'),
    url('../fonts/calluna-regular-webfont
    ➥ .svg#webfontrsodunSr') format('svg');
}
```

3. The .eot font format is used only by IE 6–8, so you can delete both references to it. Then wrap the @font-face rule in an @media rule to apply it only to devices with a minimum screen width of 700 pixels.

```
@media screen and (min-width: 700px) {
    @font-face {
    /* A font by Jos Buivenga (exljbris) ->
        www.exljbris.com */
    font-family: 'CallunaRegular';
    src: url('../fonts/calluna-regular-webfont
        ➥ .woff') format('woff'),
```

```
        url('../fonts/calluna-regular-webfont
      ⇥ .ttf') format('truetype'),
        url('../fonts/calluna-regular-webfont
      ⇥ .svg#webfontrsodunSr')
      ⇥ format('svg');
    }
}
```

4. The desktop design is based on a 980-pixel fixed-width wrapper `<div>`. However, the tablet layout needs to be flexible. So, I changed `width` to **100%**, but also set the `max-width` property to **700px**, the same width as a smaller version of the background image. The `#wrapper` style rule looks like this:

```
#wrapper {
    width: 100%;
    max-width: 700px;
    background-image: url(../images/
  ⇥ basin_bg_tab.jpg);
    background-size: contain;
}
```

The most interesting aspect of this style rule is the use of the CSS3 `background-size` property. By setting its value to `contain`, the background image scales in proportion to the page width.

5. The main heading and navigation menu need to be made smaller and repositioned to fit the narrower space. Add the following style rules to tablet.css:

```
#header h1 {
    font-size: 58px;
    text-align: center;
    padding-left: 0;
    padding-top: 10px;
    margin-bottom: 0px;
}
#nav {
    width: 660px;
    margin-left: auto;
    margin-right: auto;
}
```

**The background-size Property**

The `background-size` property allows you to scale a background image. It accepts the following values:

▶ Physical measurements, such as `px`, or percentages. If two values are given, the first controls the width and the second controls the height. If only one value is given, it controls only the width, and the image's original height is preserved.

▶ The keywords `contain` or `cover`.

The keywords preserve the image's aspect ratio while stretching or shrinking it. The difference is that `contain` scales the image to the largest size to fit the background, whereas `cover` scales it to the smallest size needed. If the background image is smaller than the element, use `cover` to fill the whole background.

The property is supported by IE 9, Firefox 4, Safari 5, Chrome 4, and Opera 10.53. Earlier browsers ignore it.

```
#nav li a {
    width: 120px;
    padding: 10px 5px;
}
```

The main heading is kept centered at all screen widths by zeroing the left padding and setting text-align to center. The navigation menu is also centered by giving the #nav style rule a fixed width of 660px and setting the horizontal margins to auto. These values will be overridden later by @media rules for smaller screens.

6. The style rules for the hero <div> in the desktop version have a fixed width. You need to override this by setting the width property to auto, leaving the left and right margins to control the overall width. The #hero rule in tozai.css also contains a fixed height for the benefit of IE 6 and min-height for other browsers. Both values need to be reset. The other changes substitute a smaller version of the background image and reposition it in relation to the text.

```
#hero {
    margin-right: 10px;
    margin-left: 10px;
    padding-right: 15px;
    padding-left: 15px;
    width: auto;
    height: auto;
    min-height: 279px;
    background-image: url(../images/
    ↪ exterior_tab.jpg);
    background-position: 265px;
}
#hero p {
    padding-right: 410px;
}
#hero h2 {
    padding-right: 0;
}
```

> **NOTES**
>
> The width of the navigation menu is calculated by adding the *width* of *#nav li a* (*120px*) plus *5px* of horizontal padding and *1px* of horizontal margin on each side. The horizontal margin is inherited from tozai.css. The final width calculation looks like this: $(120+5+5+1+1) \times 5 = 660$.

When you refresh Live view, index.html should look like **Figure 3.21**. The changes so far simply rescale the design to fit within a narrower screen.

**Figure 3.21** The styles preserve the original layout within the constraints of a tablet screen.

7. Open rooms.html, set the Document window viewport to the tablet size, and activate Live view. The page doesn't look too bad as it is, although the image of the bedroom is too big and slightly off center (**Figure 3.22**).

The design won't hold together on a tablet with a smaller screen. So, you need to make some changes. Add the following style rules to tablet.css:

```
.content-wide {
    margin-right: 15px;
    margin-left: 15px;
    padding-right: 10px;
    padding-left: 10px;
}
.floatright.img-large {
    width: 450px;
}
```

**Figure 3.22** The image looks out of proportion with the rest of the page.

This slightly changes the horizontal margins and padding for the `content-wide` class for the main content. The image of the bedroom has the `floatright` and `img-large` classes applied to it, so the compound selector overrides the width in the HTML markup and resets it to 450 pixels.

8. When you refresh Live view, the text wraps around the smaller image, but the image is distorted because its height is hard-coded in the HTML.

   Exit Live view, select the image in the Document window, and delete the height in the Property inspector (circled in **Figure 3.23**).

**Figure 3.23** To prevent the image from being distorted, you need to delete its height in the underlying HTML.

9. Reactivate Live view. The image should now be in proportion.

10. Save rooms.html, and then open dining.html in the Document window. This page contains two inline images, sashimi.jpg and sushi.jpg. Select each one in turn and delete its height in the Property inspector.

11. In the desktop layout, the main content is styled with the class content-medium, whereas the sidebar uses the class aside. The sidebar has a 720-pixel left margin into which the main content is floated left. To stack the two elements vertically, you need to cancel the float, set the main content's width to auto, and adjust the margins and padding like this:

```
.content-medium {
    float: none;
    width: auto;
}
.aside {
    margin-left: auto;
}
.content-medium, .aside {
    margin-right: 15px;
    margin-left: 15px;
    padding-right: 10px;
    padding-left: 10px;
}
```

12. When you refresh Live view, you should immediately spot a problem. The main content's background disappears, and the margins and padding aren't applied (**Figure 3.24**).

**Figure 3.24** Removing the float from the main content also affects the background.

Japanese Cuisine at Its Finest

Japanese cuisine is not only a feast for the taste buds, but for the eyes. Presentation is an important part of a chef's skills.

If you enjoy fish, you'll love the restaurant at Tozai Hotel, where our master chefs will select the choicest cuts of the day's fresh catch to serve you mouth-watering *sashimi* and *sushi*.

The clue lies in the lack of margins and padding. Switch to tozai.css, and locate the `.content-medium` style rule (around lines 143–148), which looks like this:

```
.content-medium {
    float: left;
    width: 640px;
    margin-top: 5px;
    display: inline; /* Fixes double-margin
                        bug in IE 6 & 7 */
}
```

When the <div> was floated, setting its display property to inline fixed a bug in IE 6–7 without affecting other browsers adversely. But now that the <div> is no longer floated, it destroys the layout for mobile devices.

13. Cut the line highlighted in the preceding step, and paste it into desktop.css to create a new rule for the content-medium class like this:

```
.content-medium {
    display: inline; /* Fixes double-margin
                        bug in IE 6 & 7 */
}
```

The background and margins now display correctly because desktop.css is read only by screens wider than 768 pixels.

14. In the desktop version, a background image is at the bottom of the sidebar in dining.html. Now that the sidebar is displayed the full width of the content area, you need a different approach. Add the following rules to tablet.css:

```
#sake {
    background-position: 440px bottom;
    background-repeat: no-repeat;
    background-image: url(../images/
    ➥ sake_tab.jpg);
}
#sake p {
    max-width: 400px;
}
```

CLOSE-UP

**The IE Double-margin Bug**

When you add a margin to an element and float it to the same side, IE 6 and IE 7 double the margin. The solution is to set the display property of the floated element to inline. This coaxes IE 6 and IE 7 into removing the extra margin without causing problems in other browsers.

When you refresh Live view, the sake <div> looks like **Figure 3.25**.

**Figure 3.25** A different background image is used when the sidebar is displayed full width.

### Saké—the Perfect Accompaniment

Japanese rice wine, *saké*, makes the perfect accompaniment to your meal. Although *saké* can be drunk hot, connoisseurs prefer to drink it cold or on the rocks. Drinking *saké* cold allows you to appreciate the subtle differences in taste that come from the rice variety and water used in the fermentation process.

Excepteur sint occaecat consectetur adipisicing elit, lorem ipsum dolor sit amet. Velit esse cillum dolore ullamco laboris nisi quis nostrud exercitation. Excepteur sint occaecat mollit anim id est laborum.

In reprehenderit in voluptate ut labore et dolore magna aliqua. Quis nostrud exercitation ullamco laboris nisi ut aliquip ex ea commodo consequat. Qui officia deserunt mollit anim id est laborum. Ut enim ad minim veniam, eu fugiat nulla pariatur.

Ut labore et dolore magna aliqua. Duis aute irure dolor ut aliquip ex ea commodo consequat. Mollit anim id est laborum.

The new styles position a larger image at the bottom of the <div> and 440 pixels from the left. The maximum width of a paragraph is set at 400 pixels. This ensures that the width of the text contracts on very narrow tablet screens.

15. Open garden.html, select the inline image stone-lantern.jpg, and delete its height in the Property inspector.

16. Activate Live view. The only problem is that the text overlaps the cluster of cherry blossoms in the sidebar. Add the following rule to fix it:

```
#blossom h3 + p {
    padding-right: 90px;
}
```

This uses an adjacent sibling selector (see the "Adjacent Sibling Selector" Close-Up in Chapter 2) to target just the first paragraph after the heading in the blossom <div>, giving the blossom space of its own (**Figure 3.26**).

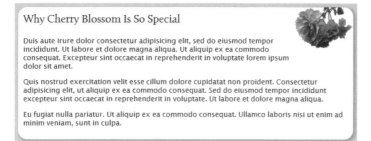

**17.** Choose File > Save All Related Files.

### Using @media rules for supplementary styles

The styles in tablet.css work fine for larger tablets, such as the iPad or the Samsung Galaxy Tab in landscape orientation. But the media query applies these styles to all devices wider than 400 pixels. When viewed on an HTC Desire in landscape orientation (533 pixels wide), the design falls apart (**Figure 3.27**).

**Figure 3.27** The HTC Desire's 533-pixel screen in landscape orientation reveals problems with the tablet layout.

The #nav style rule fixes the width of the navigation menu at 660 pixels, pushing it out of the wrapper <div>. The font size in the heading also needs to be smaller.

I have added three @media rules with media queries to tablet.css. Let's take a look at each one in turn. The first one contains most of the rules, which override previous settings and apply to all screen widths in the range of 401–680 pixels.

```
@media screen and (min-width: 401px) and
➞ (max-width: 680px) {
    #header h1 {
```

```
            font-size: 40px;
            padding-top: 7px;
        }
        #nav {
            width: 396px;
            height: 75px;
        }
        #nav li a {
            margin-bottom: 2px;
        }
        #nav li:nth-child(4) a {
            margin-left: 66px;
        }
        #hero {
            width: 87%;
            background-image: none;
            margin: 5px auto;
            min-height: 0;
        }
        #hero p {
            padding-right: 0;
        }
        #sake {
            background-position: 380px bottom;
        }
        #sake p {
            max-width: 340px;
        }
        .floatright, .floatleft {
            float: none;
            display: block;
            margin: 10px auto;
            max-width: 90%;
        }
    }
}
```

The first point of interest is the navigation menu. The #nav rule resets width to 396px, forcing the fourth and fifth navigation buttons onto a second row. Because the <li> elements used for the buttons are floated, you need to assign an explicit height to prevent the second row from overlapping the following content. The rows are separated by giving the navigation links a bottom margin of 2px.

To center the second row of buttons, the fourth one is given a left margin of 66px (132 ÷ 2) using the :nth-child() pseudo-class (see Table 1.2 in Chapter 1).

The #hero style rule sets background-image to none for smaller screens. As noted earlier, this doesn't prevent the image from being downloaded. However, flexible design inevitably involves some compromises. One way to avoid downloading this image unnecessarily would be to create separate style sheets for smaller and larger tablets, but that is likely to make maintenance more difficult.

The #sake and #sake p style rules change the position of the background image and the width of the text to fit the narrow screen better.

Finally, all inline images that use the floatleft and floatright classes are no longer floated, but are centered by setting their display property to block and their horizontal margins to auto. To prevent the images from protruding outside their containing elements, max-width is set to 90%. The percentage refers to the width of the containing block, so a 400-pixel wide image is rescaled only when the available space is less than 445 pixels.

**Figure 3.28** shows dining.html on an HTC Desire in landscape orientation after making these changes.

TIP

To center an image, set its *display* property to *block*, and set the left and right margins to *auto*. The image must have a declared width. By default, browsers use the value in the *width* attribute in the *<img>* tag, but you can override this in your style sheet.

**Figure 3.28** The heading and navigation menu now fit comfortably in the HTC Desire's 533-pixel screen.

**:last-of-type**

The :last-of-type pseudo-class selects an element that is the last of its type in the list of children of its parent element. It's fully supported by iOS, Android, and BlackBerry. The three <select> menus used for each date picker are wrapped in a paragraph. So, this rule selects the last <select> element within each paragraph.

The next @media rule fixes some problems with the alignment of form elements on screens narrower than 480 pixels.

```
@media screen and (max-width: 480px) {
    select:last-of-type {
        display:block;
        margin-left:135px;
        margin-top:5px;
    }
    #adults {
        margin-right:80px;
    }
    input + label {
        padding-left:50px;
    }
    input[type=submit] {
        margin-left:50px;
    }
}
```

**Figure 3.29** On a narrow screen the year menus are sometimes pushed onto the next line.

**Figure 3.30** The date picker menus are now neatly aligned.

The first style rule uses the CSS3 :last-of-type pseudo-class (see Table 1.2 in Chapter 1) to select the last <select> menu in each of the date pickers. Without this rule, the year menus are likely to drop to the next line and sit flush with the label on the left (**Figure 3.29**).

By setting the display property to block and setting margins, you can align the year menus with the months (**Figure 3.30**).

The other rules align the Adults and Children text input fields and the submit button.

The final @media rule simply assigns a bigger font size to the main heading when the screen width is in the range of 500–680 pixels.

```
@media screen and (min-width: 500px) and
→ (max-width: 680px) {
    #header h1 {
        font-size: 48px;
    }
}
```

*Viewing the styles at varying screen widths*

As with desktop browsers, the only reliable way to know what your designs look like is to test them on actual devices. However, even the most dedicated geek with unlimited financial resources is unlikely to possess more than a handful of tablets and mobile phones for testing. Nevertheless, you can get a good idea of what your designs will look like by using Live view and adjusting the Document window viewport in Dreamweaver CS5.5.

In addition to selecting one of the default sizes, you can create your own presets.

1. Open the list of window sizes using one of the following methods:

   ▶ Click the down arrow on the right of the Multiscreen button on the Document toolbar.

   ▶ Click the window size in the status bar at the bottom of the Document window.

   ▶ Choose View > Window Size.

2. Choose Edit Sizes to open the Window Sizes category of the Dreamweaver Preferences panel (**Figure 3.31**).

Figure 3.31 You can add your own presets and edit existing ones in the Window Sizes category of the Preferences panel.

NOTES

If you prefer, you can open the Preferences panel directly by choosing Edit > Preferences (Windows) or Dreamweaver > Preferences (on a Mac), or by pressing Ctrl+U/Command+U.

3. Click the ⊞ icon at the bottom left of the panel to add your own presets. To remove a preset, select it and click the minus button.

4. Click OK to save the changes. The new presets are immediately available in the list of window sizes.

You can also change the width of the Document window viewport dynamically like this:

1. Open the list of window sizes (*not* the Window Sizes category of the Preferences panel).

2. Choose Full Size.

3. Activate Live view.

4. Select Split view, and make sure the screen is split vertically (choose View > Split Vertically, if necessary).

5. Drag the border between Code view and Live view. Live view automatically refreshes as you drag, applying the styles dynamically in response to the changing width.

### Creating the Styles for Mobile Phones

The process of creating the styles for mobile phones is exactly the same as for tablets. The only difference is that you're dealing with a much narrower width, so it's mainly a question of adjusting margins, padding, and font sizes. A full listing of the styles in phone.css follows:

```
@charset "utf-8";
#wrapper {
    background-image: url(../images/
    ➥ basin_bg_phone.jpg);
    background-size: contain;
    width: 100%;
}
#header h1 {
    font-size: 36px;
    margin-bottom: 0px;
    padding-left: 90px;
    padding-top: 5px;
}
```

```css
/* Basic styles */
h2 {
    font-size:24px;
}
.floatleft, .floatright {
    float: none;
    max-width: 290px;
    margin: 0.5em auto;
    display: block;
}
/* Main navigation */
#nav {
    width: 308px;
    height: 95px;
    margin: 0 auto 5px auto;
}
#nav li a {
    width: 136px;
    margin: 0 6px 2px 6px;
    padding: 5px 2px;
}
#nav li: last-child a {
    margin-left: 74px;
}
/* Main content on index page */
#hero {
    width: auto;
    margin: 5px;
    padding: 10px;
    min-height: 0;
    height: auto;
}
#hero h2 {
    padding-right: 10px;
    font-size: 24px;
}
#hero p {
    padding-right: 0;
}
```

```
/* Content containers on other pages */
.content-wide, .content-medium, .aside {
    margin: 0 5px 5px 5px;
    padding: 10px;
    width: auto;
    float: none;
}
/* Form elements */
form {
    margin-left: 10px;
}
label {
    width: 100px;
}
label[for=title] {
    float: left;
}
datalist {
    float: left;
}
datalist span {
    display: block;
    margin: 5px;
}
input[name=title] {
    display: block;
    clear: left;
    margin-left: 105px;
}
select:last-of-type {
    display: block;
    margin-left: 105px;
    margin-top: 5px;
}
input[type=submit] {
    margin-left: 50px;
}
fieldset label {
    width: 80px;
    padding-left: 30px;
}
```

```
/* Alternate rules for screens wider than 360px */
@media screen and (min-width: 360px) {
    #header h1 {
        padding-left: 125px;
    }
    #nav {
        margin-left: 40px;
    }
    #hero {
        width: 87%;
        margin: 5px auto;
    }
    #hero p {
        padding-right: 0;
    }
    .floatright.img-large, img.floatleft,
 ➥ img.floatright {
        width: 330px;
    }
    #adults {
        margin-right: 80px;
    }
}
```

The screen on a BlackBerry Torch is 360 pixels wide, so an @media rule adjusts some dimensions to fit the larger screen.

After applying these styles, rooms.html looks like **Figure 3.32** on an iPod touch.

The image of the bedroom, which is 600 pixels wide in the desktop layout, is scaled down to fit in the narrower confines of a mobile phone screen.

## Assessing Media Queries

Using media queries to adapt an existing desktop design to display satisfactorily on tablets and mobile phones is a time-consuming process that involves a lot of testing and fine-tuning. However, the effort is worthwhile if you want

**Figure 3.32** The site still looks good on a 320-pixel screen.

to give visitors a similar experience regardless of their screen size. Instead of trying to reproduce the same design pixel-perfect on every browser, you need to adapt the design to fit a wide range of screen widths.

Media queries work well for tablets, but they're not necessarily the best choice for mobile phones. People who access websites on their phones are usually on the go. They're looking for quick information, not in-depth, image-heavy content. Although you can hide content by setting its `display` property to `none`, the phone still downloads it, wasting precious bandwidth for both the site owner and the phone user. Often, it makes more sense to create a dedicated, lightweight site for mobile phones and include a link to the main site for anyone who wants more in-depth coverage.

In Chapter 5, you'll explore using the jQuery Mobile framework, which is integrated in Dreamweaver CS5.5, to build dedicated mobile sites. Before doing so, the next chapter introduces the new features in HTML5 that enable users to continue interacting with a website even when offline.

# Making Your Site
# Available Offline

*You can't always get what you want,*
*But if you try sometimes,*
*You might get what you need.*

—The Rolling Stones

# Making Your Site Available Offline

Loss of signal is probably one of the most frustrating aspects of surfing the web with a mobile device. You've just clicked a link and the page is beginning to load when your train enters a tunnel. Your connection disappears. Even when the train emerges from the tunnel, your mobile has to hunt for a signal and you often need to start all over again.

HTML5 can't improve mobile connectivity, but it does make it possible to continue interacting with websites, even when no network connection is available. The secret lies in caching the necessary files. Although browsers automatically cache recently downloaded files, what's different about HTML5 is that you can instruct the browser to download files in advance of their being needed. You can also specify alternative files to be displayed if the user is offline.

In this chapter, you'll learn how to make a site available offline by creating a file that not only tells the browser which files to cache, but also specifies substitute files for offline use. To speed up this process, the download files for this chapter contain a Dreamweaver extension that I created to generate a list of all files used in a site or folder.

## How Offline Sites Work

To make a site available without a network connection— an *offline web application,* as the HTML5 specification calls it—you need to create a *manifest.* This is a list of files that the browser needs to download and store in an application cache. The first time someone visits your site, the browser checks the manifest and downloads the listed files ready for use offline. The next time the same user visits your site, the browser checks the manifest. If it detects a change, all the files are downloaded again, updating the application cache.

**Figure 4.1** shows which browsers support offline applications as reported by caniuse.com. Light green shows full support; darker green shows partial support; and pink indicates no support. Internet Explorer (IE) is the only mainstream browser with no support. Crucially, though, iOS Safari, Android, and Opera Mobile all support offline access, making it ideal for websites that you expect to be accessed on mobile devices.

**NOTES**

Firefox alerts users that the site is asking to store data on your computer for offline use and offers the option to decline. Most other browsers download the files without asking.

# Offline web applications - **Working Draft**

| Global user stats*: | |
|---|---|
| Support: | 48.77% |
| Partial support: | 1.53% |
| Total: | 50.3% |

*Method of defining web page files to be cached using a cache manifest file, allowing them to work offline on subsequent visits to the page*

Resources: Sitepoint tutorial  Dive Into HTML5 article  Mozilla Hacks article/demo

| | IE | Firefox | Safari | Chrome | Opera | iOS Safari | Opera Mini | Opera Mobile | Android Browser |
|---|---|---|---|---|---|---|---|---|---|
| Two versions back | 6.0 | 3.0 | 3.2 | 7.0 | 10.5 | 3.2 | | | 2.1 |
| Previous version | 7.0 | 3.5 | 4.0 | 8.0 | 10.6 | 4.0-4.1 | | | 2.2 |
| Current | 8.0 | 3.6 | 5.0 | 9.0 | 11.0 | 4.2 | 5.0 | 10.0 | 2.3 |
| Near Future (early 2011) | | 4.0 | | 10.0 | 11.1 | | | | |
| Future (mid/late 2011) | 9.0 | 5.0 | 6.0 | 11.0 | 11.5 | | | | |

**Note:** Currently not supported in Chrome on Linux.

Feedback

Figure 4.1 Most modern browsers apart from IE support offline access.

## Creating a Manifest

The manifest is a plain text file that must be saved with a `.manifest` filename extension. It's not important where you locate the manifest, but the most logical place is in the site root. However, if you want to make only part of a site available offline, the manifest should be located in the relevant folder and cover the files in all subfolders. The first line inside the manifest file should look like this:

```
CACHE MANIFEST
```

There should be only a single space between `CACHE` and `MANIFEST`, both of which should be in uppercase.

Following this is a list of files grouped according to how you want them to be treated when the user is offline:

▶ **Explicit section.** All files in this section are downloaded automatically, even if they're not required for the current page.

▶ **Online whitelist section.** Files in this section are never cached. The browser always tries to access the online version.

▶ **Fallback section.** This is where you specify substitute files that the browser should use when the user is offline.

The following basic rules apply to all sections:

▶ Each file must be listed on a separate line, except in the fallback section where the original and substitute files are listed on the same line with a space between them.

▶ Document-relative paths should be relative to the manifest.

▶ Paths relative to the site root (in other words, those that begin with a leading slash) or fully qualified URLs are also acceptable.

▶ The list should include not only web pages, but other assets, such as images, style sheets, and JavaScript files.

▶ Blank lines are permitted.

▶ Comments can be included, but they must be on a separate line beginning with a hash or pound sign (#) optionally preceded by spaces or tab characters.

Sections can be listed in any order and don't need to be a single block. For example, you might want to make some files available offline only for a limited period. So, it makes sense to list them separately from the core files that don't normally change.

You create sections by placing a section header on a separate line.

**NOTES**

Section headers must be written in uppercase and are followed by a colon. Headers can be preceded by spaces, but there should be nothing else on the same line.

### Specifying files that should be cached

The explicit section is the default, so files listed immediately after `CACHE MANIFEST` are automatically downloaded and cached. To switch back to the explicit section after the online whitelist or fallback section, place the following section header on a separate line:

```
CACHE:
```

NOTES

Technically speaking, you can use the CACHE: section header immediately after CACHE MANIFEST, but it's unnecessary.

### Specifying files that must always be accessed online

Server-side scripts and other files that you don't want to be cached locally should be listed in the online whitelist section. You create this by adding the following header on a separate line:

```
NETWORK:
```

Then list the path or URL of each file on a separate line in the same way as for files that you want to be downloaded.

If your site accesses resources on other domains or subdomains, you should add an asterisk (*) on a line of its own in the online whitelist section like this:

```
NETWORK:
*
```

This indicates that access to resources on other domains is not blocked.

### Specifying alternative files to use offline

To specify alternatives for files that can't be accessed offline, create a fallback section by placing the following section header on a separate line:

```
FALLBACK:
```

Each entry in the fallback section lists a file in the online site followed by the location of a substitute file to be used when offline. Both files are listed on the same line and separated by one or more spaces.

To represent any file, use a single forward slash (/) as the first part of the entry. For example:

```
FALLBACK:
/ offline.html
```

This substitutes offline.html for any file not listed elsewhere.

**Browser Caches**

Application caches are designed to make the website—or parts of it—available offline. They're separate from the normal browser cache, which speeds up the rendering of pages by avoiding the need to download files that haven't changed. When the normal cache reaches capacity, older files are deleted to make way for newer ones. The location of both types of cache is dependent on the browser.

The HTML5 specification doesn't prescribe any limit for the amount of disk space used by an application cache. The specification is equally vague about allowing users to delete specific application caches. Web developers should exercise their judgment about which files to make available offline and not fill up users' disk space unnecessarily.

*Keeping the cache up to date*

More often than not, updates to a site involve changing the contents of a file without changing its name. This presents a problem for the application cache. The browser checks only the filenames in the manifest. If they're the same, it assumes the cache doesn't need updating.

To force the browser to update the cache, you need to change the contents of the manifest. The simplest way to do this is to add a comment with a version number like this:

```
CACHE MANIFEST
# version 4
```

Increment the version number each time you make changes to the site, and upload the revised manifest after all the changes have been uploaded. You don't need to use a version number. Any unique value—such as a timestamp—in a comment will do.

### Serving the Manifest

You attach a manifest to a web page with the HTML5 `manifest` attribute in the opening `<html>` tag like this:

```
<html manifest="mysite.manifest">
```

The value of the `manifest` attribute should be a document-relative or site-root-relative path to the manifest file.

You should do this in every page in a site that you want to make available offline.

It's important to serve the manifest with the correct MIME type: `text/cache-manifest`.

Because this is a new MIME type, it might not be supported by all servers.

*Setting the correct MIME type on Apache*

If your web server runs on Apache, you should be able to configure it using an `.htaccess` file in your site root. If you already have an `.htaccess` file, add the following line to it:

```
AddType text/cache-manifest .manifest
```

If you don't have an `.htaccess` file, you can create one in Dreamweaver:

1. Choose File > New.

2. In the New Document dialog box, select Other from the list on the left, and set Page Type to Text. Click Create.

3. Type the following line of code into the new document, paying careful attention to spelling (Apache directives are case-sensitive):

    `AddType text/cache-manifest .manifest`

4. Save the file in your site root with the name **.htaccess**. The name begins with a dot. Although it's a text file, make sure it's *not* saved with a `.txt` filename extension.

    On Windows, the file will be saved as normal.

    On a Mac, you'll see a warning that files with names that begin with a dot are reserved for the system and will be hidden (**Figure 4.2**). Click Use ".". The file will be listed as normal in the Dreamweaver Files panel. However, you won't be able to see it in the Finder or any other Mac program unless it supports hidden files.

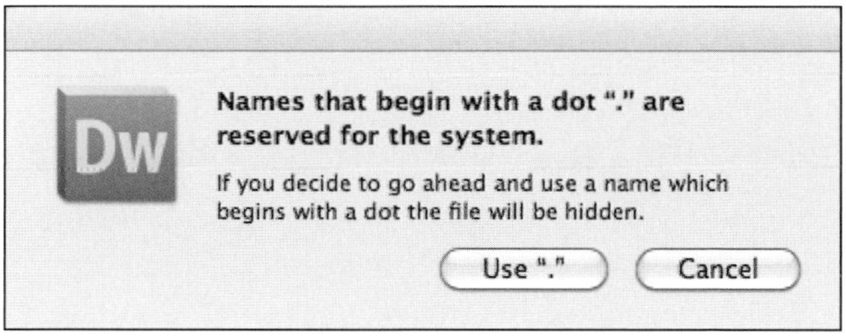

**Names that begin with a dot "." are reserved for the system.**

If you decide to go ahead and use a name which begins with a dot the file will be hidden.

Use "."    Cancel

Figure 4.2 On a Mac, Dreamweaver warns you that names beginning with a dot have special status.

5. Upload the `.htaccess` file to your website.

### Setting the MIME type on other web servers

If your website is on a server other than Apache, you need to ask the server administrator to enable the `text/cache-manifest` MIME type.

**.htaccess**

An `.htaccess` file is a mini-configuration file for the Apache web server. It has the advantage that all the settings are applied immediately without the need to restart the server. Normally, an `.htaccess` file is located in the site root and applies to the whole site. However, you can apply different settings to individual folders (directories) by placing an `.htaccess` file in the folder you want to control (the same settings apply to all subfolders unless overridden by another `.htaccess` file).

Most hosting companies configure their servers to allow site owners to fine-tune their settings with `.htaccess`. However, if you don't have permission to use `.htaccess`, you need to ask the server administrator to enable the `text/cache-manifest` MIME type.

As long as they're attached to a manifest, visited pages are stored in the application cache because a page that links to the manifest is automatically included in the explicit section. However, it's generally recommended that you list files individually rather than relying on this default behavior.

Web pages that use a server-side technology, such as PHP, ColdFusion, or ASP.NET, can also be linked to a manifest. However, the offline version stored by the application cache contains only the HTML output. For example, if the dynamic code outputs the current date, the version stored in the application cache displays the date when the online version was most recently accessed. As soon as you go back online, the stored date is updated.

### Creating a "Lazy" Manifest

The HTML5 specification includes among its examples the following extremely simple manifest:

```
CACHE MANIFEST
FALLBACK:
/ /offline.html
NETWORK:
*
```

Instead of downloading all pages immediately, the browser stores only the fallback page (offline.html) and pages that are visited while the user is online. When the user goes offline, cached pages are retrieved from the user's application cache. But if the user clicks a link to a page that hasn't previously been visited, offline.html is displayed instead.

This lazy way of caching can be very useful on a large site. However, you still need to update the manifest with a version number or other unique value each time a page is edited. Otherwise, the old version of the page remains in the application cache.

Only HTML pages can be linked to a manifest. So, other resources—such as style sheets and images—are not stored in the application cache unless they're listed in the explicit section of the manifest.

## Making the Tozai Hotel Site Available Offline

As you just learned, making a website available offline is a simple matter of generating the manifest, uploading it to your website, and making sure that it's served with the correct MIME type. The user's browser takes care of the rest. If the browser doesn't support offline web applications, it simply ignores the manifest.

The Tozai Hotel website consists of only 28 files, so typing out the manifest manually isn't a major chore, although it's important to get the spelling and path names right. However, life would be a lot easier if you could generate a file list automatically. So, I created a Dreamweaver extension to do it for you.

## Installing the Generate Site Manifest Extension

The Generate Site Manifest extension is included in the download files for this book, and it takes only a minute or so to install.

1. Launch Adobe Extension Manager CS5.5 from within Dreamweaver or directly using one of the following methods:

   ▶ Choose Commands > Manage Extensions.

   ▶ Choose Help > Manage Extensions.

   ▶ Launch the Extension Manager from the Start menu in Windows or from the Finder in Mac OS X.

2. Click the Install button in the Extension Manager title bar, and navigate to the ch04/extension folder in the download files.

3. Select GenerateSiteManifest_1_0.mxp, and click Open (Select on a Mac).

4. Read the Extension Disclaimer and choose to accept the terms. The extension should install immediately and display a brief description in the Extension Manager (**Figure 4.3**).

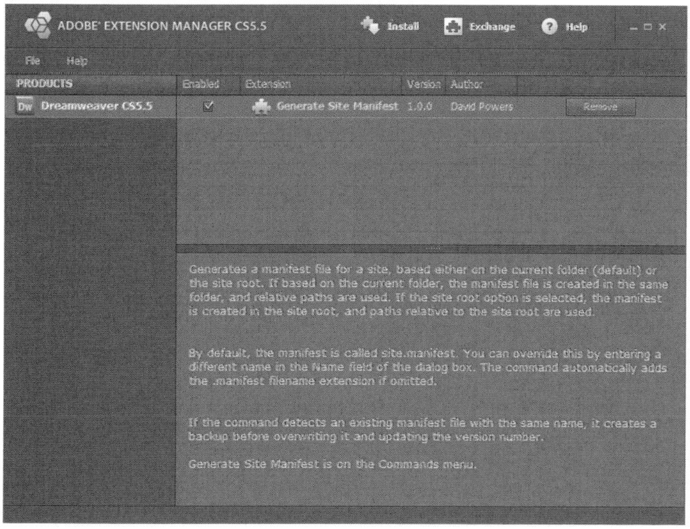

**Figure 4.3** The Generate Site Manifest extension has been successfully installed.

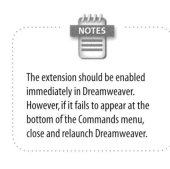

**Figure 4.4** The extension adds a new item at the bottom of the Commands menu.

**Figure 4.5** The Generate Site Manifest dialog box lets you choose the scope and name of the manifest.

**NOTES**

The extension should be enabled immediately in Dreamweaver. However, if it fails to appear at the bottom of the Commands menu, close and relaunch Dreamweaver.

**5.** The Generate Site Manifest extension should now be listed at the bottom of the Commands menu in Dreamweaver (**Figure 4.4**).

**6.** Close the Extension Manager.

### Using the Generate Site Manifest Command

The Generate Site Manifest command installed by the extension inspects the site's folder structure and builds a list of all files (except manifests and their backups, and .htaccess files), which it stores in a manifest file ready for you to edit. The command's dialog box (**Figure 4.5**) has the following options:

▶ The radio buttons let you choose whether to list files starting from the current folder or the site root.

▶ If you choose the "Current folder," all paths are relative to the folder, and the manifest is created in the same folder.

▶ If you choose "Site root," the paths are relative to the site root and the manifest is created in the root folder.

▶ By default, the manifest is saved as site.manifest. However, you can change this by entering your own value in the Name text field. The command automatically adds the .manifest filename extension to the name.

When you run the command the first time, it sets the manifest's version number to 1. If the command detects an existing manifest with the same name, it saves a backup with a .manifest.bak filename extension before generating a new manifest with an updated version number. This avoids the need to build the online whitelist and fallback sections from scratch each time you generate a new manifest file. You can copy and paste them from the backup when editing the new file.

Try out the command with the Tozai Hotel files.

**1.** Open one of the HTML files in your working copy of the Tozai Hotel site. Alternatively, open one of the HTML files in ch03/complete.

2. Choose Commands > Generate Site Manifest.

3. Leave the options in the Generate Site Manifest dialog box at their default settings, and click OK.

4. If site.manifest doesn't immediately appear in the Files panel, click the **C** icon at the top of the panel to refresh its contents. You should now see site.manifest listed in the same folder as the file you opened (**Figure 4.6**).

5. Before you can edit the manifest file in Dreamweaver, you need to make a small adjustment to the program's preferences. Choose Edit > Preferences (Dreamweaver > Preferences on a Mac), and select the File Types / Editors category from the list on the left.

6. In the "Open in code view" field, insert a space at the end of the existing list of filename extensions, and type **.manifest** (**Figure 4.7**).

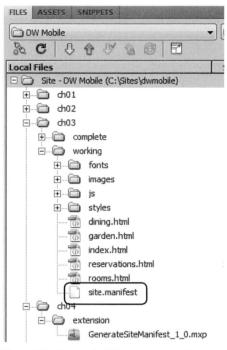

Figure 4.6 The manifest file has been created in the same folder.

**NOTES**

Don't forget the period at the beginning of .manifest.

Figure 4.7 You need to add the .manifest filename extension to the list of files that Dreamweaver can edit.

7. Click OK to close the Preferences dialog box.

8. In the Files panel, double-click site.manifest to open it in the Document window. You should see the following code:

```
CACHE MANIFEST

# version 1

dining.html
garden.html
index.html
reservations.html
rooms.html

fonts/Calluna-Regular-webfont.eot
fonts/Calluna-Regular-webfont.svg
fonts/Calluna-Regular-webfont.ttf
fonts/Calluna-Regular-webfont.woff

images/basin_bg.jpg
images/basin_bg_phone.jpg
images/basin_bg_tab.jpg
images/chef.jpg
images/cherry_blossom.png
images/exterior.jpg
images/exterior_tab.jpg
images/hotel-room.jpg
images/sake.jpg
images/sake_tab.jpg
images/sashimi.jpg
images/stone-lantern.jpg
images/sushi.jpg

js/jquery-1.5.min.js

styles/desktop.css
styles/phone.css
styles/tablet.css
styles/tozai.css
styles/tozai_mq.css
```

You now have a complete list of files ready to divide into the explicit, online whitelist, and fallback sections.

9. Edit the code by adding an online whitelist section header before the list of font files like this:

```
CACHE MANIFEST

# version 1

dining.html
garden.html
index.html
reservations.html
rooms.html

NETWORK:
fonts/Calluna-Regular-webfont.eot
```

10. Save site.manifest and close it.

11. Run the Generate Site Manifest command again and refresh the Files panel if necessary. You should now have both site.manifest and site.manifest.bak in the same folder as the HTML file you opened.

12. Double-click site.manifest to open it. The first few lines should look like this:

```
CACHE MANIFEST

# version 2

dining.html
garden.html
index.html
reservations.html
rooms.html

fonts/Calluna-Regular-webfont.eot
```

The version number has changed, and the list has been generated anew, so the online whitelist section header has disappeared.

**NOTES**

If you delete the existing manifest files, the version number reverts to 1. This is fine when experimenting before deploying a manifest file, but it could cause problems with a live site. If users have an earlier copy of the manifest with the same number, the updated files won't be downloaded.

**13.** Right-click site.manifest.bak and choose Open with > Dreamweaver from the context menu. The file contains the edit you made in step 9.

You can continue experimenting with the Generate Site Manifest command, selecting the option to list files starting from the site root, and changing the name.

### Editing the Manifest File

When deciding how to organize your manifest file, it's a good idea to look at the size of the files in your site. Unlike media queries, you can't restrict what is cached by each type of device. It's an all-or-nothing decision. Unless you're careful, you could undo all the good work of your media queries by forcing mobile phones to download files they'll never use.

Overall, the Tozai Hotel site weighs in at 696 KB, broken down as follows:

▶ **Fonts.** 212 KB

▶ **Images.** 370 KB

▶ **JavaScript (external).** 83 KB

▶ **Style sheets.** 9 KB

▶ **HTML files.** 22 KB

Quite clearly, the bulk of the weight lies in the first three categories. The fonts are used purely for aesthetic reasons, so they can easily be sacrificed offline. The styles specify alternative fonts anyway. Many of the images are decorative, but the site would be less attractive and meaningful if you got rid of all of them. However, the external JavaScript file is used only by reservations.html, which is meaningless offline. Although the form isn't connected to a processing script in the example files, in a real website users would need to be online to submit a request about the availability of rooms. So, the external JavaScript can be dispensed with; and reservations.html needs to have a fallback page for offline use.

Losing the fonts, external JavaScript, and some of the images reduces the overall download by approximately half. You can't avoid serving all the style sheets to every device, but the size is trivial and could be reduced by eliminating comments and unnecessary whitespace.

Here's my suggested version of site.manifest for the Tozai Hotel site:

```
CACHE MANIFEST

# version 1

dining.html
garden.html
index.html
rooms.html

images/basin_bg.jpg
images/chef.jpg
images/cherry_blossom.png
images/hotel-room.jpg
images/sashimi.jpg
images/stone-lantern.jpg
images/sushi.jpg

styles/desktop.css
styles/phone.css
styles/tablet.css
styles/tozai.css
styles/tozai_mq.css

FALLBACK:
images/basin_bg_phone.jpg images/basin_bg.jpg
images/basin_bg_tab.jpg images/basin_bg.jpg
reservations.html reservations_off.html

NETWORK:
fonts/Calluna-Regular-webfont.eot
fonts/Calluna-Regular-webfont.svg
fonts/Calluna-Regular-webfont.ttf
fonts/Calluna-Regular-webfont.woff

images/exterior.jpg
images/exterior_tab.jpg
images/sake.jpg
images/sake_tab.jpg
```

**NOTES**

In a real-world situation, it would make more sense to use the same background image for all devices rather than serving smaller ones through media queries. Alternatively, you could add the background images to the online whitelist section to prevent them from being cached and display the site offline without the background image.

The following points should be noted:

▶ Only one version of the background image at the top of the page, basin_bg.jpg, is in the explicit section. It's 37 KB but is required for the desktop layout.

▶ The fallback section instructs browsers to replace basin_bg_phone.jpg and basic_bg_tab.jpg with the larger image, basin_bg.jpg, when offline. The styles for tablets and phones use the CSS3 `background-size` property to scale the image, so it looks the same in all devices.

▶ The fallback section tells browsers to substitute reservations_off.html for reservations.html when offline. This tells users to go online to check the availability of rooms (**Figure 4.8**).

**Figure 4.8** When accessed offline, the reservations page displays a different message.

▶ In addition to the fonts, four images that are 183 KB in total have been added to the online whitelist section. This prevents them from being downloaded to the application cache. It means these particular images won't be available offline (**Figure 4.9**), but they're mainly decorative. However, they need to be listed explicitly here. Otherwise, they aren't displayed even when the user is online.

▶ The manifest results in browsers caching 177 KB, just 25 percent of the total size of the site.

**Figure 4.9** The exterior image isn't shown when the index page is viewed offline on a tablet.

> **TIP**
>
> Instead of listing all files that you don't want to be downloaded, you can use an asterisk (*) on a line of its own after the NETWORK: section header as a convenient shortcut.

### Attaching the Manifest File

The manifest file needs to be attached to all web pages listed in the explicit section. However, it should not be attached to any pages that you don't want to be cached, because attaching a manifest automatically adds the file to the explicit section, even if it isn't listed there.

There are two ways to attach a manifest file in Dreamweaver:

▶ Manually in Code view

▶ With the Find and Replace dialog box

To attach a manifest file in Code view:

1. Position the insertion point just before the closing angle bracket of the opening <html> tag at the top of the page.

2. Insert a space to bring up code hints. Use your keyboard down arrow key or mouse to select manifest (**Figure 4.10**), and press Enter/Return or double-click. This inserts manifest="" and moves the insertion point to between the quotes.

**Figure 4.10** Dreamweaver displays a code hint for manifest in the <html> tag.

3. Type **site.manifest** (or the name of your manifest file) between the quotes.

   Alternatively, right-click and choose Code Hint Tools > URL Browser from the context menu. Click Browse, and navigate to the manifest file. Click OK (Choose on a Mac) to insert the filename and path.

In a small site like Tozai Hotel, attaching a manifest file manually to each HTML file takes only a couple of minutes, but you need a more efficient approach on a larger site. Dreamweaver doesn't have a dedicated dialog box to handle this, but the Find and Replace dialog box does the job quickly and easily.

This is how you do it:

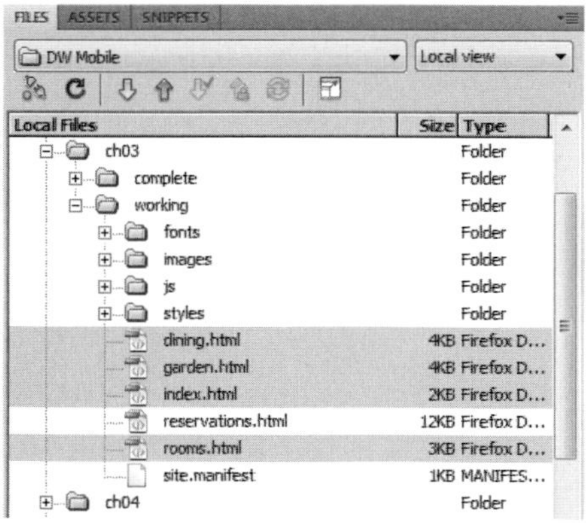

1. In the Files panel, Ctrl-click/Command-click to select the files you want to attach the manifest file to (**Figure 4.11**).

2. Choose Edit > Find and Replace or press Ctrl+F/ Command+F to open the Find and Replace dialog box.

3. Set "Find in" to **Selected Files in Site**.

4. Set Search to **Specific Tag**, and select **html** from the adjacent list.

5. If necessary, click the ⊟ icon to remove further search option menus.

6. Set Action to **Set Attribute**, and select **manifest** from the adjacent list.

7. In the To field, type the name (and path, if necessary) of the manifest file. The settings in the Find and Replace dialog box should now look like **Figure 4.12**.

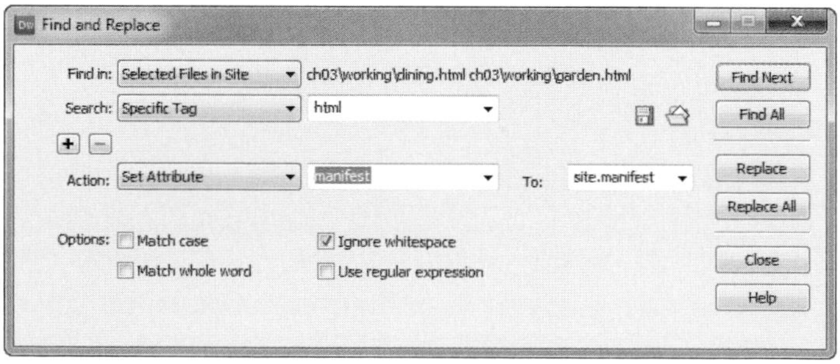

**Figure 4.11** Select only the files that you want to be cached by the manifest.

**Figure 4.12** Find and Replace offers a quick way to attach a manifest to multiple pages.

8. Click Replace All.

9. Dreamweaver warns you that the operation cannot be undone in files that are not currently open and asks you to confirm. Click Yes.

10. The Search tab of the Reports panel opens to display the changes (**Figure 4.13**).

| SEARCH | REFERENCE | W3C VALIDATION | BROWSER COMPATIBILITY | LINK CHECKER | SITE REPORTS |
|---|---|---|---|---|---|
| ▷ | File | ▲ | Matched Text | | |
| ○ | ● ch03\working\dining.html | | <html manifest="site.manifest">  <head>  <meta | | |
| ⊡ | ● ch03\working\garden.html | | <html manifest="site.manifest">  <head>  <meta | | |
| | ● ch03\working\index.html | | <html manifest="site.manifest">  <head>  <meta | | |
| | ● ch03\working\rooms.html | | <html manifest="site.manifest">  <head>  <meta | | |

Done. 4 items found, 4 replaced in 4 documents.

**Figure 4.13** The Reports panel confirms that the `manifest` attribute has been added to the selected pages.

TIP

If you attach the wrong file or make a mistake in the path name, you can use the Find and Replace dialog box to change the value of the `manifest` attribute. You can also remove the `manifest` attribute by setting Action to Remove Attribute.

Right-click the gray area to the right of the tabs, and choose Close Tab Group to close the Reports panel.

### Testing a Site Offline

As soon as you add a manifest file to the pages in a site, browsers that support offline web applications start caching the files. Once they're stored in the application cache, the browser relies on the manifest file to inform it of any changes. It's worth repeating that the manifest file needs to be updated not only when you add or remove files from the site, but also if existing pages are edited. Consequently, you should attach the manifest file only in the final stages of testing a site. Otherwise, you need to update the manifest's version number every time you make an adjustment to the site.

When you have decided the site's ready, create the manifest file, and attach it to the pages you want to make available offline. Then upload the manifest and web pages to your web server.

In theory, the application cache should be created and populated by visiting just one page. However, the time it takes for all files to be downloaded depends entirely on the browser and network conditions.

To test the application cache on a mobile device, disable all wireless connections:

▶ On iOS, choose Settings, and turn on Airplane Mode.

▶ On Android devices, choose Settings > Wireless and network(s), and tap Airplane mode or Flight mode to select it.

▶ On BlackBerry, choose Manage Connections, and tap Turn All Connections Off.

It might take a short while for the mobile device to disconnect from Wi-Fi and other networks.

Once disconnected, open the browser and navigate to the site. Usually, the browser displays a warning telling you there is no network connection (**Figure 4.14**) or telling you to turn off Airplane Mode (**Figure 4.15**).

Click OK to dismiss the alert. You should now be able to continue to the site, which should be loaded from the application cache. If you have specified an alternative page in the fallback section, it should be displayed instead of the normal page, as shown in Figure 4.8 earlier in this chapter.

If the alternative page fails to display or if images are missing, there are two likely explanations:

▶ The manifest file is not being served with the correct MIME type.

▶ The files are being served from the browser's normal cache rather than from the application cache.

A simple way to check whether the manifest file is being served with the correct MIME type is to try to load it directly in Firefox, Safari, or IE 9. If the browser asks if you want to save the file, the MIME type is probably OK. The Firefox dialog box actually confirms it as a manifest file (**Figure 4.16**). If the manifest opens in the browser as plain text, you need to check the .htaccess file or ask the server administrator to verify the MIME type.

**Figure 4.14** In Flight mode, the Samsung Galaxy Tab warns about the lack of a network connection.

**Figure 4.15** iOS tells you to turn off Airplane Mode and offers a shortcut to Settings.

**NOTES**

At the time of this writing, Opera and Chrome open manifest files as plain text, even when they are served with the correct MIME type.

The second issue is not quite as easy to check. In my experiments on a small number of mobile devices, browsers appeared to use the application cache only if a file couldn't be found in the normal cache. For example, my iPad continued to display the online version of reservations.html, even offline. However, going back online and visiting several other sites cleared it out of the cache. Only then did the offline version display correctly.

Generally speaking, the fact that browsers store files in their local cache is beneficial. It avoids unnecessary downloads, saving bandwidth and speeding up the user's experience. However, you might want to add the following line to the <head> of pages that you don't want to be available offline:

```
<meta http-equiv="expires" content="-1">
```

This doesn't prevent the page from being cached, but it expires the page immediately, so the browser always fetches a new version. The downside of using this technique is that the page will always be downloaded afresh.

## Going Offline

It doesn't take a great deal of effort to make a website available offline, although it's important to update the manifest file by adding a version number or another unique identifier each time you make any changes to the site's content. However, just because you can make a site available offline doesn't necessarily mean that you should. Ask yourself whether the site makes sense offline. Remember that a manifest forces the browser to download all files listed in the explicit section, taking up bandwidth and valuable disk space on the user's device. Firefox asks the user's permission to create an application cache, but most other browsers don't.

When creating a manifest, give careful thought to the size and importance of files you add to the explicit section. Are they really vital to the offline version of the site? If not, add them to the online whitelist section or specify substitutes in the fallback section.

All the techniques explored in Chapters 2–4 can be used in websites designed for a wide range of devices from desktops to mobile phones. The rest of the book is devoted to building websites and apps designed specifically for modern smartphones using the jQuery Mobile framework, which has been integrated into Dreamweaver CS5.5.

SECTION III

# jQuery Mobile and PhoneGap

CHAPTER

# Introducing jQuery Mobile

*Round round get around*
*I get around, yeah*

—The Beach Boys

# Introducing jQuery Mobile

Websites are traditionally made up of individual pages, each stored in a separate HTML file. Even if the site is generated by a content management system, such as WordPress or Drupal, loading a new page usually involves a round trip to the web server. The need to fetch the HTML for each new page is a bottleneck for mobile devices, particularly on a slow or unreliable connection. To overcome this problem, jQuery Mobile stores the HTML markup for multiple pages in a single file and uses JavaScript to manipulate the file's document object model (DOM) to display only the first page. Tapping a link hides the page and replaces it with another. But jQuery Mobile does much more. It's a sophisticated JavaScript and CSS framework designed to build websites that act and feel like mobile apps.

Pages glide in and out or flip. Each page has a back button, and JavaScript keeps track of visited pages to ensure smooth navigation. Less frequently visited pages can be stored in separate files to reduce the size of the initial download. There's also a wide range of user interface (UI) and form widgets, such as navigation bars, accordions, check box and radio button groups, and sliders.

Dreamweaver CS5.5 not only supports jQuery Mobile, but two of its engineers, Kin Blas and Jorge Taylor, have been actively involved in the development of the framework, with Kin contributing significant parts of the JavaScript code. As the name suggests, jQuery Mobile is based on the extremely popular jQuery JavaScript framework. You don't need to know JavaScript or jQuery to use jQuery Mobile, although you'll get a lot more out of it if you do.

Sites built with jQuery Mobile work in all current browsers, including Internet Explorer 7 and later, not just on mobile devices.

In this chapter, you'll learn how to create a simple jQuery Mobile site and navigate between pages. You'll also insert a couple of widgets and learn some of the basic principles underlying jQuery Mobile. Although the starter pages and Insert panel do a lot of the coding for you, it's important to understand what the code means, so you can edit or customize the widgets.

## Creating a Basic Site with jQuery Mobile

To help you get started with jQuery Mobile, Dreamweaver CS5.5 provides three sample pages, which you access through the New Document dialog box.

1. Choose File > New to open the New Document dialog box.

2. Select Page from Sample in the list on the left.

3. In the Sample Folder column, select Mobile Starters (**Figure 5.1**).

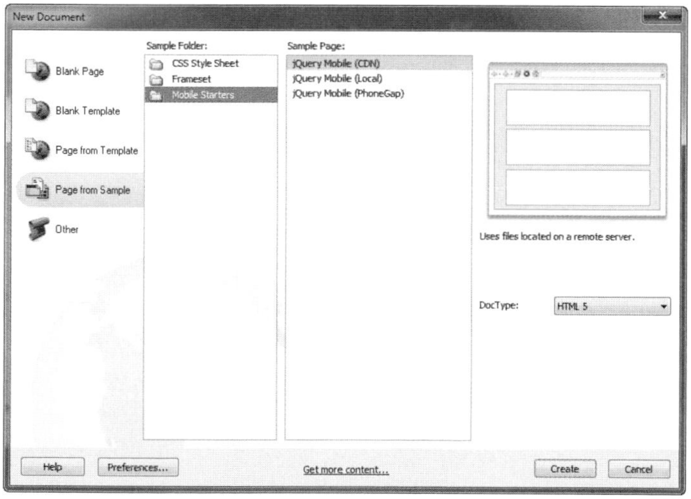

**Updating jQuery Mobile**

When Dreamweaver CS5.5 was released, work on version 1.0 of the jQuery Mobile framework was at an advanced stage, but still incomplete. Check www.adobe.com/support/dreamweaver to see if a Dreamweaver extension is available to update the jQuery Mobile files and Mobile Starter pages.

Also refer to the Close-Up titled "Changing the Library Source" later in this chapter for details of how to obtain and link to the most up-to-date versions of the jQuery Mobile files.

**Figure 5.1** The starter pages create a jQuery Mobile site with placeholders for four pages.

You are not restricted to using static HTML pages. You can also use jQuery Mobile with pages dynamically generated by a server-side technology, such as PHP, ColdFusion, or ASP.NET.

Although there are three sample pages, they all create an identical skeleton site. The difference lies in the external JavaScript and CSS files they attach to the HTML page. When you select Mobile Starters, you're presented with the following choices:

▶ **jQuery Mobile (CDN).** This version links to files served by the jQuery content distribution network (CDN). The potential advantage of using the CDN is that visitors to your site might already have the files in their cache if they have visited other sites that also use the CDN. This speeds up the display and reduces the amount of bandwidth used. The disadvantages are that there's a small possibility the CDN might be down, and that you need to be online when testing your files in Dreamweaver.

▶ **jQuery Mobile (Local).** This version creates a folder called jquery-mobile in your site root, copies all the necessary files and images to it, and links to the local versions of the files. When deploying the site on the Internet, you need to upload the jquery-mobile folder and all its contents to your web server.

▶ **jQuery Mobile (PhoneGap).** This is the same as the local version with the addition of a link to an extra JavaScript file, which is required for accessing the mobile device's native features—such as accelerometer, camera, and geolocation—through the PhoneGap framework. You'll learn more about PhoneGap in Chapter 7.

## Using a Starter Page

The best way to understand how jQuery Mobile works is to create a basic site using a starter page. It's not necessary to define a new Dreamweaver site unless you want to; you can just save the starter page in a separate working folder. However, *don't* call the folder jquery-mobile, because that's the name Dreamweaver uses for the local files that it installs.

The jQuery Mobile framework makes extensive use of HTML5 features. It's important to use the correct DOCTYPE to ensure browsers handle the pages correctly.

1. Choose File > New to open the New Document dialog box, and select Page from Sample. Then select Mobile Starters in the Sample Folder column and jQuery Mobile (Local) in the Sample Page column.

2. Check that DocType is set to **HTML 5** (the setting is on the right of the New Document dialog box under the thumbnail image). Change the setting if necessary.

3. Click Create. Dreamweaver inserts in Design view the basic structure for what will become a four-page site when viewed on a mobile phone or in a browser. It's a single HTML page with four jQuery Mobile page blocks (**Figure 5.2**).

4. Choose File > Save, and save the file as **index.html** in your working folder or in the site root if you created a new Dreamweaver site.

5. When you click Save, Dreamweaver displays the Copy Dependent Files dialog box (**Figure 5.3**). Click Copy to save the jQuery Mobile files to your Dreamweaver site root.

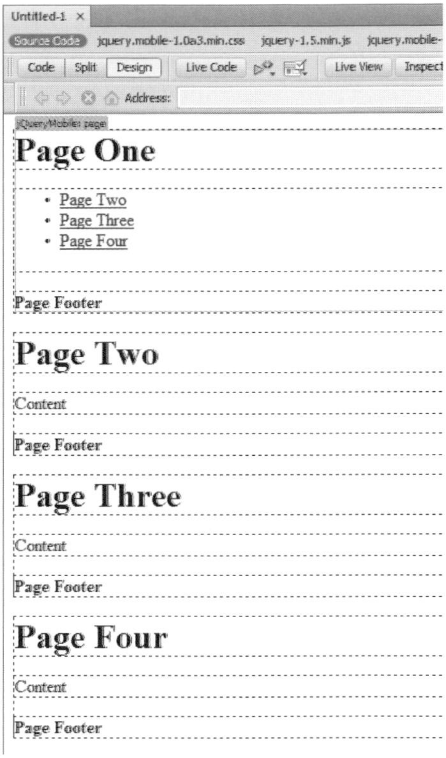

Figure 5.2 The starter page contains only the bare bones of a mobile site.

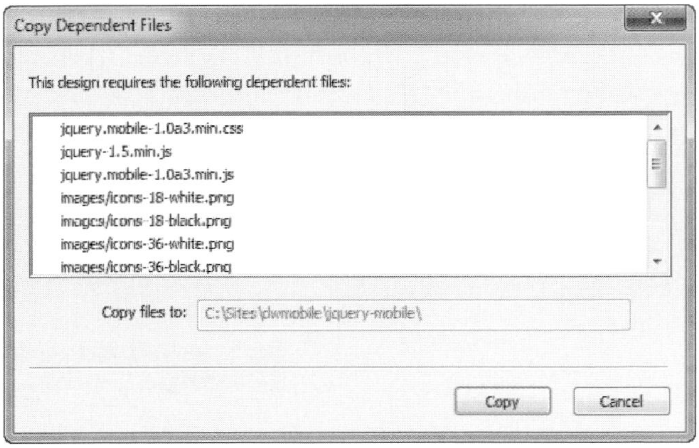

Figure 5.3 Dreamweaver creates local copies of all the files required by jQuery Mobile.

| FILES | ASSETS | SNIPPETS | | | |
|---|---|---|---|---|---|

Local Files | Size | Type | Modified

| | | | |
|---|---|---|---|
| Site - DW Mobile (C:\Sites\dw... | | Folder | 20/03/2011 17: |
| ch01 | | Folder | 01/02/2011 23: |
| ch02 | | Folder | 06/02/2011 14: |
| ch03 | | Folder | 23/02/2011 14: |
| ch04 | | Folder | 08/03/2011 08: |
| ch05 | | Folder | 20/03/2011 14: |
| begin | | Folder | 20/03/2011 14: |
| complete | | Folder | 20/03/2011 16: |
| images | | Folder | 13/03/2011 10: |
| source | | Folder | 11/03/2011 18: |
| working | | Folder | 20/03/2011 17: |
| index.html | 6KB | Firefox... | 15/03/2011 17: |
| ch06 | | Folder | 17/03/2011 18: |
| ch07 | | Folder | 20/03/2011 17: |
| ch08 | | Folder | 20/03/2011 17: |
| ch09 | | Folder | 20/03/2011 17: |
| jquery-mobile | | Folder | 12/03/2011 16: |
| images | | Folder | 09/03/2011 13: |
| ajax-loader.png | 1KB | PNG File | 09/03/2011 13: |
| form-check-off.png | 1KB | PNG File | 09/03/2011 13: |
| form-check-on.png | 1KB | PNG File | 09/03/2011 13: |
| form-radio-off.png | 1KB | PNG File | 09/03/2011 13: |
| form-radio-on.png | 1KB | PNG File | 09/03/2011 13: |
| icon-search-black... | 2KB | PNG File | 09/03/2011 13: |
| icons-18-black.png | 1KB | PNG File | 04/02/2011 13: |
| icons-18-white.png | 1KB | PNG File | 04/02/2011 13: |
| icons-36-black.png | 2KB | PNG File | 04/02/2011 13: |
| icons-36-white.png | 2KB | PNG File | 04/02/2011 13: |
| jquery-1.5.min.js | 83KB | JScript ... | 09/03/2011 13: |
| jquery.mobile-1.0a3.... | 41KB | Cascad... | 09/03/2011 21: |
| jquery.mobile-1.0a3.... | 55KB | JScript ... | 09/03/2011 13: |

**Figure 5.4** The jquery-mobile folder is always created in the site root.

**TIP**

Normally, you need to hold down the Ctrl/Command key while clicking links in Live view. However, jQuery Mobile links appear to work without the need to do so. If nothing happens when you try to click a link, try holding down the appropriate key. Alternatively, choose View > Live View Options > Follow Links Continuously. This option works only with the current file and needs to be reselected each time you activate Live view.

**6.** In the Files panel, expand the jquery-mobile folder. It contains two JavaScript files, a style sheet, and an images folder with several .png files (**Figure 5.4**). The actual number of image files varies according to the version of jQuery Mobile.

To reduce the number of files that need to be downloaded, jQuery Mobile uses CSS3 rather than images for many effects, such as gradients and rounded corners. Many of the icons are stored as CSS sprites and displayed using background positioning.

**7.** Resize Design view by clicking the down arrow next to the Multiscreen button in the Document toolbar and choosing 320 × 480 Smart Phone from the list of window sizes.

Alternatively, choose View > Window Sizes or click the window size in the status bar at the bottom of the Document window to open the list of window sizes.

**8.** Activate Live view. The previously unstyled skeleton is transformed with only Page One displayed and the unordered list converted into a series of buttons with right-facing arrows indicating they're links (**Figure 5.5**).

**9.** The whole area of each button is clickable. Click a link to one of the other pages. As you click, you should notice the button turn light blue before the existing page is replaced by the one you selected. The new page has a Back button at the top left of the header (**Figure 5.6**).

| Page One |
|---|
| Page Two |
| Page Three |
| Page Four |
| Page Footer |

| ‹ Back | Page Three |
|---|---|
| Content | |
| Page Footer | |

**Figure 5.5** The first page is turned into a navigation menu.

**Figure 5.6** Each page block is displayed as a separate page, even though the underlying HTML is in the same file.

**CSS Sprites**

A CSS sprite is an image that contains several smaller images. For example, icons-18-black.png (**Figure 5.7**) combines 18 icons in a single file. Each icon is 18 pixels wide, so CSS is used to apply the image as the background to an 18-pixel-wide element. The horizontal position of the background image is adjusted to move the correct icon into view. To display the right-facing arrow, `background-position` is set to -54px 0, moving the background image 54 pixels to the left and zero pixels down.

**Figure 5.7** Storing multiple icons as a single image reduces the number of downloads.

Creating CSS sprites can be time-consuming because the background positioning needs to be very accurate. However, they significantly reduce the number of resources that the browser needs to download, and they're supported by all mainstream browsers in current use.

**10.** Click the Back button to return to the first page block. The transition in Live view might seem jerky, but it's normally very smooth when viewed in a browser or on a mobile device.

Because the starter page contains only placeholder text, the content is far from exciting. But once you start filling the page blocks with your own content and adding widgets, you'll begin to appreciate the power of the jQuery Mobile framework. First, let's take a closer look at the HTML markup.

### Inspecting the Structure of a jQuery Mobile Site

When you activate Live view or load index.html into a browser, jQuery Mobile manipulates the DOM, dynamically adding classes to most HTML elements. In some cases, this styles the elements and hides or reveals a section of the file. In other cases, it injects new elements, such as the Back button, into the DOM. The JavaScript also binds event handlers to many elements. Because jQuery Mobile is specifically designed for mobile devices, the events respond not only to clicks, but also to touch gestures. Consequently, a jQuery Mobile site should work equally well on a smartphone, tablet, or desktop browser.

Let's take a look at the code inserted by the starter page to see how a jQuery Mobile site is structured.

**NOTES**

Not all browsers are equal. The jQuery Mobile team is concentrating its efforts on the most widely used mobile platforms, giving top priority to Android, iOS, BlackBerry 6, Palm WebOS, and Windows Phone 7. There are plans to extend support to BlackBerry 5 and Nokia. Details of mobile device support can be found at http://jquerymobile.com/gbs.

1. Open the starter page that you created in the previous section in the Document window, and click the Split button to reveal the underlying code.

2. The code at the top of the page looks like this:

```
<!DOCTYPE html>
<html>
<head>
<meta charset="utf-8">
<title>jQuery Mobile Web App</title>
<link href="../../jquery-mobile/jquery.mobile-
➥ 1.0a3.min.css" rel="stylesheet" type=
➥ "text/css"/>
<script src="../../jquery-mobile/jquery-1.5.
➥ min.js" type="text/javascript"></script>
<script src="../../jquery-mobile/jquery.mobile
➥ -1.0a3.min.js" type="text/javascript">
➥ </script>
</head>
```

The page begins with an HTML5 DOCTYPE declaration and sets the character set to Unicode (UTF-8). The highlighted lines of code attach the jQuery Mobile style sheet and two external JavaScript files: the jQuery core library and the jQuery Mobile script.

Recent best practice recommends against loading JavaScript files in the <head> of a document because it blocks all other activity until the JavaScript has been parsed. However, it's essential to load these three files first because jQuery Mobile applies many markup enhancements before the document.ready event fires. Don't move the <script> tags to the bottom of the page.

> **TIP**
>
> The jQuery Mobile team is likely to release regular updates to the JavaScript files and style sheet. I'll show you in "Creating and linking to an external file with a single page block" later in this chapter how to keep your versions up to date.

**3.** Scroll down to the `<body>` section. The code used to build the first two page blocks of the jQuery Mobile site looks like this:

```
<div data-role="page" id="page">
    <div data-role="header">
        <h1>Page One</h1>
    </div>
    <div data-role="content">
        <ul data-role="listview">
            <li><a href="#page2">Page Two
            ➥ </a></li>
            <li><a href="#page3">Page Three
            ➥ </a></li>
            <li><a href="#page4">Page Four
            ➥ </a></li>
        </ul>
    </div>
    <div data-role="footer">
        <h4>Page Footer</h4>
    </div>
</div>

<div data-role="page" id="page2">
    <div data-role="header">
        <h1>Page Two</h1>
    </div>
    <div data-role="content">
        Content
    </div>
    <div data-role="footer">
        <h4>Page Footer</h4>
    </div>
</div>
```

Your initial impression is likely to be that someone has run riot with `<div>` elements. Each page block is wrapped in a `<div>`, as are the headers, footers, and content sections. Although this sounds contrary to HTML5's aims of a more meaningful, semantic structure, the reality is somewhat different, as you'll see in a moment.

The other points to note in this basic structure are

▸ Most elements contain a `data-role` attribute that describes the element's role within the structure. This attribute is one of the most important features of jQuery Mobile. It's what the HTML5 specification calls a *custom data attribute*. So, it's a perfectly valid markup.

▸ Each `<div>` that represents a page within the site is identified by `data-role="page"`.

▸ Each page block has a unique ID. By default, Dreamweaver assigns `page` to the first one, `page2` to the second, and so on.

▸ The links that load these internal page blocks point to named anchors—in other words, the ID preceded by a hash sign. For example, the link to the second page block uses `href="#page2"`. It's only DOM manipulation that makes it appear to be a separate page. As you'll see later in this chapter, links to external pages point to the filename or URL.

4. Click the Live Code button to see the HTML code generated by jQuery Mobile when the page is loaded in a browser (**Figure 5.8**).

The generated code is considerably more complex than the raw HTML. The jQuery Mobile framework uses the `data-role` attributes to assign classes to each element according to its function in the page. To make the site accessible to visually impaired people using a screen reader, it also injects WAI-ARIA `role` and `aria-level` attributes (see Table 2.2 in Chapter 2). As Figure 5.8 shows, the `<div>` with the `data-role` value `content` is assigned the WAI-ARIA `main` role, indicating that it contains the main content of the page.

```
9   <div data-role="page" id="page" data-url="page" class="ui-page ui-body-c
    ui-page-active">
10      <div data-role="header" class="ui-bar-a ui-header" role="banner">
11          <h1 class="ui-title" tabindex="0" role="heading" aria-level="1">
    Page One</h1>
12      </div>
13      <div data-role="content" class="ui-content" role="main">
14          <ul data-role="listview" class="ui-listview" role="listbox">
15              <li role="option" tabindex="0" data-theme="c" class="ui-btn
    ui-btn-icon-right ui-li ui-btn-up-c"><div class="ui-btn-inner"><div class=
    "ui-btn-text"><a href="#page2" class="ui-link-inherit">Page Two</a></div>
    <span class="ui-icon ui-icon-arrow-r"></span></div></li>
16              <li role="option" tabindex="-1" data-theme="c" class="ui-btn
    ui-btn-icon-right ui-li ui-btn-up-c"><div class="ui-btn-inner"><div class=
    "ui-btn-text"><a href="#page3" class="ui-link-inherit">Page Three</a></div>
    <span class="ui-icon ui-icon-arrow-r"></span></div></li>
17              <li role="option" tabindex="-1" data-theme="c" class="ui-btn
    ui-btn-icon-right ui-li ui-btn-up-c"><div class="ui-btn-inner"><div class=
    "ui-btn-text"><a href="#page4" class="ui-link-inherit">Page Four</a></div>
    <span class="ui-icon ui-icon-arrow-r"></span></div></li>
18          </ul>
19      </div>
20      <div data-role="footer" class="ui-bar-a ui-footer" role="contentinfo">
21          <h4 class="ui-title" tabindex="0" role="heading" aria-level="1">
    Page Footer</h4>
22      </div>
23  </div>
```

**Figure 5.8** The jQuery Mobile framework makes sites accessible by injecting WAI-ARIA roles into the HTML elements.

5. With Live code still active, pass your mouse pointer over the page link buttons in Live view. As the pointer moves from one button to the next, you should see the class names highlighted in pink as they change dynamically (**Figure 5.9**).

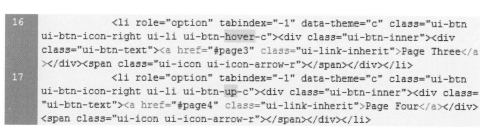

```
16              <li role="option" tabindex="-1" data-theme="c" class="ui-btn
    ui-btn-icon-right ui-li ui-btn-hover-c"><div class="ui-btn-inner"><div
    class="ui-btn-text"><a href="#page3" class="ui-link-inherit">Page Three</a
    ></div><span class="ui-icon ui-icon-arrow-r"></span></div></li>
17              <li role="option" tabindex="-1" data-theme="c" class="ui-btn
    ui-btn-icon-right ui-li ui-btn-up-c"><div class="ui-btn-inner"><div class=
    "ui-btn-text"><a href="#page4" class="ui-link-inherit">Page Four</a></div>
    <span class="ui-icon ui-icon-arrow-r"></span></div></li>
```

**Figure 5.9** As you move the mouse pointer over the buttons, the classes switch between hover and up.

**TIP**

If you want to inspect the changes to the code during the transition to another page, press F6 to freeze the JavaScript. Pressing F6 again normally toggles JavaScript back on, but disrupting jQuery Mobile is likely to prevent the page from responding further. Exit Live view and then reactivate it to restore normal functionality.

**6.** Keep your eye on Live code as you click one of the links in Live view. You should see several sections of code highlighted in pink (**Figure 5.10**).

As Figure 5.10 shows, the <base> tag in the <head> of the document is updated to show the name of the page being navigated to, and the <body> tag is assigned the ui-mobile-viewport-transitioning class. The clicked button is also assigned the ui-btn-active class.

These classes are applied for less than a second during the transition from one page to the next. When the new page loads, further dynamic changes to the classes display it within the viewport.

```
1   <!DOCTYPE html><html class="ui-mobile-nosupport-boxshadow ui-mobile
    portrait min-width-320px min-width-480px max-width-768px max-width-1024px"
    ><head><base href="file:///C|/Sites/dwmobile/ch05/working/page3"><meta
    name="viewport" content="width=device-width, minimum-scale=1,
    maximum-scale=1">
2   <meta charset="utf-8">
3   <title>jQuery Mobile Web App</title>
4   <link href="../../jquery-mobile/jquery.mobile-1.0a3.min.css" rel=
    "stylesheet" type="text/css">
5   <script src="../../jquery-mobile/jquery-1.5.min.js" type="text/javascript"
    ></script>
6   <script src="../../jquery-mobile/jquery.mobile-1.0a3.min.js" type=
    "text/javascript"></script>
7   </head><body class="ui-mobile-viewport ui-mobile-viewport-transitioning">
8
9   <div data-role="page" id="page" data-url="page" class="ui-page ui-body-c
    ui-page-active slide out">
10      <div data-role="header" class="ui-bar-a ui-header" role="banner">
11          <h1 class="ui-title" tabindex="0" role="heading" aria-level="1">
    Page One</h1>
12      </div>
13      <div data-role="content" class="ui-content" role="main">
14          <ul data-role="listview" class="ui-listview" role="listbox">
15              <li role="option" tabindex="0" data-theme="c" class="ui-btn
    ui-btn-icon-right ui-li ui-btn-up-c"><div class="ui-btn-inner"><div class=
    "ui-btn-text"><a href="#page2" class="ui-link-inherit">Page Two</a></div>
    <span class="ui-icon ui-icon-arrow-r"></span></div></li>
16              <li role="option" tabindex="0" data-theme="c" class="ui-btn
    ui-btn-icon-right ui-li ui-btn-up-c ui-btn-active"><div class=
    "ui-btn-inner"><div class="ui-btn-text"><a href="#page3" class=
    "ui-link-inherit">Page Three</a></div><span class="ui-icon
    ui-icon-arrow-r"></span></div></li>
```

**Figure 5.10** Clicking a link results in multiple changes to the CSS classes.

You don't need to understand the minute details of how jQuery Mobile handles the page transitions, but it's useful to be able to inspect the code generated by the browser. As you just learned, jQuery Mobile applies multiple classes to most HTML elements. Knowing which classes are applied at any particular time helps you customize the styles to give your site an individual look (styling a jQuery Mobile site is the subject of Chapter 7).

### Adding Content to the Starter Page

Now that you understand the basic structure of a jQuery Mobile multiple-page file, let's flesh out the starter page with some content. For a dedicated mobile site, it's generally a good idea to pare down the content to avoid visitors having to scroll through long pages on a small screen. The download files for this chapter contain a shorter version of the text in the Tozai Hotel case study from Chapters 2–4. Of course, feel free to use your own content if you prefer.

1. With the starter page open in the Document window, exit Live view if necessary. In the Document toolbar, replace the default value in the Title field with **Tozai Hotel**.

2. Select the Page One heading in Design view, and replace it with **Tozai Hotel**.

3. Select each of the links in the unordered list in turn, and replace them with **Guest Rooms**, **Dining**, and **Garden**.

4. Position the insertion point after Garden in the final list item, and press Enter/Return to insert a new list item. Type **Reservations**.

5. Select the text you have just typed in the new list item, and type **reservations.html** in the Link field of the Property inspector. The page you're linking to doesn't exist yet; you'll create it later.

**6.** Open Split view, and click the turquoise "jQuery Mobile: listview" tab at the top left of the unordered list of links to select the underlying HTML code (**Figure 5.11**).

**Figure 5.11** Each jQuery Mobile widget has a turquoise tab that can be used to select the HTML code.

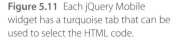

> **TIP**
>
> If you can't see the turquoise tab when you move your mouse pointer over a jQuery Mobile widget, choose View > Visual Aids and make sure there's a check mark next to Invisible Elements. If there isn't, select Invisible Elements to turn on the option.

**7.** Press the keyboard right arrow key once to deselect the unordered list and move the insertion point outside the closing </ul> tag.

**8.** The text for the Tozai Hotel site is available in three formats in the ch05/source folder. Open index.docx, index.doc, or index.txt; copy the Where East Meets West heading; and the following two paragraphs.

**9.** If you used one of the Microsoft Word documents, choose Edit > Paste Special or press Ctrl+Shift+V/ Shift+Command+V. In the Paste Special dialog box, select the "Text with structure (paragraphs, lists, tables, etc.)" radio button and the "Clean up Word paragraph spacing" check box. Then click OK to paste the text into the page.

If you used the plain text version, simply copy and paste the text. Instead of wrapping the heading and paragraphs in the appropriate HTML tags, Dreamweaver inserts line breaks (<br> tags). You need to format the text manually.

**10.** Click anywhere inside the Where East Meets West heading, and format it as a level 2 heading using the Format menu in the Property inspector in HTML mode or by pressing Ctrl+2/Command+2.

11. Click anywhere inside the Page Footer heading in the first page block, and select Paragraph from the Format menu in the Property inspector. Replace the placeholder text by copying and pasting the address from the Word document or text file that you opened in step 8.

12. Save index.html and change the Document window size by choosing View > Window Size > 320 × 480 Smart Phone.

13. Activate Live view. The page should look like **Figure 5.12**.

14. Click the Reservations button. You should briefly see an animated Loading image followed by an error alert (**Figure 5.13**).

    In this case, the target page, reservations.html, doesn't exist. But on a mobile device, a page might fail to load because of connectivity problems. Whatever the reason, jQuery Mobile gracefully abandons the attempt to load the file and automatically displays a warning for a couple of seconds.

### Fixing the look of the footer

Customizing the default styles of a jQuery Mobile site is the subject of Chapter 7, but the address in the footer section needs to be in a smaller font size and better aligned. So, let's fix that now.

1. Create a new CSS file called **custom.css**, and save it a new folder called **styles** within your working folder.

2. Open the CSS Styles panel, click the ▦ icon to open the Attach External Style Sheet dialog box, and link styles/custom.css to index.html.

   Dreamweaver automatically attaches new style sheets just before the closing </head> tag, so any styles you add to custom.css are lower in the cascade than the jQuery Mobile default styles, allowing you to override them.

3. Activate Live view, and click the Inspect button in the Document toolbar. As you move your mouse pointer over the page in Live view, Dreamweaver highlights the current element showing margins in yellow and

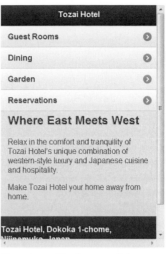

**Figure 5.12** The first page links to the other sections and displays some short text.

**Figure 5.13** An error message is displayed when the page can't be found.

TIP

Using the CSS Styles panel is the most efficient way to attach an external style sheet when working with jQuery Mobile. If you choose Format > CSS Styles or open the Class menu in the Property inspector, you need to scroll through a list of approximately 200 jQuery Mobile classes to get to the Attach Style Sheet option.

**Figure 5.14** CSS Inspect mode in Live view reveals the margins surrounding an element.

**Figure 5.15** The status bar lists the classes applied to the footer `<div>`.

**Figure 5.16** The footer paragraphs are now in better proportion to the rest of the page.

padding in magenta. With the mouse pointer over one of the paragraphs in the footer, you can see that it has big top and bottom margins (**Figure 5.14**).

4. To style the paragraphs inside the footer, you need to find out which rules have already been applied to the footer. As long as you don't click anywhere in Live view, you can climb up the document hierarchy by pressing the left arrow key. Pressing once selects the `<div>` that contains the footer (**Figure 5.15**).

5. You can now read the names of the classes applied dynamically to the footer: `ui-bar-a` and `ui-footer`. The main purpose of the `ui-bar-a` class is to define the color scheme, and it isn't exclusive to the footer. However, there's no doubt about the meaning of `ui-footer`. You can base a new style rule for the footer paragraphs on this class.

6. Add the following style rule to custom.css:

```
.ui-footer p {
    font-size: 12px;
    margin: 0;
    padding: 3px 15px;
}
```

This uses a descendant selector that applies to all paragraphs nested inside elements with the class `ui-footer`. It changes the font size, zeroes the margins, and adds 3 pixels of vertical padding and 15 pixels of horizontal padding.

7. Save custom.css and refresh Live view. The first page now looks much smarter (**Figure 5.16**).

### Adding text to the other pages

Replacing the placeholder text in the other jQuery Mobile page blocks is a straightforward cut-and-paste job. Just use the `data-role` of each `<div>` to determine what goes where. The page heading has a `data-role` of `header`; for the main content, it's `content`; and for the footer, it's `footer`.

You need to be careful how much text you put in the header. In a website designed for a desktop, it's normal to have a banner heading with the site or company name. The heading that describes the page's content usually comes below. When designing for a small screen, though, space is at a premium. For example, let's say you decide to combine the site name with the subject of the page in the second page block like this:

```
<div data-role="page" id="page2">
    <div data-role="header">
        <h1>Tozai Hotel Guest Rooms</h1>
    </div>
```

**Figure 5.17** shows what happens when the header is viewed on a screen that's only 320 pixels wide.

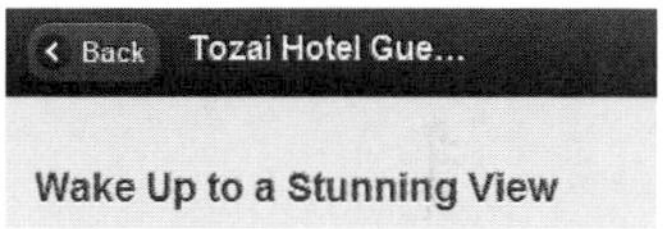

The default jQuery Mobile styles for headers, footers, and most list items use the white-space and overflow properties to keep the text on a single line and hide the overflow, adding an ellipsis to indicate that the text has been truncated.

If you use the default layout, you need to keep headers and footers short.

**Figure 5.17** Long text is truncated in the header.

### Using headings to preserve the document structure

The recommended best practice for search engine optimization and accessibility is to build web pages with headings organized in a logical structure. The most important heading at the top of the page should be wrapped in <h1> tags, the next most important level of headings should be in <h2> tags, and so on.

The multiple-page structure is merely an illusion created by jQuery Mobile manipulating the DOM. Search engines and screen readers see only a single page, so your heading levels should be organized accordingly. There should be one <h1> heading at the top of the file, and subsequent header sections should use <h2> headings. Headings in the content sections should use <h3> tags.

**Figure 5.18** The font size of <h1> through <h6> is always the same in a header or footer.

**TIP**

To save you time, index_text.html in ch05/begin contains the text for the remaining page sections copied from the Word document with the headings formatted to reflect the file's logical structure.

**TIP**

When inserting jQuery Mobile widgets, it's extremely important to make sure the insertion point is in the right place. Unfortunately, Dreamweaver CS5.5 does not automatically move the insertion point outside the current element. For example, if the insertion point is just before a closing paragraph tag, the widget is inserted inside the paragraph, generating invalid code.

The jQuery Mobile team anticipated the need to use different level headings to maintain a logical file structure while at the same time presenting the visual illusion of separate pages. All levels of headings from <h1> through <h6> are styled identically in headers, footers, and other elements that have a specific data-role, such as the headings of collapsible blocks and accordions. **Figure 5.18** shows the second page's header with shorter text and using <h2> tags instead of <h1>.

### Inserting a List View widget

The List View widget is one of the most versatile jQuery Mobile components and is useful for navigating to other parts of the site. It's not only styled automatically, but you can also add images, which are automatically rescaled as icons (**Figure 5.19**).

**Figure 5.19** A List View widget can make an attractive navigation device.

1. With index.html open in the Document window, deactivate Live view if necessary, and open Split view. Make sure the Document window viewport is fully expanded (View > Window Size > Full Size). Setting up the workspace like this makes it easier to add new elements accurately.

2. In Design view, locate the third page block, and click at the end of the second paragraph following the heading Japanese Cuisine at Its Finest.

3. Check the position of the insertion point in Code view. Dreamweaver puts it just before the closing </p> tag (**Figure 5.20**).

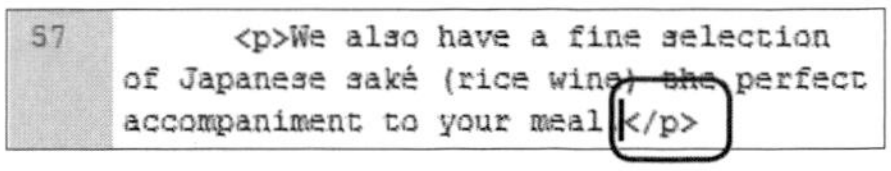

4. It's vital to move the insertion point so that it's between the closing </p> tag and the opening <p> tag of the next paragraph. The simplest way is to move into Code view and click to the right of the closing </p> tag.

   The alternative is to click the <p> in the Tag selector at the bottom of the Document window to select the entire paragraph (**Figure 5.21**). Then press the right arrow key once to move the insertion point to the right of the closing </p> tag (**Figure 5.22**).

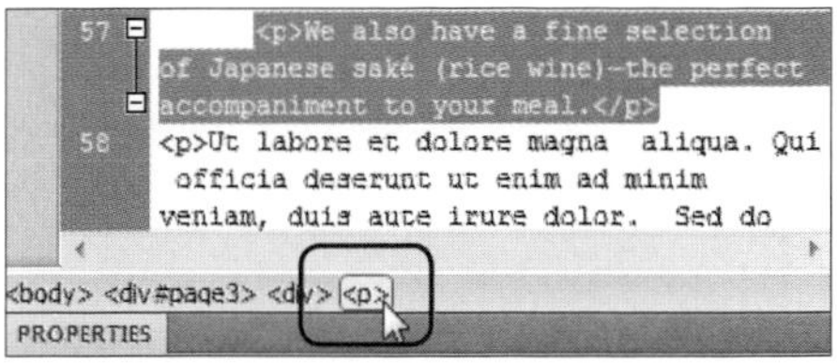

5. In the Insert panel, select the jQuery Mobile category, and click List View to open the jQuery Mobile List View dialog box.

   Alternatively, choose Insert > jQuery Mobile > List View.

6. In the dialog box, set List Type to **Unordered**, Items to **4**, and select the Inset check box, as shown in **Figure 5.23**.

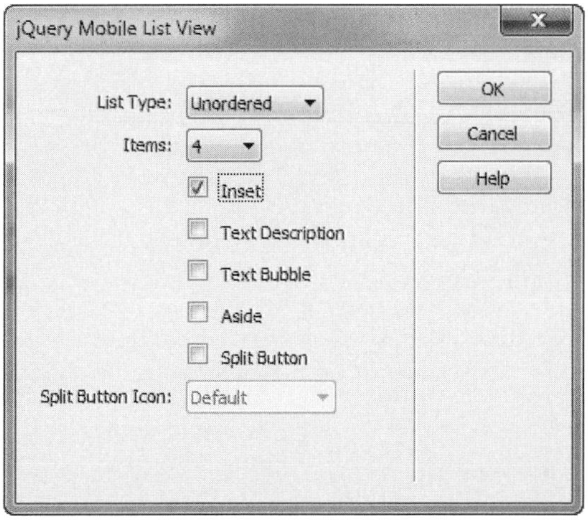

**Figure 5.20** Pay close attention to the position of the insertion point.

**Figure 5.21** Use the Tag selector to select the whole paragraph.

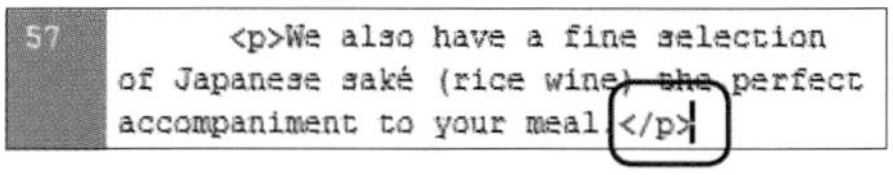

**Figure 5.22** The insertion point is now in the correct position.

**Figure 5.23** The options can be combined to produce different types of lists.

159

**7.** Click OK to insert the List View widget. If the insertion point was in the correct place, you should see an unordered list with four list items after the closing </p> tag in Code view. In Design view, you should see a List View widget with four placeholder links (**Figure 5.24**).

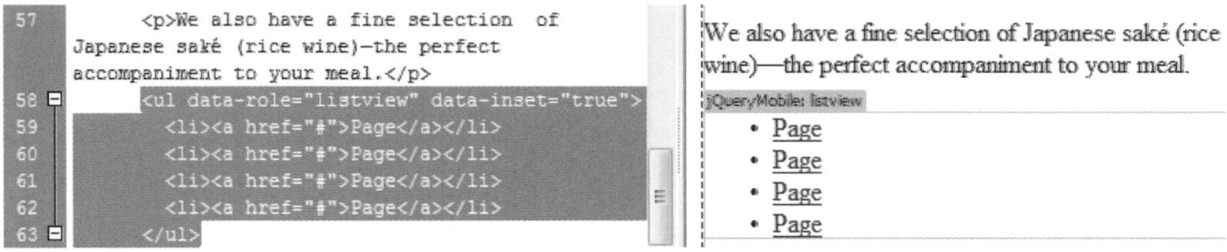

```
57          <p>We also have a fine selection of         We also have a fine selection of Japanese saké (rice
     Japanese saké (rice wine)—the perfect               wine)—the perfect accompaniment to your meal.
     accompaniment to your meal.</p>
58 ☐          <ul data-role="listview" data-inset="true">    jQueryMobile: listview
59            <li><a href="#">Page</a></li>                 • Page
60            <li><a href="#">Page</a></li>                 • Page
61            <li><a href="#">Page</a></li>                 • Page
62            <li><a href="#">Page</a></li>                 • Page
63 ☐          </ul>
```

**Figure 5.24** Check that the widget has been inserted in the correct location.

**8.** You'll convert the first placeholder link into a title bar for the widget by removing the link and assigning the list item the data-role of list-divider.

In Design view, right-click in the first placeholder link, and choose Remove Tag <a> from the context menu. Replace the text with **Japanese Food & Drink**.

**9.** With the insertion point inside the text you just typed, open the Tag Inspector panel (Window > Tag Inspector or F9/Option+Shift+F9). Make sure that the Attributes button and Category view icon at the top left of the panel are selected, and that the current tag is <li>, as shown in **Figure 5.25**.

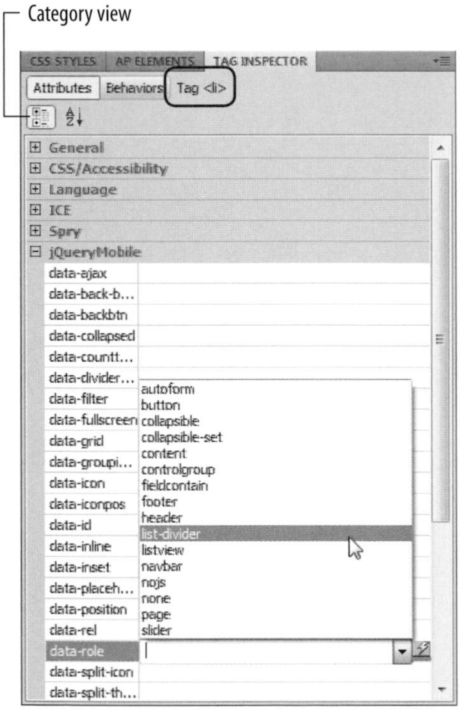

**10.** Expand the jQuery Mobile category, and select list-divider from the data-role options.

**11.** Replace the three other placeholders with **Sashimi**, **Sushi**, and **Sake**. The underlying code for the List View widget should now look like this:

```
<ul data-role="listview" data-inset="true">
    <li data-role="list-divider">Japanese Food
    ↳ &amp; Drink</li>
    <li><a href="#">Sashimi</a></li>
    <li><a href="#">Sushi</a></li>
    <li><a href="#">Sake</a></li>
</ul>
```

Category view

**Figure 5.25** The Tag Inspector gives you access to all the jQuery Mobile attributes.

At the moment, the last three items are only dummy links. You'll fix that later.

12. Activate Live view and click the Dining link. The List View widget should now look like **Figure 5.26**. Adding the list-divider data-role to the first item turns it into a heading. The other three items are displayed as buttons with right-facing arrows, and the widget is inset from the edge of the page with rounded corners.

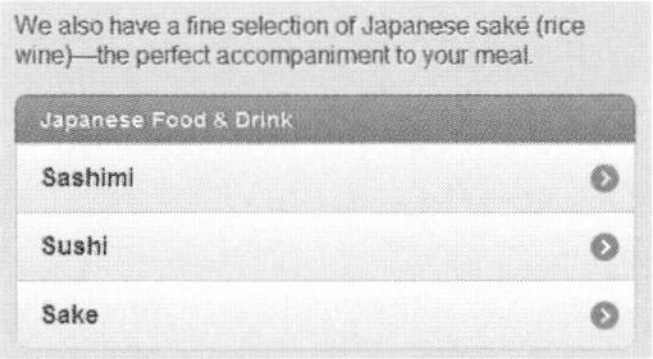

**Figure 5.26** The widget is automatically styled by jQuery Mobile.

### Adding icons to a List View widget

You can add icons to each item in a List View widget. This not only makes it more attractive, but it also gives the user an indication of what each item links to. Creating custom icons is time-consuming and increases the number of resources that need to be downloaded. So, jQuery Mobile automatically rescales a full-sized image that's used elsewhere in the site. All you need to do is to insert the image as the first child of the <li> item; jQuery Mobile handles the rest for you.

1. Exit Live view if it's still enabled.

2. The images need to be inserted between the opening <li> and <a> tags. As you did earlier, you can either click directly in Code view to position the insertion point, or select the <a> tag in the Tag selector and press the left arrow key.

3. With the insertion point between the <li> and <a> tags of the second list item, choose Insert > Image, navigate to ch05/images, and select sashimi.jpg.

4. When you click OK (Choose on a Mac), the Image Tag Accessibility Attributes dialog box appears. Select <empty> from the "Alternate text" menu, and click OK.

The image is inserted in front of the link and looks completely out of proportion in Design view (**Figure 5.27**). Don't worry. As long as the image is the first child of the `<li>` element, jQuery Mobile styles it dynamically in a browser or Live view.

**Figure 5.27** The image is displayed full size in Design view.

5. Repeat steps 2–4 to insert sushi.jpg and sake_380.jpg in the other two list items. The underlying code now looks like this:

```
<ul data-role="listview" data-inset="true">
    <li data-role="list-divider">Japanese Food
    ➥ &amp; Drink</li>
    <li><img src="../images/sashimi.jpg" width
    ➥ ="400" height="244" alt=""><a href="#">
    ➥ Sashimi</a></li>
    <li><img src="../images/sushi.jpg" width
    ➥ ="400" height="241" alt=""><a href="#">
    ➥ Sushi</a></li>
    <li><img src="../images/sake_380.jpg"
    ➥ width="380" height="279" alt=""><a href
    ➥ ="#">Sake</a></li>
</ul>
```

**NOTES**

The jQuery Mobile styles scale the images to a maximum width and height of 80 pixels without preserving the original aspect ratio. This results in the images being slightly distorted, but I decided it was acceptable at this size. However, square images or those with approximately equal width and height scale better. Customizing the CSS to preserve the aspect ratio involves editing not only the style rules for the images, but also for the List View widget.

6. Save index.html, activate Live view, and click the Dining link. The List View widget should now look like Figure 5.19.

You can check your code against index_listview.html in ch05/complete.

## Creating and Linking to External Pages

The danger of storing multiple pages in a single file is that the file might become difficult to maintain. It also forces visitors to download your whole site, even though they might be interested in only a specific section. Therefore, it's a good idea to split up a jQuery Mobile site into several files. You can link to external files that contain either one or multiple page blocks. Let's start by looking at a file with a single page block because it's easier to handle.

### Creating and linking to an external file with a single page block

The final link on the first page of index.html points to reservations.html, which hasn't yet been created. The following steps describe how to create a file with a single page block and link to it.

1. Choose File > New > Blank Page. Set Page Type to **HTML** and Layout to **<none>**. Make sure DocType is set to **HTML 5**, and click Create.

2. Save the new file as **reservations.html** in the same folder as index.html, and set the page title to **Tozai Hotel: Reservations**.

3. In the jQuery Mobile category in the Insert panel, click Page. Alternatively, choose Insert > jQuery Mobile > Page. This opens the jQuery Mobile Files dialog box (**Figure 5.28**).

4. Select the Local radio button to use the local versions of the jQuery Mobile files.

5. When you click OK, the jQuery Mobile Page dialog box appears. Type **reservations** in the ID field, select the

**Figure 5.28** Dreamweaver gives you the choice of using remote or local versions of the jQuery Mobile files.

The jQuery Mobile Updates link at the bottom of the jQuery Mobile Files dialog box takes you to a web page where extensions to update the jQuery Mobile library assets will be posted when new versions are released.

Normally, IDs should be unique within a page but can be reused in other pages. However, jQuery Mobile uses DOM manipulation to load content from external pages into the current page, so IDs should be unique within the site rather than just within the current page.

Header and Footer check boxes, and click OK to insert the skeleton code for a single jQuery Mobile page block.

6. Replace the placeholder text with a header, content, and footer like this:

```
<div data-role="page" id="reservations">
    <div data-role="header">
        <h1>Reservations</h1>
    </div>
    <div data-role="content">
        <h2>Check Availability</h2>
    </div>
    <div data-role="footer">
        <p>Tozai Hotel, Dokoka 1-chome,
        ➥ Nijinomuko, Japan</p>
        <p>Phone: 012-345 678 </p>
    </div>
</div>
```

7. Save reservations.html, and switch to index.html as the active document.

8. Activate Live view and click the Reservations button to load the page you just created. As **Figure 5.29** shows, a Back button is automatically created to the left of the header.

9. Click the Back button to return to the first page, and exit Live view.

**Figure 5.29** The new page creates an automatic link back to the previous page.

### Linking to an external file from a page block other than the first

In the preceding section, you linked to reservations.html from the first page block in index.html. However, linking to an external file from a subsequent page block within a file with multiple page blocks is slightly more complex. The following instructions explain how to insert a jQuery Mobile Button widget to link to reservations.html from the second page block within index.html.

1. In Design view, locate the second page block, and click at the end of the first paragraph following the Wake Up to a Stunning View heading. Press Enter/Return to insert an empty paragraph.

2. In the jQuery Mobile category in the Insert panel, click Button. Alternatively, choose Insert > jQuery Mobile > Button.

3. In the jQuery Mobile Button dialog box (**Figure 5.30**), set Buttons to **1**, Button Type to **Link**, and Icon to **None**. Then click OK to insert the Button widget.

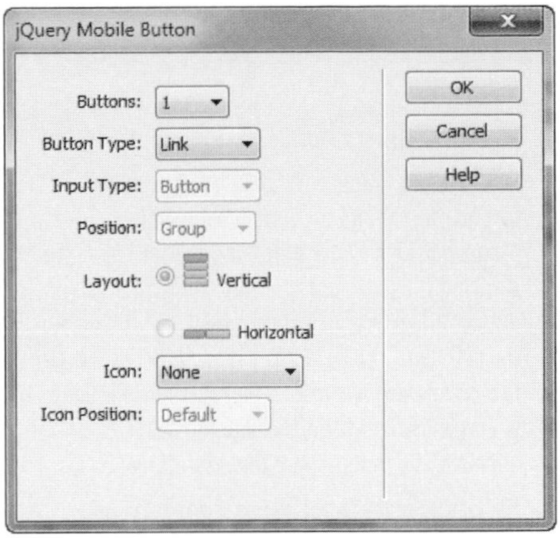

4. Replace the placeholder text with **Check Room Availability**, and link to reservations.html. The HTML code should look like this:

```
<p><a href="reservations.html" data-role=
➥ "button">Check Room Availability</a></p>
```

When you set the Button Type to Link, Dreamweaver simply inserts an ordinary link with `data-role="button"` in the opening `<a>` tag.

5. Activate Live view, and click the Guest Rooms button to navigate to the second page. The link is styled as a button that stretches the full width of the paragraph (**Figure 5.31**).

6. Click the Check Room Availability button. You should see a Loading widget followed by the yellow error alert (see Figure 5.13 earlier in this chapter). See the "jQuery Mobile Navigation" Close-Up on the next page to understand why the page can't be loaded.

7. Chose Site > Manage Sites, select the name of your current site, and click Edit to open the Site Setup dialog box.

8. Expand Advanced Settings in the column on the left, and select Local Info. Select the Site Root radio button for "Links relative to," and type **http://www.example.com/** in the Web URL field. Of course, if you're building a real site, use the actual domain name.

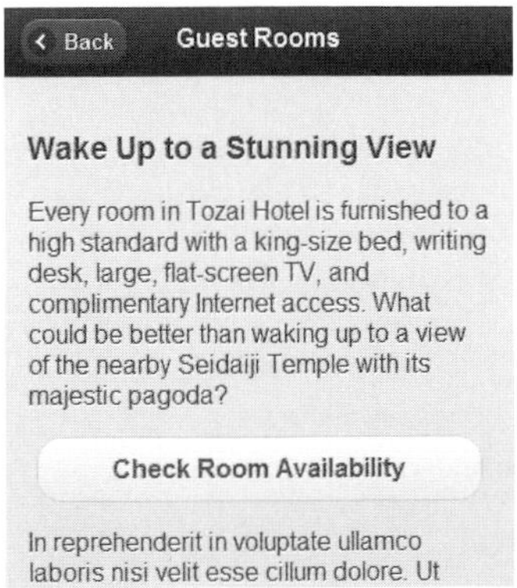

**Figure 5.30** The jQuery Mobile Button widget has many options.

**TIP**

You might need to delete the ` ` HTML entity for a non-breaking space after the opening `<p>` tag. Dreamweaver normally deletes it automatically when you start typing in an empty paragraph, but it doesn't always do so when you insert a widget. Failure to remove the nonbreaking space adds an extra line of space above the widget.

**Figure 3.31** Styling a link as a button makes it easier to tap on a mobile phone.

**jQuery Mobile Navigation**

Links in jQuery Mobile use DOM manipulation to load content into the current page, and the framework keeps track of where you have been, allowing you to retrace your steps through the Back button. When you linked to reservations.html from the first page, jQuery Mobile sent an Ajax request to the external file and loaded the jQuery Mobile Page widget into index.html. Clicking the Back button unloaded the content from the external file.

Navigating to the Guest Rooms section of index.html changes the URL to index.html#page2. When you try to navigate to reservations.html from this location using a document-relative link, the browser can no longer find it. To make the link work, it must be relative to the site root rather than relative to the document.

Linking to multiple-page files requires special handling, as described in "Creating and linking to a file with multiple page blocks."

Even though custom.css isn't attached to reservations.html, the footer is styled the same way as in index.html. This is because the content of reservations.html is loaded into the DOM of index.html, so it picks up the same styles. If you load reservations.html directly in Live view, the footer uses a larger font size and is flush against the left margin.

9. Click Save and Done to close the Site Setup and Manage Sites dialog boxes.

10. Changing the setting in the Site Setup dialog box affects only future links. You need to change existing links manually to be relative to the site root.

Exit Live view, and relink the Button widget to reservations.html using a site-root-relative link:

```
<a href="/ch05/working/reservations.html" data
↪ -role="button">Check Room Availability</a>
```

11. Save index.html and reactivate Live view. Click the Guest Rooms link and then the Check Room Availability button. This time the reservations page should load correctly, and you should be able to use the Back button to get back to the Guest Rooms page and then to the first page.

### *Creating and linking to a file with multiple page blocks*

There are two ways to create a file with multiple page blocks:

▶ Use a mobile starter page and delete any elements you don't want.

▶ Create a blank HTML page and use the Insert panel or Insert menu to add as many jQuery Mobile page blocks as you need. The jQuery Mobile Files dialog box (see Figure 5.28 earlier in this chapter) appears only when you insert the first page block.

The most important aspect of linking from one file with multiple page blocks to another is that you need to tell the browser to clear the history of visited links. Otherwise, you rapidly run into navigation problems. Unfortunately, clearing the history of visited links prevents the Back button from being added automatically to the header. Still, it's simple to add it manually.

To save you time, I have created a file called food.html in ch05/begin. It contains three jQuery Mobile page blocks with the IDs sashimi, sushi, and sake. You'll link to this page from the List View widget that you created earlier in this chapter.

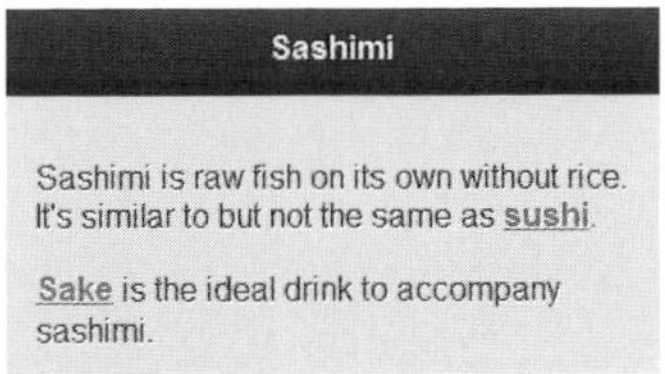

1. Copy food.html from ch05/begin and save it in your working folder.

2. With food.html the active document, activate Live view to load the first page, which contains internal links to the other two page blocks (**Figure 5.32**).

3. Click one of the links to load one of the other internal page blocks. When the next page loads, a Back button automatically appears in the header. You can use this to return to the first page, or you can click one of the other internal links. Whenever you return to the first page, the Back button disappears.

4. Switch to index.html in the Document window. Locate the List View widget you created earlier in this chapter, and link to food.html, adding a hash or pound sign (#) and the ID of the appropriate jQuery Mobile Page widget at the end of each URL. The HTML code for the List View widget should look like this:

Sashimi is raw fish on its own without rice. It's similar to but not the same as sushi.

Sake is the ideal drink to accompany sashimi.

**Figure 5.32** Only the first page block shows when the file is loaded in Live view.

```
<ul data-role="listview" data-inset="true">
    <li data-role="list-divider">Japanese Food
    ↵ &amp; Drink</li>
    <li><img src="../images/sashimi.jpg" width
    ↵ ="400" height="244" alt=""><a href="
    ↵ /ch05/working/food.html#sashimi">
    ↵ Sashimi</a></li>
    <li><img src="../images/sushi.jpg" width
    ↵ ="400" height="241" alt=""><a href="
    ↵ /ch05/working/food.html#sushi">Sushi
    ↵ </a></li>
    <li><img src="../images/sake_380.jpg"
    ↵ width="380" height="279" alt=""><a
    ↵ href="/ch05/working/food.html#sake">Sake
    ↵ </a></li>
</ul>
```

5. Activate Live view and click the Dining button to load the third page block in index.html.

6. Click one of the links in the List View widget. The appropriate page block of food.html loads, complete with a Back button.

**7.** Click the Back button. You are taken back to the Dining page of index.html.

**8.** Click another link in the List View widget to load food. html again. This time click one of the internal links in food.html. You should see the error alert. The page can't be loaded.

As explained earlier, when you navigate to an external page, jQuery Mobile fetches the content of the external page and loads it into the DOM of the current page. So, when you try to navigate to an internal link, jQuery Mobile looks for a page with that ID in the current document. But the page block with the ID you're trying to load is still in the external document, and jQuery Mobile can't find it.

**9.** When linking to an external file with multiple page blocks, you need to tell jQuery Mobile to clear its history and load the page directly. You do this by adding `rel="external"` to the opening <a> tag of the link.

Exit Live view. Then click anywhere in the Sashimi link in the List View widget in the third page block of index.html, open the Tag Inspector, and expand the Uncategorized category. Type **external** in the `rel` attribute field (**Figure 5.33**).

Alternatively, add the `rel` attribute manually in Code view:

```
<a href="/ch05/working/food.html#sashimi"
→ rel="external">Sashimi</a>
```

**10.** Add `rel="external"` to the other two links in the List View widget.

**11.** Activate Live view and navigate to the Dining page. Click one of the links in the List View widget. The appropriate page block in food.html should load. Click one of the internal links. This time the correct page block should load.

**12.** Click the Back button to return to the page block in food.html that originally loaded from the Dining page. There's no Back button because jQuery Mobile cleared its navigation history when it loaded food.html.

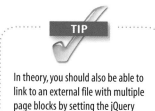

**Figure 5.33** When linking to a multiple-page file, set `rel` to `external`.

> **TIP**
>
> In theory, you should also be able to link to an external file with multiple page blocks by setting the jQuery Mobile custom data attribute `da-ta-ajax` to `false` in the opening <a> tag. However, in my tests, I found `data-ajax="false"` often resulted in the site freezing, whereas `rel="external"` was consistently reliable.

You can use the Back button in the Browser Navigation toolbar (**Figure 5.34**) to return to the Dining page, but it would be more consistent to add a jQuery Mobile Back button.

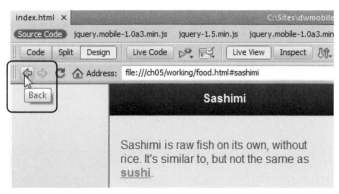

**Figure 5.34** You can use Dreamweaver's Browser Navigation toolbar to navigate in Live view.

### Adding Back and Home buttons to page headers

If you add a link inside a header, jQuery Mobile automatically turns it into a button and places it to the left of the heading. A second link is automatically located on the right. The following instructions describe how to add two buttons to the headers in food.html. The first one mimics the Back button, whereas the other links back to the home page.

1. Open food.html in the Document window, and exit Live view if necessary.

2. Click anywhere in the Sashimi heading, and then click <h1> in the Tag selector at the bottom of the Document window to select the entire element.

3. Press the left arrow key once to move the insertion point to the left of the opening <h1> tag, and type **Back**.

4. Select the text you just typed, and create a site-root-relative link to index.html#page3 (the Dining page block).

5. To mimic the browser's Back button, you need to use another jQuery Mobile custom data attribute, `data-rel` and set its value to `back`. With the link still selected,

In this and the following section, you'll encounter several new jQuery Mobile custom data attributes. They're described in detail in Chapter 6.

It's recommended to link to a named page for the benefit of mobile browsers that are not fully supported by jQuery Mobile.

expand the jQuery Mobile category in the Tag Inspector, and type **back** in the `data-rel` field.

Alternatively, add `data-rel="back"` manually in the opening `<a>` tag in Code view.

The link should look like this:

```
<a href="/ch05/working/index.html#page3"
➥ data-rel="back">Back</a>
```

**6.** Select the `<h1>` tag again, and press the right arrow key to move the insertion point to the right of the closing `</h1>` tag.

**7.** Type **Home** and convert the text into a link to index. html.

**8.** You want this link to reload the main page, so add `rel="external"` to the opening `<a>` tag in the same way as in the previous section.

The code in the header should now look like this:

```
<div data-role="header">
    <a href="/ch05/working/index.html#page3"
    ➥ data-rel="back">Back</a>
    <h1>Sashimi</h1>
    <a href="/ch05/working/index.html"
    ➥ rel="external">Home</a>
</div>
```

**9.** Add the same links to the other two headers in food. html.

**10.** Save food.html and test the new links by switching to index.html and activating Live view. Click the Dining link, and then click one of the links to food.html. You should now see Back and Home buttons on either side of the header (**Figure 5.35**).

**11.** Test the links thoroughly. When you click one of the internal links in food.html, jQuery Mobile is savvy enough to realize there's a Back button hard-coded into the header, so it doesn't add another one.

**TIP**

Because the code in the links is identical in each page block, it's quicker to copy and paste the links rather than going through all the steps again.

Sashimi is raw fish on its own, without rice. It's similar to, but not the same as sushi.

Sake is the ideal drink to accompany sashimi.

**Figure 5.35** The Back and Home links make the external page user friendlier.

Even though the link in the Back button points to the Dining page, clicking the button always takes you back one step in the navigation history. Clicking the Home button takes you to the first page block in index.html and clears the navigation history so you can continue moving around the site normally.

**12.** There's just one fly in the ointment: When you click the Back button to return to the Dining page, there's no way to navigate to the rest of the site. You need to hard-code a Back button that links back to the home page in this page block too. Amend the header section of the Dining page block like this:

```
<div data-role="page" id="page3">
    <div data-role="header">
        <a href="#page">Back</a>
        <h2>Dining at Tozai</h2>
</div>
```

**13.** This hard-coded Back button uses an internal link, so jQuery Mobile automatically inserts a Back button in the first page block when you return there. It seems counterintuitive to have a Back button on the site's home page, but it's easy to suppress with the data-backbtn custom data attribute.

Select the <div> that contains the header for the first page, and use the Tag Inspector to set the value of data-backbtn to false. The code looks like this:

```
<div data-role="page" id="page">
    <div data-backbtn="false" data-role="header">
        <h1>Tozai Hotel</h1>
    </div>
```

This prevents the Back button from appearing on the home page.

### Adding icons to the Back and Home buttons

At the moment, the hard-coded Back and Home buttons are text only. You can also add icons to them with the `data-icon` and `data-iconpos` custom data attributes by following these steps.

1. Exit Live view, and switch to food.html.

2. Click inside one of the Back links, and expand the jQuery Mobile category in the Tag Inspector. Select `arrow-l` from the `data-icon` list (**Figure 5.36**) to add a left-facing arrow icon to the button.

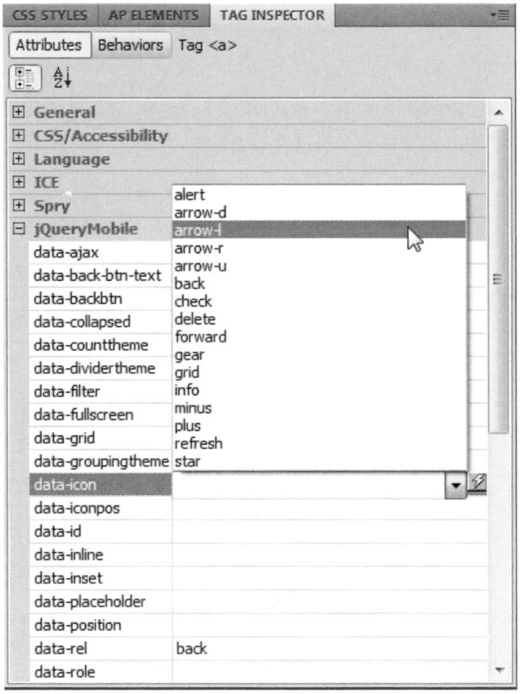

**Figure 5.36** You can choose from a wide range of icons.

As Figure 5.36 shows, there is also an attribute called `data-iconpos`, which determines the position of the icon. The default position is on the left of the button, so there's no need to add `data-iconpos` to the Back link.

3. Click inside one of the Home links, and select home from the data-icon list in the Tag Inspector. To place the icon on the right of the button, select right from the data-iconpos list.

4. Repeat steps 2 and 3 for the other Back and Home links, including the Back link in the Dining page block in index.html.

5. Test the links as before by switching to index.html and activating Live view. When you click one of the links in the Dining page, you should see that icons have been added to the Back and Home buttons (**Figure 5.37**).

   You can compare your code with index.html and food. html in ch05/complete.

## Building on a Solid Foundation

This chapter has provided you with an overview of building a dedicated mobile site with jQuery Mobile using one of the Mobile Starter pages in Dreamweaver CS5.5. The starter page speeds up development by creating a file with multiple page blocks complete with a List View widget to navigate to the other pages. You also learned how to create and link to external jQuery Mobile files, which can contain single or multiple page blocks. Navigation to and from external files that contain only a single jQuery Mobile page block is straightforward, but external files with multiple page blocks require more complex handling.

In addition, you learned how to insert List View and Button widgets. The next chapter explores the other jQuery Mobile widgets in Dreamweaver CS5.5 and delves deeper into the many custom data attributes, such as data-role, that lie at the heart of the jQuery Mobile framework.

The jQuery Mobile team added home and search to the list of default icons at a late stage in the Dreamweaver CS5.5 development cycle. If home is not listed in the code hints for data-icon, enter the value manually.

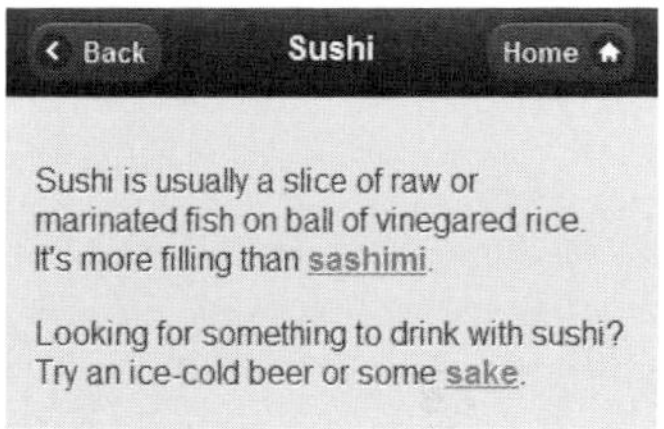

Figure 5.37 Icons can be added on either side or above or below the text.

# CHAPTER

# 6

# Diving Deeper
# into jQuery Mobile

*If this be magic, let it be an art*
*Lawful as eating.*

—William Shakespeare

# Diving Deeper into jQuery Mobile

The jQuery Mobile framework weaves its magic through a combination of JavaScript and CSS. When a page initially loads, the JavaScript analyzes the custom data attributes in each HTML element and uses them to assign CSS classes, bind event handlers, and insert page elements. Tapping a link or button triggers an event, showing or hiding content, or loading a new page block. Each time this happens, jQuery Mobile dynamically updates the CSS classes applied to each element.

Under the hood are more than 12,000 lines of JavaScript and approximately 2,000 lines of CSS. Using the custom data attributes mercifully hides this complexity from the web designer. Dreamweaver's jQuery Mobile widgets automatically insert the appropriate custom data attributes into the HTML. Even so, you need to know what they mean to troubleshoot problems and customize the default settings. What's more, the widgets don't exploit every feature in jQuery Mobile. You miss out on a lot if you rely solely on the widgets.

This chapter begins with a reference guide to jQuery Mobile attributes to help you unleash more of the framework's power. The rest of the chapter is devoted to showing you how to use Dreamweaver's prebuilt jQuery Mobile widgets. There are 13 altogether, which you can access through the Insert panel or Insert menu. Many of them are designed for use in forms. You'll learn how to build a simple form and handle the response. In addition, you'll explore the many options offered by the List View and Button widgets that you used in the previous chapter.

## A Guide to jQuery Mobile Custom Data Attributes

Let's start the exploration of the custom data attributes with the most important one: `data-role`.

### Designating an Element's Role

The `data-role` attribute assigns the role that an HTML element plays in the jQuery Mobile framework. Page blocks have a `data-role` of `page`; a page block's main content is in a `<div>` that has a `data-role` of `content`, and so on. **Table 6.1** lists the `data-role` values and describes their meaning.

TABLE 6.1 jQuery Mobile data-role Values

| VALUE | DESCRIPTION |
| --- | --- |
| autoform | Not documented. |
| button | Converts an `<a>` tag into a button. |
| collapsible | Creates a collapsible block of content consisting of a heading (h1–h6) and other HTML elements. Clicking the heading toggles the remaining elements open and closed. |
| collapsible-set | Creates an accordion when applied to a `<div>` wrapped around a set of collapsible blocks. |
| content | Designates the main content section of a page block. |
| controlgroup | Groups buttons, radio buttons, and check boxes. |
| fieldcontain | Styles and aligns form elements. Wrap each form element in a `<div>` or `<fieldset>` and apply this `data-role`. |
| footer | Designates the footer element of a page block. |
| header | Designates the header element of a page block. |
| list-divider | Converts an `<li>` element into a divider styled differently from the rest of the list. |
| listview | Converts an ordered or unordered list into a series of buttons. |
| navbar | Converts an unordered list into a navigation bar. Apply to a `<div>` wrapped around the list. |
| nojs | If JavaScript is disabled, the browser displays only the content in elements with this `data-role`. JavaScript-enabled browsers hide these elements. |
| none | When applied to an individual form element, this prevents jQuery Mobile from styling it, leaving the browser to display it normally. |
| page | Designates a page block. |
| slider | In spite of its name, this does not create a slider widget. It converts a `<select>` element with two `<options>` into a flip toggle switch, such as an on/off switch. Slider widgets are automatically created by using an `<input>` element with the HTML5 `range` type. |

Many of these `data-role` values are inserted automatically by Dreamweaver's jQuery Mobile widgets, which are described later in this chapter. The following sections concentrate on those that aren't handled by widgets.

### Creating a collapsible block

A collapsible block consists of a heading, which can be any level from <h1> through <h6>, followed by content that you want to toggle open and closed. In its collapsed state, only the heading is displayed (**Figure 6.1**).

When the user taps the heading, the hidden content is revealed, moving the remaining content farther down the page (**Figure 6.2**).

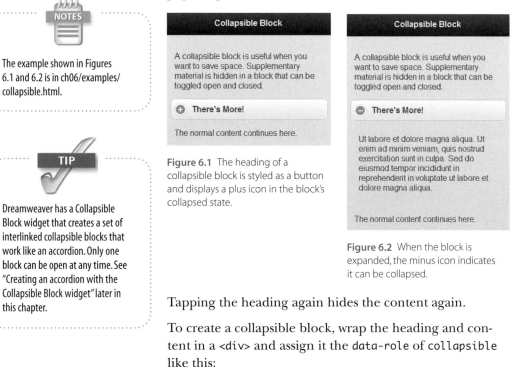

**Figure 6.1** The heading of a collapsible block is styled as a button and displays a plus icon in the block's collapsed state.

**Figure 6.2** When the block is expanded, the minus icon indicates it can be collapsed.

Tapping the heading again hides the content again.

To create a collapsible block, wrap the heading and content in a <div> and assign it the `data-role` of `collapsible` like this:

```
<div data-role="collapsible">
    <h2>There's  More!</h2>
        <p>Ut labore et dolore magna aliqua. . .</p>
</div>
```

**NOTES**

The example shown in Figures 6.1 and 6.2 is in ch06/examples/collapsible.html.

**TIP**

Dreamweaver has a Collapsible Block widget that creates a set of interlinked collapsible blocks that work like an accordion. Only one block can be open at any time. See "Creating an accordion with the Collapsible Block widget" later in this chapter.

This example uses a single paragraph, but you can put any HTML elements inside a collapsible block. By default, the block is displayed open. To show it initially closed, add the `data-collapsed` attribute to the opening `<div>` tag and set its value to `true`:

```
<div data-collapsed="true" data-role="collapsible">
    <h2>There's More!</h2>
    <p>Ut labore et dolore magna aliqua. . .</p>
</div>
```

Collapsible blocks are independent of each other, allowing the user to open and close them in different combinations.

### Creating a navigation bar

Wrapping an unordered list in a `<div>` that has the `data-role` of `navbar` creates a navigation bar with the following characteristics:

▶ The bar can be nested in a header or footer `<div>` or in the main content.

▶ It fills the entire width of its parent element.

▶ Up to a maximum of five items can be displayed horizontally.

▶ All items are equal width.

▶ Text in each item is kept on a single line and truncated if the text is too wide to fit.

The basic code for a navigation bar looks like this:

```
<div data-role="navbar">
    <ul>
        <li><a href="#">One</a></li>
        <li><a href="#">Two</a></li>
    </ul>
</div>
```

**Figure 6.3** shows examples of a five-item navigation bar nested in the header, plus navigation bars with two to six items in the main content section.

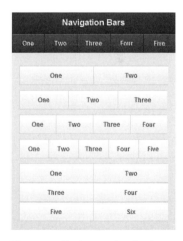

**Figure 6.3** The layout of navigation bars is controlled automatically.

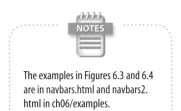

**Figure 6.4** Use `data-grid` to control the layout for navigation bars with more than five items.

NOTES

The examples in Figures 6.3 and 6.4 are in navbars.html and navbars2.html in ch06/examples.

As Figure 6.3 shows, unordered lists that contain more than five items default to displaying two items in each row. However, you can override this default behavior by adding the `data-grid` attribute to the opening `<div>` tag. This attribute accepts as its value a letter in the range a–d. The default value of `data-grid` is a, which results in two cells in each row. Incrementing the letter increases the number of cells in each row by one, up to a maximum of five (d).

**Figure 6.4** shows two navigation bars, each with ten items. The top one uses the default layout, so it has two items in each row. The bottom one is laid out five items to a row because `data-grid` is set to d like this:

```
<div data-role="navbar" data-grid="d">
    <ul>
        <li><a href="#">One</a></li>
        . . .
        <li><a href="#">Ten</a></li>
    </ul>
</div>
```

*Providing content for browsers with JavaScript disabled*

The jQuery Mobile framework depends entirely on JavaScript being enabled in the browser. The `data-role` of `nojs` performs a similar function to the HTML `<noscript>` tag. Content is hidden from JavaScript-enabled browsers and displayed only when JavaScript is disabled.

The file nojs.html in ch06/examples is a copy of collapsible.html with the addition of the following `<div>`:

```
<div data-role="nojs">
    <p><strong>WARNING:</strong> JavaScript needs
    to be enabled. . .</p>
</div>
```

**WARNING**: JavaScript needs to be enabled in the browser to view this site for mobile devices. Please enable JavaScript. Alternatively, visit our main site, which remains accessible without JavaScript.

**Figure 6.5** It's a good idea to redirect visitors who have JavaScript disabled.

When you load nojs.html into Live view, it looks identical to Figure 6.1. However, if you choose View > Live View Options > Disable JavaScript, you'll see the warning message instead (**Figure 6.5**).

## Attributes that Control Behavior and Style

In addition to the `data-role` attribute, jQuery Mobile has many other custom data attributes that control the behavior and style of individual elements. **Table 6.2** describes each one and lists the values it expects.

**TABLE 6.2** jQuery Mobile Custom Data Attributes

| ATTRIBUTE | VALUES | DESCRIPTION |
|---|---|---|
| `data-ajax` | true/false | Determines whether Ajax is used to load content. The default is `true`. |
| `data-back-btn-text` | Text | Sets custom text for the Back button. The default is "Back." |
| `data-backbtn` | true/false | Set this attribute to `false` to prevent a Back button from being generated in a header. |
| `data-collapsed` | true/false | Determines whether a collapsible block is closed or open on initial display. The default is `false`. Set to `true` to hide content. |
| `data-counttheme` | a–f | Sets the theme for count bubbles in a List View widget. |
| `data-direction` | reverse | Reverses the direction of a page transition. See "Controlling page transitions" later in this chapter. |
| `data-dividertheme` | a–f | Sets the theme for elements with the `data-role` of `list-divider`. |
| `data-filter` | true/false | Adds a search box above a List View widget when set to `true`. See "Creating a searchable List View widget" later in this chapter. |
| `data-fullscreen` | true/false | When added to a page block and set to `true`, the page is displayed full screen. Headers and footers are toggled on and off by tapping the screen. See "Creating persistent headers and footers" later in this chapter. |
| `data-grid` | a–d | Controls the number of cells in each row of a navigation bar. See "Creating a navigation bar" earlier in this chapter. |
| `data-groupingtheme` | a–f | Sets the theme for dividers in a List View widget. The default is b. |
| `data-icon` | See Figure 6.7 | Adds an icon to a button using either jQuery Mobile's default icons or custom icons. When specifying a custom icon, this generates a CSS class using the specified name prefixed by `ui-icon-`. |
| `data-iconpos` | See Table 6.3 | Specifies the position of an icon in relation to the button text. |
| `data-id` | Text | Applies a common identity to elements in different page blocks. See "Creating persistent headers and footers" later in this chapter. |

*Table continues on next page*

**TABLE 6.2** jQuery Mobile Custom Data Attributes *(continued)*

| ATTRIBUTE | VALUES | DESCRIPTION |
|---|---|---|
| data-inline | true/false | When set to `true`, displays buttons as inline elements only as wide as their content. The default is `false`, which displays buttons the full width of their containing element. |
| data-inset | true/false | When set to `true`, insets a List View widget from the margins. The default is `false`, which stretches the List View widget the full width of its containing element. |
| data-native-menu | true/false | When set to `false`, jQuery Mobile styling is applied to `<select>` menus. |
| data-placeholder | true/false | Set this attribute to `true` in an `<option>` element to prevent it from being selected in a `<select>` menu. Works only if `data-native-menu` is set to `false`. |
| data-position | fixed/inline/ fullscreen | Determines how headers and footers are displayed. The default is `inline`, which displays headers and footers in the normal flow of the document. See "Creating persistent headers and footers" later in this chapter. |
| data-rel | back/dialog | Setting this attribute to `back` on a link mimics the browser's Back button. Setting it to `dialog`, opens the new page as a dialog box suspended above the existing page. See "Creating a dialog box" later in this chapter. |
| data-role | See Table 6.1 | Assigns the role of an element. See "Designating an Element's Role" earlier in this chapter. |
| data-split-icon | See Figure 6.7 | Adds an icon to a split button in a List View widget. |
| data-split-theme | a–f | Sets the theme for a split button in a List View widget. |
| data-state | collapsed/ horizontal/ vertical | Originally in Alpha 1, but no longer appears to be used. Replaced by `data-collapsed` and `data-type`. |
| data-theme | a–f | Sets the theme for an element and its children. |
| data-track-theme | a–f | Not documented. |
| data-transition | See description | Determines how the transition to the next page block is handled, as described in "Controlling page transitions" later in this chapter. |
| data-type | horizontal/ vertical | Determines whether grouped buttons, radio buttons, and check boxes are displayed horizontally or vertically. |

*Creating persistent headers and footers*

By default, the header scrolls out of view as you move down the page, and the footer scrolls into view only when you get to the bottom. However, it's often useful to keep the header and/or footer in view all the time, particularly if one of them contains a navigation bar. To make a header or footer persistent, add the `data-position` attribute to its opening <div> tag and set the value to fixed like this:

```
<div data-position="fixed" data-role="header">
    <a href="#page" data-icon="arrow-l">Back</a>
    <h2>Dining at Tozai</h2>
</div>
```

If you use the same footer on each page, you should also give it a common ID. However, because you can't reuse a normal ID within a single document, jQuery Mobile provides the custom `data-id` attribute. Add it to the opening <div> tag of each footer like this:

```
<div data-id="myfooter" data-position="fixed"
➥ data-role="footer">
    <p>Tozai Hotel, Dokoka 1-chome, Nijinomuko,
    ➥ Japan</p>
    <p>Phone: 012-345 678</p>
</div>
```

While the user is scrolling the page, the header and footer disappear temporarily, but they reappear when the page comes to a halt (**Figure 6.6**).

To toggle on and off the display of fixed headers and footers, add `data-position` to the opening <div> tag of the page block and set it to fullscreen like this:

```
<div data-role="page" id="page3"
➥ data-position="fullscreen">
    <div data-position="fixed" data-role="header">
```

When the page loads, the fixed header and footer appear as usual, but tapping the screen causes them to disappear. They come back into view when you tap the screen again.

**Figure 6.6** When `data-position` is set to `fixed`, the header and footer reappear after you scroll down the page.

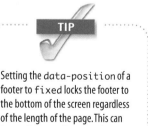
TIP

Setting the `data-position` of a footer to `fixed` locks the footer to the bottom of the screen regardless of the length of the page. This can leave a large gap between the content and the footer when a short page is viewed on a large screen, such as an iPad.

### Adding icons to buttons

As you learned in Chapter 5, adding `data-icon` to the opening <a> tag of a link inserts an icon. **Figure 6.7** shows the icons displayed by each of the 18 preset values.

Figure 6.7 To add an icon to a button, set `data-icon` to the appropriate value.

By default, icons are displayed on the left of the button. To display the button on a different side, set `data-iconpos` to one of the values in **Table 6.3**.

**NOTES**

The examples in Figures 6.7 and 6.8 are in icons.html and iconpos.html in ch06/examples.

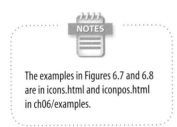

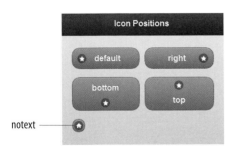

Figure 6.8 Icons can be displayed in four different positions around a button.

TABLE 6.3  Specifying the Position of an Icon

| Value | Description |
| --- | --- |
| bottom | Positions the icon below the button text. |
| left | Positions the icon to the left of the button text. This is the default, so setting it is optional. |
| notext | Hides the button text onscreen but adds it as a title attribute to provide context for screen readers. |
| top | Positions the icon above the button text. |
| right | Positions the icon to the right of the button text. |

**Figure 6.8** shows the effect of the different values of `data-iconpos`.

The code for the icon-only button at the bottom left of Figure 6.8 looks like this:

```
<a href="#" data-icon="home" data-iconpos="notext"
➥ data-role="button">Home</a>
```

Setting the value of `data-iconpos` to `notext` adds `title="Home"` to the link, and suppresses the text onscreen.

### Creating a dialog box

A dialog box is an ordinary jQuery Mobile page block but is displayed as an inset panel with rounded corners against a dark background, giving the impression of a modal window (**Figure 6.9**).

You don't need to apply any special styling to a dialog box; jQuery Mobile does it automatically when you add the `data-rel` attribute to a link and set it to `dialog`.

To distinguish a dialog box from an ordinary page, it's a good idea to use a different type of transition, such as `pop` or `flip` (page transitions are covered in the next section).

By default, a dialog box has an X-shaped icon at the top left of the header, which can be used to close it. However, it's a good idea to add a button to dismiss the dialog box. Add the `data-rel` attribute to the link and set its value to `back`.

The following brief exercise demonstrates how to create a dialog box and link to it.

1. Choose File > New > Page from Sample. In the Sample Folder column, select Mobile Starters, and then select jQuery Mobile (Local) in the Sample Page column.

2. Click Create, and save the file in your working folder as **dialog.html**.

3. Delete the link to Page Four in the unordered list under the Page One heading.

4. Scroll down to the content section under the Page Two heading, and type **Terms of Use**.

5. Select the text, and create a link to *#page4*.

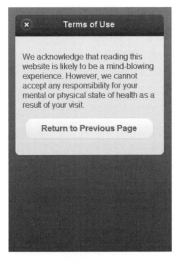

**Figure 6.9** Dialog boxes are styled differently and are not added to the navigation history.

Dreamweaver CS5.5 fails to detect the existing jquery-mobile folder and presents you with the Copy Dependent Files dialog box again. You need to click Copy, even though the files already exist. If you click Cancel, the file isn't saved. Hopefully, this problem will be fixed in an updated version.

**Figure 6.10** Use a different page transition when linking to a dialog box.

NOTES

In Live view, the flip transition to and from the dialog box looks very jerky. It's usually very smooth in Android or iOS.

6. With your insertion point inside the link, expand the jQuery Mobile category in the Attributes view of the Tag Inspector and set the following attributes (**Figure 6.10**):

 ▶ **data-rel.** dialog

 ▶ **data-role.** button

 ▶ **data-transition.** flip

7. Change the Page Four heading to **Terms of Use**.

8. In the content area under the new heading, type **Return to Previous Page**, and create a dummy link by typing # in the Link field of the Property inspector.

9. Set the link's data-rel attribute to back and data-role to button.

10. Save the page, and activate Live view to test it. Click the link to Page Two, and then click the Terms of Use button to load the dialog box. It should look similar to Figure 6.9.

11. Click the Return to Previous Page button to return to Page Two. When you click the Back button in Page Two, you should be returned to the first page, not the dialog box.

 You can compare your code with dialog.html in ch06/ examples.

### Controlling page transitions

By default, page blocks slide in from the right. To give your site some variety, you can change the transition from one page block to the next by adding the data-transition attribute to the opening <a> tag of a link and setting it to one of the following values:

 ▶ **fade**. This fades in the new page.

 ▶ **flip**. This uses a 3D transition to flip the page horizontally like a revolving panel, revealing the next page on the reverse as it passes beyond 90 degrees.

 ▶ **pop**. This displays the new page expanding from the center of the screen.

- ▶ **slide**. This is the default behavior, sliding the new page in from the right.

- ▶ **slidedown**. The new page slides down from the top of the screen.

- ▶ **slideup**. The new page slides up from the bottom of the screen.

To reverse the transition direction, add `data-direction` to the opening `<a>` tag and set its value to `reverse`. For example, using `data-direction="reverse"` in combination with `data-transition="pop"` results in the existing page shrinking toward the center, revealing the new page behind.

### Controlling the look of page elements with themes

Table 6.2 lists several custom data attributes that incorporate the word "theme." The most important of these is `data-theme`, which controls the look of elements by applying styles from the default jQuery Mobile style sheet. Dreamweaver code hints for `data-theme` and related attributes offer the choice of a lowercase letter from a to f. The letter refers to the names of classes in the style sheet. For example, setting an element's `data-theme` to `a` applies classes ending in `-a`, such as `ui-body-a` and `ui-btn-up-a`, to the element and all its children. Setting `data-theme` to `b` applies classes ending in `-b`, and so on. **Figure 6.11** shows the effect of applying themes `a`–`e` to individual list items in a List View widget.

When you apply a theme to a page block, jQuery Mobile adjusts the color of buttons and page backgrounds to blend with the theme, as **Figure 6.12** shows.

### Creating your own themes

The jQuery Mobile style sheet defines only themes a to e. Adding the code hint for theme f is to encourage you to devise your own theme. This is how you do it:

**1.** Open the jQuery Mobile style sheet.

**2.** The line breaks have been removed to reduce the file size, so choose Commands > Apply Style Formatting to make the style sheet more readable.

**Figure 6.11** The data-theme attribute changes the default color of elements.

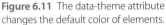

**Figure 6.12** Applying a theme to a page block gives it a unified look.

**3.** Copy the classes for the *a* theme. At the time of this writing, there are 16 of them beginning with `ui-bar-a`. You can easily find the end of the theme by choosing Edit > Find and Replace, and searching for `ui-bar-b`, which is the first class in the next theme.

**4.** Close the jQuery Mobile style sheet without saving. This reverts the file to its minified state.

**5.** Paste the classes into your own style sheet, and run Find and Replace to change all instances of `-a` to `-f`.

**6.** Change the colors and other properties to suit your taste.

**7.** Attach your style sheet to your jQuery Mobile pages, and set `data-theme` to f in elements or page blocks in which you want to use your custom theme.

Creating custom themes will be even easier when the jQuery Mobile ThemeRoller tool becomes available. Similar to the jQuery UI ThemeRoller (http://jqueryui.com/themeroller), it should provide a simple web interface, where you can choose your own color combinations and effects, and automatically generate a custom style sheet. The ThemeRoller tool for jQuery Mobile is expected to be released shortly after this book is published. Check the jQuery Mobile website at http://jquerymobile.com for up-to-date information.

## Rapid Deployment with jQuery Mobile Widgets

Mastering custom data attributes unlocks the jQuery Mobile framework's power, but it requires a lot of effort. Fortunately, Dreamweaver CS5.5 eases the learning curve with prebuilt widgets, which allow you to select the available options through a dialog box. Many of the widgets are form input elements that are designed to respond in a way that's familiar to smartphone users. The form elements are also aligned automatically.

### Exploring Dreamweaver's Prebuilt Widgets

The jQuery Mobile category in the Insert panel (**Figure 6.13**) offers a choice of 13 prebuilt widgets. The same options

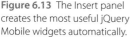

**TIP**

You can create 21 custom themes (f to z).

**NOTES**

The examples in Figure 6.14 are in listviews.html in ch06/examples.

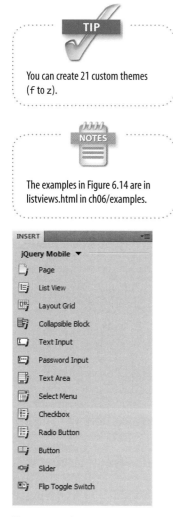

**Figure 6.13** The Insert panel creates the most useful jQuery Mobile widgets automatically.

are also available by choosing Insert > jQuery Mobile and selecting from the submenu that appears.

The following widgets are available:

▶ **Page.** This inserts a single page block. It can be used to add extra pages to a file with multiple page blocks or to create a single page block in an empty document. The dialog box gives you the option to omit the header and/or footer.

▶ **List View.** This inserts an ordered or unordered list, which can be styled in multiple ways (**Figure 6.14**). The options in the widget's dialog box can be combined for different effects.

▶ **Layout Grid.** This creates a layout grid with two to five columns of equal width.

▶ **Collapsible Block.** This creates a set of three collapsible blocks similar to an accordion widget.

▶ **Text Input.** This inserts a text input field wrapped in a container that displays a label and aligns the widget with other form elements. All form-related widgets, apart from Button, are similarly wrapped.

▶ **Password Input.** This inserts a password field.

▶ **Text Area.** This inserts a `<textarea>` element that expands and contracts automatically depending on the amount of user input.

▶ **Select Menu.** This inserts a `<select>` element.

▶ **Checkbox.** This inserts a group of check boxes. The dialog box has options for assigning the group's name, the number of check boxes to insert, and whether to lay them out horizontally or vertically.

▶ **Radio Button.** This inserts a group of radio buttons. The widget's dialog box has the same options as for a check box group.

▶ **Button.** On mobile sites, links are often converted to buttons because they are easier to tap than ordinary text links. This widget can insert one to ten buttons in a single operation, offering a wide range of options, including button type, layout, and whether to include an icon and the icon's position. In addition to displaying

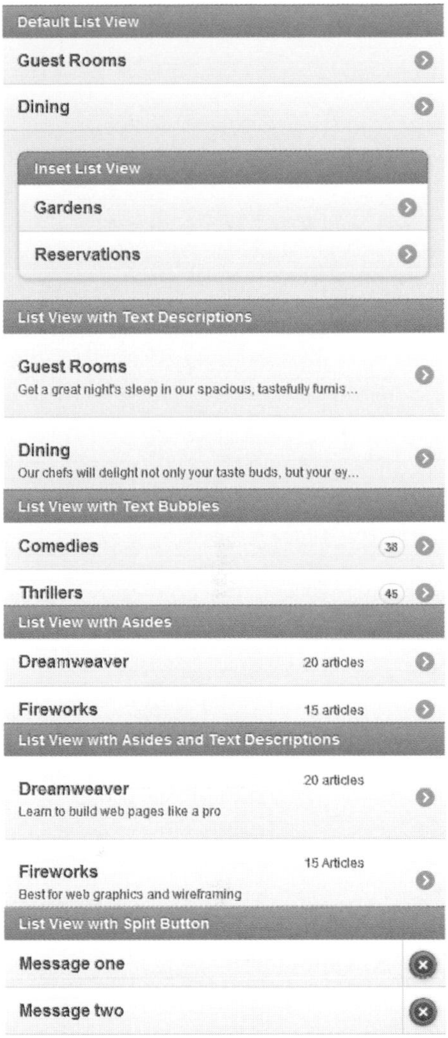

**Figure 6.14** Some of the many options for the List View widget.

189

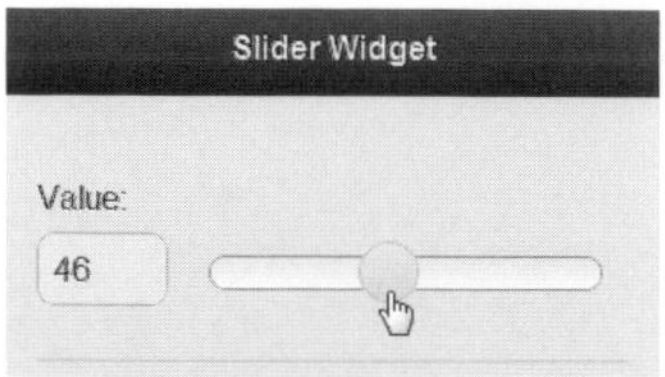

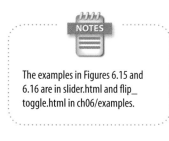

**Figure 6.15** The Slider widget is useful for entering numeric values within a specified range.

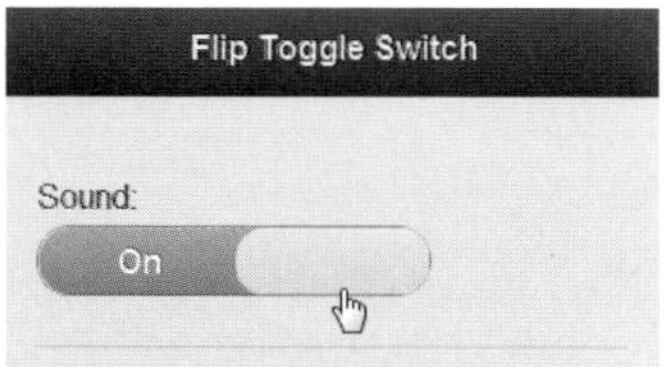

**Figure 6.16** A flip toggle switch is used mainly for mutually exclusive options, such as On/Off.

**NOTES**

The examples in Figures 6.15 and 6.16 are in slider.html and flip_toggle.html in ch06/examples.

links as buttons, the widget has options for standard form buttons.

▶ **Slider.** This inserts an <input> element with the range type, which is displayed as a horizontal slider (**Figure 6.15**). The default range is 0–100, but this can be changed by editing the <input> element's min and max attributes.

▶ **Flip Toggle Switch.** This creates a sliding switch with two options (**Figure 6.16**).

Chapter 5 described how to insert a page block using the Insert panel, so I won't repeat the same information here. The following sections describe the options available for the other widgets.

### Choosing options for a List View widget

The List View widget is very versatile. You can combine the options in the jQuery Mobile List View dialog box (**Figure 6.17**) in many ways to produce different effects. Figure 6.14 shows some of the combinations you can use.

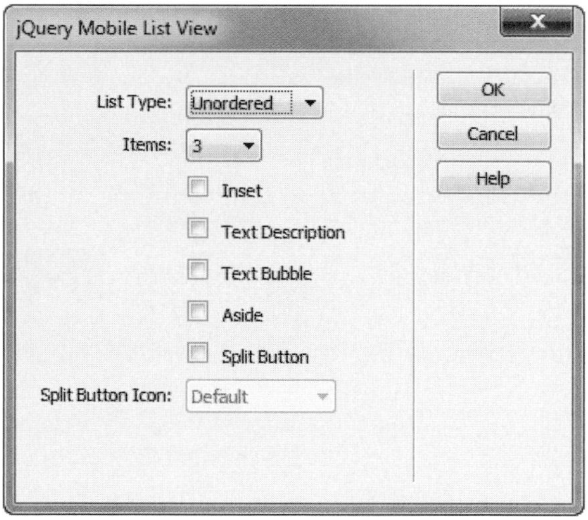

**Figure 6.17** Most options for the List View widget can be combined with each other.

The dialog box offers the following options:

▶ **List Type.** The default is Unordered. Selecting Ordered inserts a number before the text in each item.

▶ **Items.** The maximum is ten. To insert more, you need to copy and paste extra list elements manually.

▶ **Inset.** This insets the List View widget and adds rounded corners. The default is to display the widget the full width of the parent element.

▶ **Text Description.** This adds a single line of text under the item heading. Text that is too wide is truncated.

▶ **Text Bubble.** This is primarily intended to display numbers, but you can use any text. Because the bubble uses absolute positioning, you need to edit the text in Code view.

▶ **Aside.** This inserts a short section of text floated to the right of the item heading. Because the text is floated, it's difficult to identify the list item that it relates to in Design view. To make sure you select the correct text for editing, it's better to work in Code view.

▶ **Split Button.** This option creates two separate clickable areas, one for text and the other for an icon. The underlying code for the icon is a text link, but the text is automatically hidden and converted into a `title` attribute in the same way as if you set `data-iconpos` to `notext`.

▶ **Split Button Icon.** This menu is activated when you select the Split Button check box. Selecting Default displays a right-facing arrow.

### Creating a searchable List View widget

The jQuery Mobile List View dialog box doesn't include the option to make the List View widget searchable, but this is an awesome enhancement—and it's incredibly easy to implement. Just add the `data-filter` attribute to the List View widget's opening `<ul>` or `<ol>` tag and set its value to `true` like this:

```
<ul data-filter="true" data-role="listview">
```

The example in Figures 6.18 through 6.20 is in listview_search.html in ch06/examples.

This automatically adds a search field at the top of the List View widget (**Figure 6.18**). As you start typing in the search field, the widget displays only those items that contain the text you have entered. For example, **Figure 6.19** shows what happens when the letter **d** is entered in the search field. The search is case-insensitive and matches the text anywhere in the list items, not just the first letter. As you continue typing, the widget narrows down the options until you find the entry you're looking for (**Figure 6.20**).

| Searchable List |
|---|
| Q Filter results... |
| Acrobat |
| After Effects |
| AIR |
| Audition |
| BrowserLab |
| Business Catalyst |
| Captivate |
| ColdFusion |
| ColdFusion Builder |

**Figure 6.18** Searchable List View widgets are useful for long lists.

| Searchable List |
|---|
| Q d |
| Audition |
| ColdFusion |
| ColdFusion Builder |
| Digital Publishing Suite |
| Dreamweaver |
| Flash Builder |
| InDesign |

**Figure 6.19** The widget narrows down the options as soon as you begin typing in the search field.

| Searchable List |
|---|
| Q dr |
| Dreamweaver |

**Figure 6.20** The search is case-insensitive.

### Understanding the Layout Grid widget

The Layout Grid widget inserts a series of `<div>` elements that create a borderless grid with two to five columns of equal width. Although mobile screens are usually too narrow for a grid layout, this widget is useful in situations where you want to align buttons or text in a uniform way. The examples of icons and icon positions in Figures 6.7 and 6.8 earlier in the chapter were created using the Layout Grid widget.

The widget's dialog box (**Figure 6.21**) has just two options: the number of rows and columns in the grid. The maximum for both is five. In the case of columns, this limit is imposed by jQuery Mobile. To add extra rows, you need to copy and paste the underlying code.

When you insert a Layout Grid widget, Dreamweaver inserts placeholder text in each <div> indicating its row and column number (**Figure 6.22**).

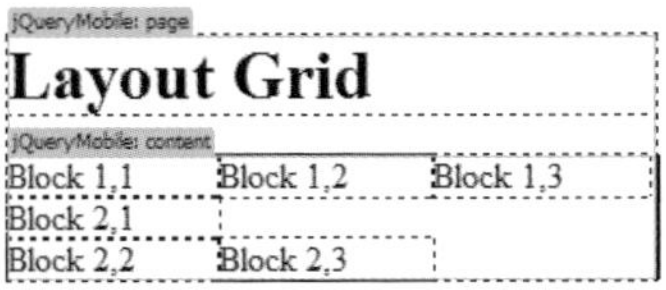

Unfortunately, if the grid has more than two rows, some <div> elements are superimposed on top of others in Design view, forcing you to work directly in the code. That's why it's essential to understand how a Layout Grid widget is constructed. Unlike other widgets, it uses classes instead of custom data attributes. The following code is for a grid with two rows and three columns:

**Figure 6.21** The Layout Grid widget has only two options.

**Figure 6.22** Design view has difficulty displaying the layout grid accurately.

```
<div class="ui-grid-b">
    <div class="ui-block-a">Block 1,1</div>
    <div class="ui-block-b">Block 1,2</div>
    <div class="ui-block-c">Block 1,3</div>
    <div class="ui-block-a">Block 2,1</div>
    <div class="ui-block-b">Block 2,2</div>
    <div class="ui-block-c">Block 2,3</div>
</div>
```

The final letter in the class assigned to the outer <div> determines the number of columns as follows:

▶ **ui-grid-a**. Two-column grid.

▶ **ui-grid-b**. Three-column grid.

▶ **ui-grid-c**. Four-column grid.

▶ **ui-grid-d**. Five-column grid.

Similarly, the final letter in the class assigned to each <div> within the grid indicates which column it belongs to as follows:

▶ **ui-block-a**. Column 1.

▶ **ui-block-b**. Column 2.

▶ **ui-block-c**. Column 3.

▶ **ui-block-d**. Column 4.

▶ **ui-block-e**. Column 5.

The structure of a Layout Grid widget is easy to understand, although the naming of the classes would be more intuitive if numbers were used instead of letters. It's confusing that *a* represents 2 when preceded by ui-grid-, but it's 1 when preceded by ui-block-.

However, the main problem with the Layout Grid widget is that you need to change nearly all the class names if you change your mind about the number of columns in a grid. You can't just change the class in the outer <div>. The inner <div> elements must be in the correct *a–e* sequence depending on the number of columns in each row. Unlike HTML tables, Dreamweaver CS5.5 doesn't have menu options to add or delete columns or rows in a Layout Grid widget. You need to edit the code manually or delete the widget and start again.

### Creating an accordion with the Collapsible Block widget

Dreamweaver's jQuery Mobile Collapsible Block widget is misleadingly named. Instead of inserting a single collaps-ible block (see "Creating a collapsible block" earlier in this chapter), it inserts three collapsible blocks wrapped in an outer <div> with the data-role of collapsible-set. This creates what is commonly called an accordion widget—a set of collapsible blocks in which only one block can be open at any time.

The Dreamweaver widget doesn't have any options; it simply inserts the following HTML structure:

```
<div data-role="collapsible-set">
    <div data-role="collapsible">
        <h3>Header</h3>
        <p>Content</p>
    </div>
    <div data-role="collapsible" data-collapsed=
    ↪ "true">
        <h3>Header</h3>
        <p>Content</p>
    </div>
    <div data-role="collapsible" data-collapsed=
    ↪ "true">
```

```
        <h3>Header</h3>
        <p>Content</p>
    </div>
</div>
```

**Figure 6.23** shows what this produces in Live view. By default, the first collapsible block is displayed open. However, you can override this by adding the `data-col-lapsed` attribute to the opening `<div>` tag of the first block and setting its value to `true`.

After inserting the widget, replace the placeholder text with your own content. The heading inside each inner `<div>` is automatically converted into the collapsible block's label. All other HTML inside an inner `<div>` is treated as the collapsible block that is toggled open and closed by clicking the heading. Although Dreamweaver uses `<h3>` tags, the headings can be any level from `<h1>` through `<h6>`. As explained in "Using headings to preserve the document structure" in Chapter 5, all levels of headings in elements that have a specific `data-role` are styled identically. Change the level of the headings to fit your document structure.

To increase the number of blocks within the accordion, just copy and paste one of the inner `<div>` elements to create as many blocks as you need.

### Inserting a Text Input widget

In common with other jQuery Mobile form widgets, the Text Input widget is wrapped in a `<div>` with a `data-role` of `fieldcontain`. This ensures that the element's label and input field are styled and aligned uniformly. Inside the `<div>`, the widget consists of a `<label>` element and an `<input>` element with the `type` attribute set to `text`. The HTML code looks like this:

```
<div data-role="fieldcontain">
    <label for="textinput">Text Input:</label>
    <input type="text" name="textinput"
    ↪ id="textinput" value=""  />
</div>
```

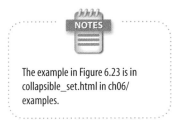

**Figure 6.23** Only one block of a collapsible set can be open at any given time.

NOTES

The example in Figure 6.23 is in collapsible_set.html in ch06/examples.

NOTES

Form widgets must be inside an HTML `<form>` element. Dreamweaver CS5.5 does not add the `<form>` tags automatically. You need to add them yourself by choosing Insert > Form > Form.

By default, Dreamweaver names the element `textinput`. If you insert more Text Input widgets, Dreamweaver automatically names them `textinput2`, `textinput3`, and so on. However, you should assign your own names to form elements to match your processing script. Because the same value is applied to the `for`, `name`, and `id` attributes, all three need to be changed. The simple way to do so is to select the `<input>` element in Design view and change the name in the field on the left of the Property inspector (circled in **Figure 6.24**).

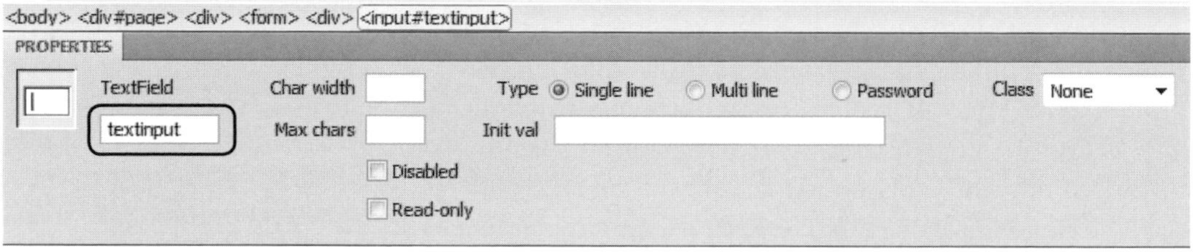

**Figure 6.24** Changing the input element's name in the Property inspector automatically updates the **id** and **for** attributes.

For example, if you change the name in the Property inspector to `first_name`, Dreamweaver updates all three values simultaneously:

```
<label for="first_name">Text Input:</label>
<input type="text" name="first_name"
↬ id="first_name" value=""  />
```

Although the Text Input widget sets the `<input>` tag's `type` attribute to `text`, you're not limited to using the default value. In fact, I strongly recommend changing the `type` to match the expected input (see Table 2.4 in Chapter 2 for a complete list of types). You can change the `type` attribute manually in Code view or through the Tag Inspector (see Figure 2.22 in Chapter 2).

---

**TIP**

Never use spaces in form names. Separate words with an underscore or use camel case, for example `first_name` or `firstName`. Spaces in form names are a common cause of errors in form-processing scripts.

If you set type to number, recent mobile devices automatically display a numeric input pad when you tap in the input field (**Figure 6.25**).

Setting type to tel brings up the same numeric pad on an Android device; in iOS it brings up a dedicated phone number keypad (**Figure 6.26**).

Unfortunately, at the time of this writing, setting type to date does not bring up a date picker. The input field is treated simply as text.

**Figure 6.25** Choosing the appropriate type of input element brings up the relevant keypad.

**Figure 6.26** A tel input type prevents users from entering invalid characters in a phone number in iOS.

### Inserting a Password Input widget

A jQuery Mobile Password Input widget is identical to a Text Input widget except the type attribute is set to password. In most modern phones, the most recently input character is displayed briefly to allow the user to verify that the correct one was chosen. The character is then displayed as a dot to prevent revealing the password to anyone looking over the user's shoulder.

The `cols` and `rows` attributes in the opening `<textarea>` tag specify the width and height of the text area in browsers that don't support CSS. They are required by the HTML 4.01 specification but are optional in HTML5. You can delete them if you want, but leaving them in does no harm.

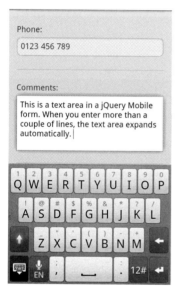

**Figure 6.27** The Text Area widget is a great example of jQuery Mobile's responsive design.

### Inserting a Text Area widget

A Text Area widget inserts a `<label>` and a `<textarea>` tag wrapped in a `<div>` like this:

```
<div data-role="fieldcontain">
    <label for="textarea">Textarea:</label>
    <textarea cols="40" rows="8" name="textarea"
    ➥ id="textarea"></textarea>
</div>
```

The jQuery Mobile style sheet initially displays the Text Area widget with sufficient space for two lines of text, but the height automatically expands as the user enters more (**Figure 6.27**).

You can change the default name of the Text Area widget through the Property inspector in the same way as for a Text Input widget.

### Choosing options for a Select Menu widget

A Select Menu widget inserts a `<div>` containing a `<label>` and a `<select>` menu with three `<option>` elements like this:

```
<div data-role="fieldcontain">
    <label for="selectmenu" class="select">
    ➥ Options:</label>
    <select name="selectmenu" id="selectmenu">
        <option value="option1">Option 1</option>
        <option value="option2">Option 2</option>
        <option value="option3">Option 3</option>
    </select>
  </div>
```

You change the name of the <select> menu in the Property inspector in the same way as for a Text Input widget. You change the <option> elements in the same way as for an ordinary <select> menu; namely, select the menu in Design view and click the List Values button in the Property inspector (**Figure 6.28**).

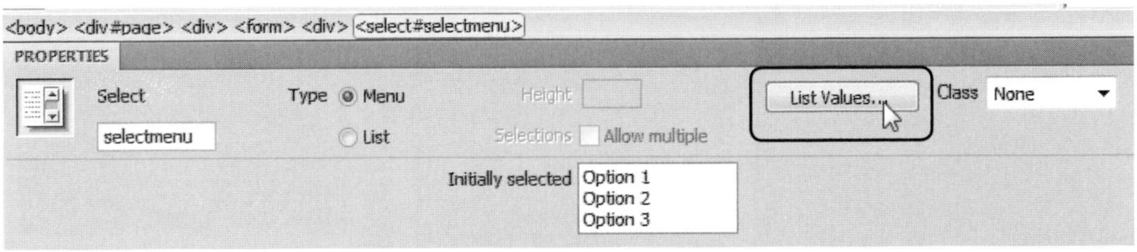

**Figure 6.28** Access the List Values dialog box through the Property inspector.

This opens the List Values dialog box (**Figure 6.29**). Text entered in the Item Label column is inserted between a pair of <option> tags and is displayed onscreen when the <select> menu is activated. Text entered in the Value column is assigned to the value attribute of the opening <option> tag. Use the plus and minus buttons at the top left of the dialog box to add or remove options. Use the up and down arrows at the top right of the dialog box to reorder the options.

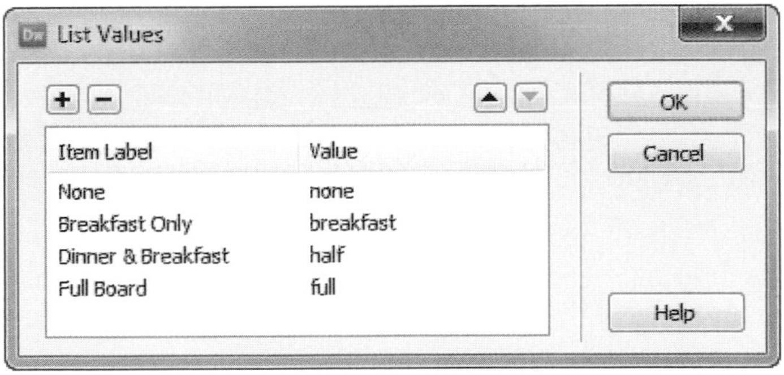

**Figure 6.29** Use the List Values dialog box to set the options in a Select Menu widget.

After setting the options, select one of the values in the "Initially selected" field in the Property inspector to add Selected to its opening <option> tag.

When a `<select>` menu gains focus, jQuery Mobile displays the options using the platform's default style (**Figures 6.30** and **6.31**).

**Figure 6.30** In iOS, a Select Menu widget is displayed as a rolling barrel.

**Figure 6.31** In Android, the screen is darkened and the menu is presented as a radio button group.

**Figure 6.32** The Select Menu widget can also be styled to look the same on all platforms.

However, if you prefer the menu options to be displayed in a uniform style on all platforms, as shown in **Figure 6.32**, add the `data-native-menu` attribute to the opening `<select>` tag and set its value to `false` like this:

```
<select name="meals" id="meals" data-native-menu=
↪ "false">
```

It's common practice to use the first `<option>` tag in a `<select>` menu to invite users to make a selection. To prevent that option from being selected, add `data-place-holder` to the opening `<option>` tag and set its value to `true` like this:

```
<select name="meals" id="meals" data-native-menu=
↪ "false">
    <option data-placeholder="true">Choose One
    ↪ </option>
    <option value="none">None</option>
```

**Figure 6.33** Setting `data-placeholder` to `true` prevents a menu option from being selected.

As **Figure 6.33** shows, the first item is displayed as a heading, not as an option.

It's important to note that when setting `data-placeholder` to `true`, you must also set `data-native-menu` to `false`.

The default style for `<select>` menus leaves the first option selectable.

### Offering multiple choices with a Checkbox widget

To insert a Checkbox widget, click Checkbox in the jQuery Mobile category in the Insert panel, or choose Insert > jQuery Mobile > Checkbox. This opens the jQuery Mobile Checkbox dialog box (**Figure 6.34**).

The dialog box has the following options:

▶ **Name.** This sets the `name` attribute that is shared by all check boxes in the same group. Dreamweaver also uses this value to assign a unique ID to each `<input>` element. For example, if you enter **meals** in this field, the check boxes are assigned the IDs `meals_0`, `meals_1`, and so on.

▶ **Checkboxes.** Select the number of check boxes you want in the group. The dialog box permits a maximum of ten. If you want more, you need to add them manually to the HTML code later.

▶ **Layout.** In a vertical layout, the check boxes are stacked on top of each other with labels on the right. The horizontal layout presents only the labels as a horizontal bar (**Figure 6.35**).

**Figure 6.34** The Checkbox widget has options for vertical and horizontal layout.

**TIP**

If the form-processing script uses PHP, you need to append an empty pair of square brackets to the name, for example `meals[]`. This tells the processing script to treat the selected values as an array. Because brackets are illegal characters in IDs, Dreamweaver ignores them when assigning the IDs to each check box, keeping your code valid.

**NOTES**

The examples in Figure 6.35 are in checkbox.html in ch06/examples.

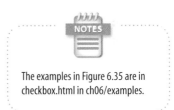

**Figure 6.35** The Checkbox widget has options for vertical and horizontal layout.

The horizontal option is suitable only for two or three items with short labels. Otherwise, the bar is broken over two lines. Also, it might not be immediately obvious to users that multiple choices are possible unless you say so explicitly.

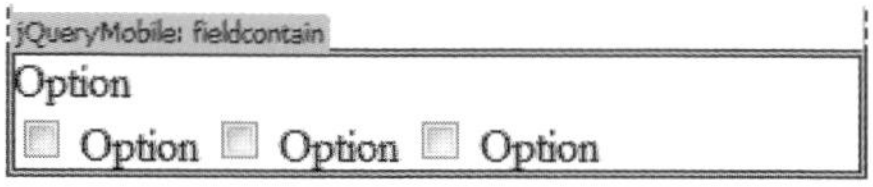

When you insert a jQuery Mobile Checkbox widget, the check boxes are always displayed horizontally in Design view, even if you choose the option for vertical layout. This is because the classes that control the layout are added dynamically only when the page is loaded in a browser. **Figure 6.36** shows what a widget with three check boxes looks like when it's first inserted in a page.

**Figure 6.36** A new Checkbox widget contains placeholders for the heading and labels.

The underlying HTML inserted by the widget looks like this:

```
<div data-role="fieldcontain">
    <fieldset data-role="controlgroup">
        <legend>Option</legend>
        <input type="checkbox" name="meals"
        ➥ id="meals_0" class="custom" value="" />
        <label for="meals_0">Option</label>
        <input type="checkbox" name="meals"
        ➥ id="meals_1" class="custom" value="" />
        <label for="meals_1">Option</label>
        <input type="checkbox" name="meals"
        ➥ id="meals_2" class="custom" value="" />
        <label for="meals_2">Option</label>
    </fieldset>
</div>
```

Because each check box requires a separate `<label>` tag, the check box group is wrapped in a `<fieldset>`. The heading is wrapped in `<legend>` tags.

In addition to replacing the Option placeholder text in the `<legend>` and `<label>` tags, you also need to set the `value` attribute for each check box. This is the value that is passed to the form-processing script if a check box is selected. You can do this directly in Code view or by selecting the check box in Design view and entering the value in the "Checked value" field in the Property inspector (**Figure 6.37**).

**Figure 6.37** You can set the properties for each check box in the Property inspector.

If you want a check box to be selected by default, set the "Initial state" radio button in the Property inspector to Checked.

If you change your mind about the orientation of a Checkbox widget, it's very easy to switch. To convert a vertical widget to a horizontal one, add the data-type attribute to the opening <fieldset> tag and set its value to horizontal like this:

```
<fieldset data-role="controlgroup"
→ data-type="horizontal">
```

To convert a horizontal Checkbox widget to a vertical one, just delete the data-type attribute or set its value to vertical.

### Inserting a Radio Button widget

A radio button group is similar to a check box group, but it allows only one item to be selected. The options in the jQuery Mobile Radio Button dialog box are identical to those for a Checkbox widget. You also edit the HTML code in the same way. Refer to the preceding section for details.

### Selecting the options for a Button widget

Buttons play a big role in jQuery Mobile because they offer a bigger target than ordinary links for users to tap on a small screen. Some links are automatically converted to buttons—for example, links in header sections. You can also convert other links into buttons by adding the data-role attribute to the link's opening <a> tag and setting it to button. The jQuery Mobile Button widget in the Insert panel and menu opens up even more options.

**NOTES**

Editing the value in the field labeled "Checkbox name" affects only the selected check box. If you want to change the name for the whole group, you need to edit each one separately.

**TIP**

If your form-processing script uses PHP, do not add an empty pair of square brackets after the name. Only one value can be selected in a Radio Button widget, so the user's selection should not be transmitted as an array.

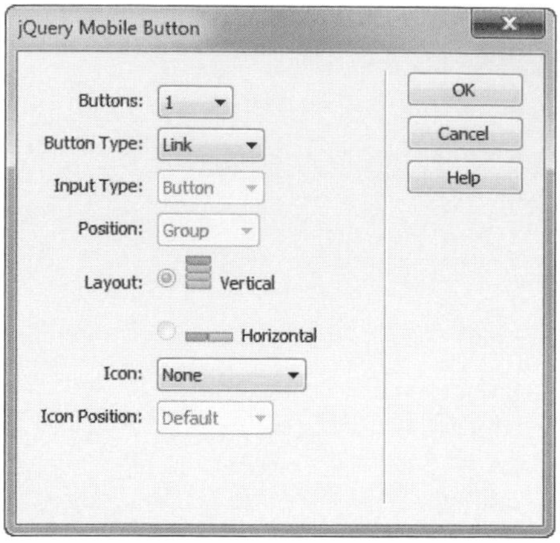

**Figure 6.38** The range of options in the jQuery Mobile Button dialog box reflects the importance of buttons in a mobile site.

The jQuery Mobile Button dialog box (**Figure 6.38**) has the following settings:

▶ **Buttons.** This allows you to create 1–10 buttons at the same time.

▶ **Button Type.** This option offers three choices:

**Link.** This inserts <a> tags styled as buttons.

**Button.** This inserts <button> tags, allowing you to add a greater amount of content, including images, between the opening and closing tags.

**Input.** This inserts <input> tags.

▶ **Input Type.** This option is available only when Button Type is set to Input. It sets the type attribute of the <input> tag to button, submit, reset, or image.

▶ **Position.** This option is grayed out for single buttons. When Buttons is set to more than 1, there are two choices:

**Group.** The buttons are grouped together as a continuous block vertically or horizontally depending on the Layout setting (**Figure 6.39**).

**Inline.** The buttons are displayed inline independent of each other. As Figure 6.39 shows, buttons drop to the next line if there isn't sufficient room to display them next to each other.

---

NOTES

The examples in Figure 6.39 are in buttons.html in ch06/examples.

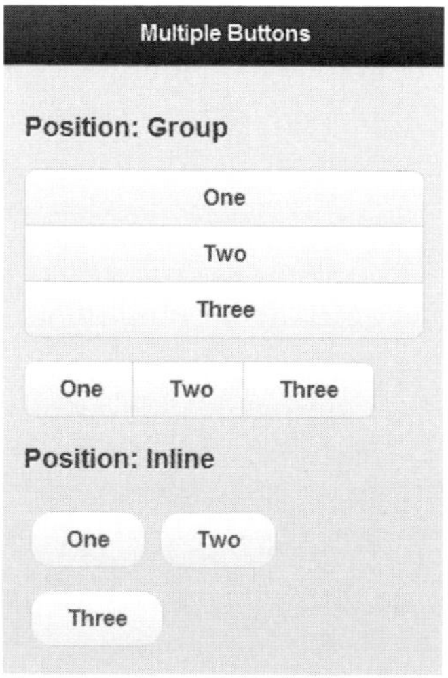

---

**Figure 6.39** Buttons can be displayed as a continuous group or independent of each other.

- ▶ **Layout.** This option is available only when Buttons is set to more than 1 and Position is set to Group.
- ▶ **Icon.** This allows you to add an icon to the buttons. The same icon is applied to all buttons created at the same time. See Figure 6.7 earlier in this chapter for the range of available icons.
- ▶ **Icon Position.** This sets the position of the icon in relation to the button text. See Table 6.3 for the options available.

The Home and Search icons are missing from the Icon menu in the jQuery Mobile Button dialog box. Hopefully, they will be added in an updated version of Dreamweaver CS5.5.

### Inserting a Slider widget

There's no dialog box for the jQuery Mobile Slider widget. It simply inserts the following HTML code:

```
<div data-role="fieldcontain">
    <label for="slider">Value:</label>
    <input type="range" name="slider" id="slider"
    ➥ value="0" min="0" max="100" />
</div>
```

The <input> tag uses the HTML5 range type. The value attribute sets the initial value displayed in a text field next to a horizontal slider (see Figure 6.13 earlier in this chapter) that changes the value within the range set by the min and max attributes.

To change the values of the for, name, and id attributes, select the input field in Design view, and edit the "Input name" field on the left of the Property inspector (**Figure 6.40**).

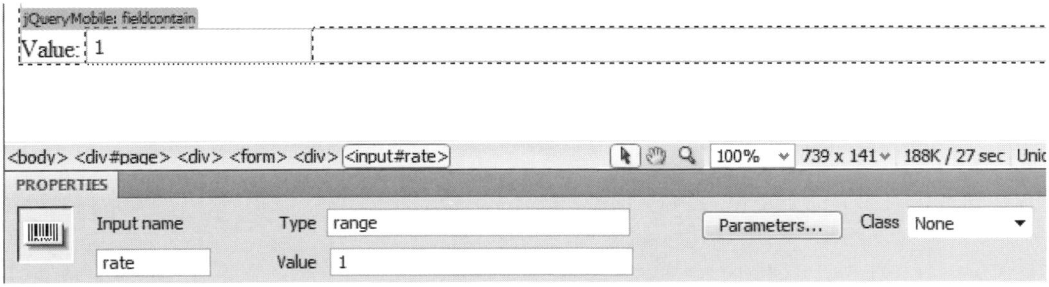

**Figure 6.40** The Property inspector displays only some attributes of a Slider widget.

In the Value field, enter the initial value that you want the widget to display. Alternatively, edit the value attribute through the Tag Inspector or in Code view. The value *must* be a number. The Slider widget cannot handle a range of letters, such as A–F.

By default, the widget displays a range of 0–100. To change this, edit the min and max attributes in one of the following ways:

▶ Edit the values directly in Code view.

▶ With the <input> element selected, edit the attributes in the Uncategorized category in the Tag Inspector.

▶ With the <input> element selected, click the Parameters button in the Property inspector and edit the values in the Parameters dialog box (**Figure 6.41**).

**Figure 6.41** The Parameters dialog box lets you set other attributes.

| Parameters | | |
|---|---|---|
| + − | ▲ ▼ | OK |
| | | Cancel |
| Parameter | Value | |
| id | rate | |
| MAX | 5 | |
| MIN | 1 | |
| | | Help |

The Parameters dialog box displays the values of the id, max, and min attributes. In addition to editing their values, you can add other attributes, such as step, by clicking the plus icon at the top left of the dialog box and entering the attribute name in the Parameter column and its value in the Value column. The Parameter column is case-insensitive. Dreamweaver automatically converts attributes to lowercase when it inserts them in the <input> tag.

**TIP**

The step attribute sets the increment between numbers in the range. For example, in a range of 0–100, setting step to 10 displays 10, 20, 30, and so on. If omitted, the default is to increment the numbers by 1.

*Inserting a Flip Toggle Switch widget*

The jQuery Mobile Flip Toggle Switch widget is a stylized <select> menu with two <option> tags. There is no dialog box. Dreamweaver inserts the following HTML code into the page:

```
<div data-role="fieldcontain">
    <label for="flipswitch">Option:</label>
    <select name="flipswitch" id="flipswitch"
    ➥ data-role="slider">
        <option value="off">Off</option>
        <option value="on">On</option>
    </select>
</div>
```

Confusingly, the data-role attribute of the Flip Toggle Switch widget has a value of slider. This converts the <select> menu into a horizontal set of buttons designed primarily for selecting mutually exclusive options, such as On/Off (see Figure 6.16 earlier in this chapter).

You edit the options for a Flip Toggle Switch widget in the same way as for a <select> menu or directly in Code view.

## Case Study: Creating a Reservation Form

After all that theory, let's put some of it into practice by building a reservation form for the Tozai Hotel case study. In most respects, creating a form with jQuery Mobile is no different from any other web form. However, jQuery Mobile's use of dynamic styling presents some challenges when working in Design view. The next few pages offer some hints on how to overcome these challenges.

You'll also learn how to dynamically replace a <select> menu with a text input field when the user chooses an option that calls for direct input.

### Building the Form with jQuery Mobile Widgets

The following instructions assume you have read the previous sections describing how to edit the options for the various jQuery Mobile widgets.

Selecting the heading and using the right arrow key to position the insertion point prevents Dreamweaver from inserting an unwanted empty paragraph.

*Configuring a Select Menu widget*

Continue working with reservations.html from the previous chapter. Alternatively, copy reservations.html from ch06/begin and save it in a working folder.

1. With reservations.html open in the Document window, put the insertion point in the Check Availability heading, and click <h2> in the Tag selector to select the whole element. Press the right arrow key once to move the insertion point outside the closing </h2> tag.

2. Insert a form by choosing Insert > Form > Form.

3. Click Select Menu in the jQuery Mobile category in the Insert panel to insert a Select Menu widget inside the form.

4. Select the <select> menu element and change its name in the Property inspector from selectmenu to title.

5. Click the List Values button, add two extra options to the <select> menu, and set their values to **Choose**, **Mr.**, **Mrs.**, **Ms.**, and **Other**.

6. In Code view, add the data-native-menu attribute to the opening <select> tag and set its value to false.

7. Set the value attribute in the first <option> element to an empty string, add the data-placeholder attribute, and set its value to true.

8. Change the menu's label to **Title**. The HTML code should now look like this:

```
<form name="form1" method="post" action="">
    <div data-role="fieldcontain">
        <label for="title" class="select"
        ↪ data-native-menu="false">Title:
        ↪ </label>
        <select name="title" id="title">
            <option value="" data-placeholder=
            ↪ "true">Choose</option>
            <option value="Mr.">Mr.</option>
            <option value="Mrs.">Mrs.</option>
            <option value="Ms.">Ms.</option>
```

```
        <option value="Other">Other
      ↳ </option>
    </select>
  </div>
</form>
```

### Configuring Text Input widgets

The next stage in building the form is to insert several Text Input widgets.

1. In Design view, click the turquoise tab labeled "jQuery Mobile: fieldcontain" at the top left of the Select Menu widget to select the entire `<div>`. Then press the right arrow key once to move the insertion point to the right of the closing `</div>` tag.

   Alternatively, position the insertion point manually in Code view.

2. You need two text input fields for first and last names. Click jQuery Mobile Text Input in the jQuery Mobile category in the Insert panel to insert the first one, press the right arrow key once to move the insertion point to the correct position, and insert another Text Input widget. Your page should now look like **Figure 6.42** in Design view.

3. Because jQuery Mobile styles elements dynamically, the classes that insert vertical space between the widgets aren't applied in Design view, making it extremely difficult to edit the first Text Input widget.

   One way to deal with this problem is to turn off the display of invisible elements by choosing View > Visual Aids > Invisible Elements. This hides the widgets' turquoise tabs (choosing the same option toggles them back on). However, the tabs are useful for selecting widgets not only to move the insertion point, but also to copy and paste, move, or delete them.

   My preferred solution is to create a style rule to add some vertical space between widgets in Design view. Scroll up to the `<head>` of the page in Code view and

> **TIP**
>
> It's worth repeating how important it is to move the insertion point outside an existing HTML element before inserting a new jQuery Mobile widget. Failure to do so results in the new widget being nested inside the existing element.

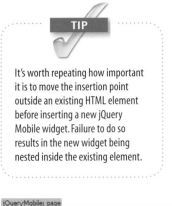

**Figure 6.42** The second Text Input widget's tab obscures the previous widget.

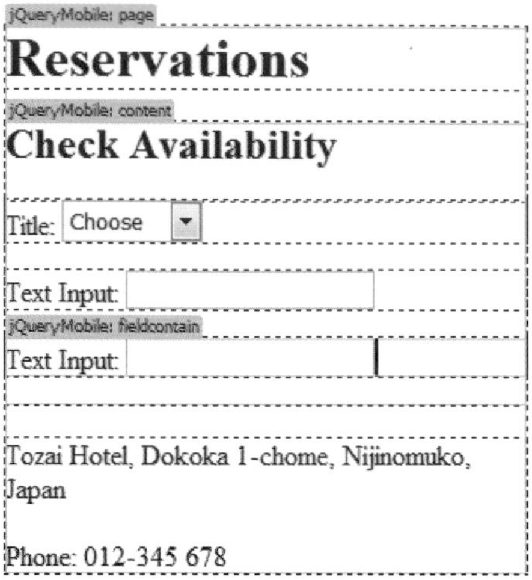
jQueryMobile: page
Reservations
jQueryMobile: content
Check Availability
Title: Choose
Text Input:
jQueryMobile: fieldcontain
Text Input:
Tozai Hotel, Dokoka 1-chome, Nijinomuko, Japan
Phone: 012-345 678

**Figure 6.43** The style rule makes it easier to edit the form widgets.

add the following `<style>` block just before the closing `</head>` tag:

```
<style>
div[data-role=fieldcontain] {
    margin: 1em inherit;
}
</style>
```

This uses an attribute selector (see Table 1.1 in Chapter 1) to select all `<div>` elements that have a `data-role` of `fieldcontain`—in other words, all form widgets. The style rule applies top and bottom margins of one em but leaves the horizontal margins untouched. Adding this rule has the effect of pushing the form widgets one line apart (**Figure 6.43**).

An added bonus of this style rule is that it doesn't increase the vertical margins between form widgets when viewed in a browser, so it doesn't matter if you forget to delete it when you have finished editing the form.

TIP

Select the `<style>` block created in step 3, right-click, and choose Create New Snippet. Give the snippet a name, such as `jQuery Mobile Widget Separator`, and click OK to save it in the Snippets panel ready for reuse in other pages.

CLOSE-UP

**The placeholder and data-placeholder Attributes**

HTML5 and jQuery Mobile have similarly named attributes—`placeholder` and `data-placeholder`—that are also similar in purpose but work very differently. In browsers that support the HTML5 `placeholder` attribute, the attribute's value is displayed as a text hint inside a text input field. The text hint is usually dimmed, and it disappears as soon as the input field has focus (**Figure 6.44**).

On the other hand, the jQuery Mobile `data-placeholder` attribute turns an `<option>` element in a `<select>` menu into a heading that can't be selected, normally prompting the user to select one of the other options. See Figure 6.33 in "Choosing options for a Select Menu widget" earlier in this chapter for an example.

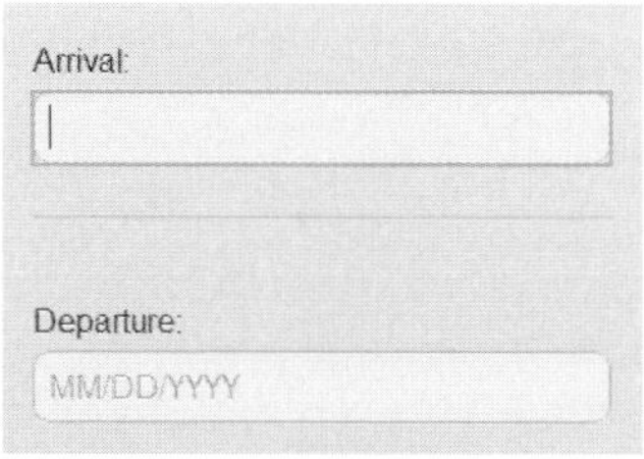
Arrival:
Departure:
MM/DD/YYYY

**Figure 6.44** The `placeholder` attribute reminds users what to enter in a form field.

**4.** Edit the Text Input widgets, changing their labels to **First Name** and **Family Name**, and their names to first_name and family_name respectively.

**5.** Make sure the insertion point is after the closing </div> tag of the second Text Input widget and insert two more Text Input widgets. Change the labels to **Arrival** and **Departure**. Also change the names in the Property inspector to arrival and departure, respectively.

**6.** With the arrival text input element selected, open the Tag Inspector panel, expand the Uncategorized category, type **MM/DD/YYYY** in the placeholder field, and set required to (Yes), as shown in **Figure 6.45**.

**7.** Repeat the previous step with the departure text input element selected. Also, set required to (Yes) for the first_name and family_name input fields.

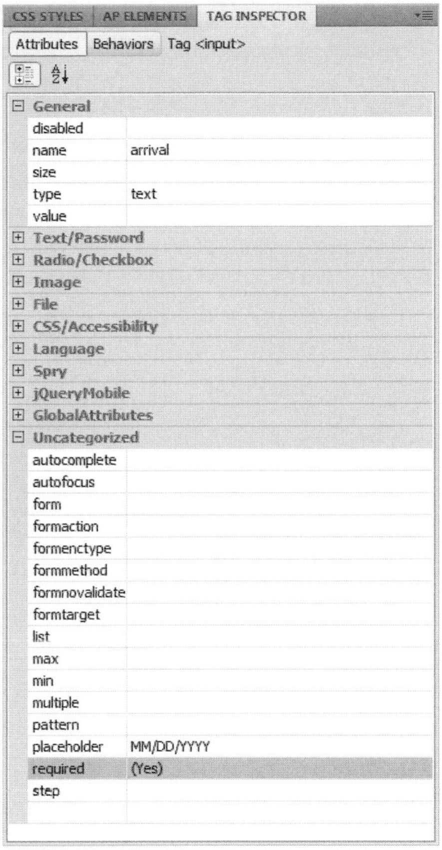

### Adding Radio Button and Slider widgets

The final part of the form asks the user to enter the number of adults and children. Normally, you would use the same input elements for both fields, but this example shows how different widgets can be used for similar purposes.

**1.** Move the insertion point to after the closing </div> tag for the departure input field, and click Radio Button in the jQuery Mobile category of the Insert panel. Use the following settings in the jQuery Mobile Radio Button dialog box:

- ▸ **Name.** adults
- ▸ **Radio buttons.** 4
- ▸ **Layout.** Horizontal

**2.** Change the <legend> text to **Adults:** and edit the labels for the radio buttons to read **1, 2, 3, 4**. You also need to select each radio button in turn, and enter the relevant number in the "Checked value" field in the Property inspector. A hotel booking requires a minimum of one adult, so set "Initial state" of the first radio button to Checked.

**Figure 6.45** The Tag Inspector exposes all HTML5 attributes for the selected element.

**Figure 6.46** The unstyled form elements look disorganized in Design view.

TIP

The Submit button is not wrapped in a `<div>` like other form elements, but jQuery Mobile styles it to blend with the rest of the form.

**Figure 6.47** The form demonstrates alternative ways of selecting a number with the Radio Button and Slider widgets.

3.  Move the insertion point outside the Radio Button widget's closing `</div>` tag, and insert a jQuery Mobile Slider widget in the form. Edit the Slider widget to change its name to `children` and set `max` to 3. Also change the label to **Children**.

4.  Move the insertion point outside the Slider widget's closing `</div>` tag, and click Button in the jQuery Mobile category in the Insert panel. Use the following settings in the jQuery Mobile Button dialog box:

    ▶ **Buttons.** 1

    ▶ **Button Type.** Input

    ▶ **Input Type.** Submit

    ▶ **Icon.** None

5.  Click OK to insert the Submit button. Dreamweaver doesn't automatically give it a name, so enter **send** in the "Button name" field on the left of the Property inspector. The completed form should look like **Figure 6.46** in Design view.

6.  Save reservations.html and activate Live view. The jQuery Mobile styles automatically align the previously disorganized form elements. Depending on the window size you choose, the labels are displayed above or to the left of the elements.

7.  Scroll down to the bottom of the form. The radio buttons are displayed as a horizontal group with rounded corners, and the slider offers a choice of 0–3 (**Figure 6.47**).

    You can compare your code with reservations_noscript. html in ch06/complete.

### Improving the Form with jQuery

Although the form is perfectly functional, it needs to be improved before it can be deployed. The first issue that needs to be fixed is providing a text input field if the user selects Other in the Title `<select>` menu.

*Dynamically loading a text input field to replace a Select Menu widget*

In Chapter 2 you learned how to create an editable drop-down menu using the HTML5 `<datalist>` element. The jQuery Mobile framework doesn't offer the same functionality, but it's quite simple, as you'll see in this exercise, to remove a Select Menu widget and replace it with a text input field when the user selects a specific option.

1. In Code view, scroll down to the bottom of reservations.html and insert a `<script>` block with a jQuery document-ready function like this:

```
    </div>
<script>
$(function() {

});
</script>
</div>
</body>
```

   Pay particular attention to the location of the `<script>` block. It must be *inside* the page block `<div>`. Otherwise, the JavaScript code you're going to add won't be available to the form when it's loaded dynamically into the browser.

2. On the blank line inside the document-ready function, type `$(` followed by an opening quotation mark. Dreamweaver CS5.5's built-in jQuery code hinting displays a list of HTML tags. Choose `select` and type #. This triggers the jQuery code hints again to offer you a list of all IDs on the page (**Figure 6.48**).

3. Choose `title` from the list of IDs. Dreamweaver automatically adds a closing quotation mark, so move the insertion point outside the quotes and add a closing parenthesis. This selects the `<select>` element with the ID `title` as a jQuery object.

4. You need to bind an `onchange` event handler to the selected element using the jQuery `live()` method like

**TIP**

Because jQuery Mobile uses DOM manipulation to load content into the current page, custom jQuery functions need to be inside the jQuery Mobile page block that requires access to them. They aren't loaded if you locate custom functions outside the page block.

**Figure 6.48** The jQuery code hints help you avoid spelling mistakes by presenting a list of IDs on the current page.

this (Dreamweaver provides code hints as you continue typing):

```
$(function() {
    // Change handler for Select Menu widget
    $('select#title').live('change',
    ➥ function(e) {
        // Check selected value
    });
});
```

5. You want to replace the Select Menu widget with a text input field only if the user selects Other. So, add a condition inside the event handler like this:

```
$('select#title').live('change', function(e) {
    // Check selected value
    if ($(this).val() == 'Other') {
        // Replace with text input field
    }
});
```

Inside the event handler, $(this) refers to the element that the function is bound to—in other words, the <select> menu. The val() method gets the selected value. The double equal sign compares the selected value with "Other." The code inside the curly braces will be executed only if the values match.

6. To work out how to replace the Select Menu widget with a text input field, you need to call on the assistance of Live Code. Click the Live Code button in the Document toolbar or choose View > Live Code.

Locate the dynamically generated code for the widget. **Figure 6.49** shows what it looks like.

**Figure 6.49** You need to inspect the widget's dynamically generated code to style the replacement appropriately.

```
23      <div class="ui-select"><a href="#" role="button" aria-haspopup="true"
     data-theme="c" class="ui-btn ui-btn-icon-right ui-btn-corner-all ui-shadow
     ui-btn-hover-c"><span class="ui-btn-inner ui-btn-corner-all"><span class=
     "ui-btn-text">Choose</span><span class="ui-icon ui-icon-arrow-d ui-icon-shadow">
     </span></span></a><select name="title" id="title" data-native-menu="false"
     tabindex="-1">
24          <option data-placeholder="true">Choose</option>
25          <option value="Mr.">Mr.</option>
26          <option value="Mrs.">Mrs.</option>
27          <option value="Ms.">Ms.</option>
28          <option value="Other">Other</option>
29      </select></div>
```

Although the code looks complex, it can be simplified like this:

```
<div><a>Link to hidden pop-up</a>
    <select></select>
</div>
```

So, to replace the Select Menu widget with a text input field, you need to replace the `<select>` menu's parent `<div>` rather than just the `<select>` element. Removing only the `<select>` element leaves an unwanted jQuery Mobile button in the DOM.

**NOTES**

Use the line numbers in Figures 6.49 and 6.51 only as a guide to the approximate location of the code. It might be different in your file.

7. To replace one element with another, jQuery provides the appropriately named `replaceWith()` method, which takes as its argument the replacement element. Exit Live view and add the following code between the curly braces of the conditional block that you added in step 4:

```
if ($(this).val() == 'other') {
    // Replace with text input field
    $(this).parent().replaceWith('<input type=
➥ "text" name="title" id="title">');
}
```

This chains the `parent()` method to `$(this)` to select the `<select>` menu's parent `<div>` and then chains the `replaceWith()` method. The argument passed to `replaceWith()` is a string containing the HTML for a text input field with the same name and ID as the element it's replacing.

8. Save reservations.html and activate Live view. Click the Select Menu widget and test it by changing to any value except Other. The value should be selected. Next, change the value to Other. The Select Menu widget should be replaced by a text input field (**Figure 6.50**).

9. To match the style of other text input fields, activate Live Code again, locate the dynamically generated markup for the First Name field, and copy its class definition (**Figure 6.51**).

**Figure 6.50** The widget has been replaced, but the input field needs to be styled to match the rest of the form.

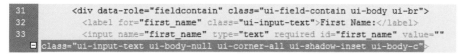

**Figure 6.51** Live Code reveals the class definition for the Text Input widget.

215

**10.** Exit Live view and paste the class definition into the HTML markup that's passed as an argument to `replaceWith()`. The complete script now looks like this:

```
$(function() {
    // Change handler for Select Menu widget
    $('select#title').live('change',
    ➥ function(e) {
        // Check selected value
        if ($(this).val() == 'Other') {
            // Replace with text input field
            $(this).parent().replaceWith(
            ➥ '<input type="text" name="title"
            ➥ id="title" class="ui-input-text
            ➥ ui-body-null ui-corner-all
            ➥ ui-shadow-inset ui-body-c">');
        }
    });
});
```

Replacing the `<select>` menu with a text input field has a disadvantage: It prevents the user from returning to the menu if Other is selected by accident, which could easily happen on a touch-sensitive device. However, the user is left with a normal text input field, so the form remains functional.

**11.** Test the Select Menu widget in Live view again. This time the new text input field should be styled the same as the others.

You can compare your code with reservations_select. html in ch06/complete.

The form would also benefit from the addition of scripts to validate the date format and to check that all required fields have been filled in. For space reasons, detailed instructions are not included here, but the completed scripts are in reservations.html in the ch06/complete folder. See http://foundationphp.com/dwmobile for more information about the scripts.

## Submitting a Form and Displaying the Response

Although the jQuery Mobile framework has all the components necessary to create and submit an online form, it cannot process data input. That's the responsibility of a server-side technology, such as PHP, ColdFusion, ASP. NET, or Perl. Writing form-processing scripts is beyond the scope of this book.

Among the many books that deal with form processing, you might find my Adobe Dreamweaver CS5 with PHP: Training from the Source (Adobe Press, 2010) helpful. Alternatively, if your server supports ColdFusion, consult ColdFusion 9 Web Application Construction Kit by Ben Forta and others (Adobe Press, 2010).

By default, jQuery Mobile attempts to submit the form input using Ajax. All that's necessary is to set the value of the form's `action` attribute to the URL of the file that processes the form input. If the form-processing script outputs the response as a jQuery Mobile page block, it's loaded automatically like any other content, complete with a Back button.

However, sending and loading the response by Ajax has the following limitations:

▶ Using Ajax results in the form being submitted directly, thereby sidestepping any validation.

▶ The Back button takes the user back to the same form.

▶ At the time of this writing, using Ajax works only when the form is submitted using the GET method.

To set up a form for submission in jQuery Mobile:

1. Select the form by clicking its red border in Design view. Alternatively, click anywhere in the form and select <form> in the Tag selector at the bottom of the Document window.

2. Enter the URL of the form-processing script in the Action field of the Property inspector.

3. Set Method to GET or POST.

   If you select Default, Dreamweaver removes the `method` attribute from the <form> tag, which results in the form being submitted by the GET method.

4. If you select the POST method, expand the jQuery Mobile category in the Tag Inspector and set `data-ajax` to `false`. Alternatively, add `data-ajax="false"` to the opening <form> tag in Code view.

The script that processes the form should output a jQuery Mobile page block or redirect the user to such a page.

If the form was submitted by the GET method, the response page automatically adds a Back button to the header. Clicking the button returns the user to the page that contains the form.

**GET and POST**

The `method` attribute in the opening <form> tag determines how the browser handles user input when the form is submitted. When the attribute is set to GET (the value is case-insensitive) or omitted, the form appends the data to the URL as a *query string*—a question mark followed by a series of name/value pairs. The GET method is normally used in search forms because the URL can be bookmarked. Browsers also try to cache the results.

When the `method` attribute is set to POST, the data is sent in the background and cannot be bookmarked. The POST method should be used when the form is intended to update a database, upload files, or send the input by email. It should also be used when a large amount of data needs to be transmitted, because Internet Explorer limits the amount of data that can be sent by the GET method to approximately 2,000 characters.

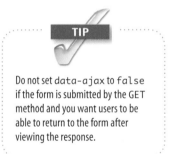

**TIP**

Do not set `data-ajax` to `false` if the form is submitted by the GET method and you want users to be able to return to the form after viewing the response.

When you set `data-ajax` to `false`, you need to hard-code navigation buttons into the response page's header in the same way as described in "Adding Back and Home buttons to page headers" in Chapter 5.

## Getting Your Hands Dirty with Code

As this chapter has demonstrated, the jQuery Mobile widgets in Dreamweaver CS5.5 speed up development. But you still need a good understanding of the code they use, and you need to be prepared to dive into the code to achieve the results you want. In the next chapter, you'll learn how to convert a jQuery Mobile site into a native app for Android and iOS using the PhoneGap framework, which is integrated into Dreamweaver CS5.5. It's another code-heavy chapter, so take a well-earned rest before diving in.

# Building a Native App with PhoneGap

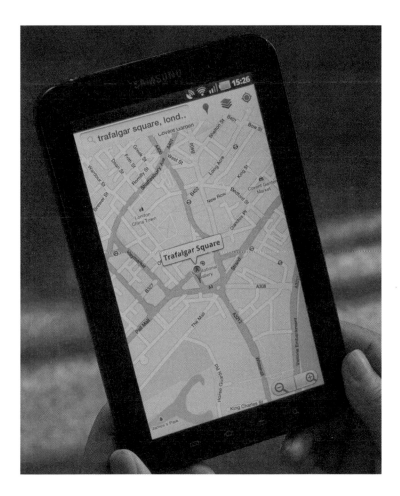

*Receipted bills and invitations*
*To inspect new stock or to visit relations*
*And applications for situations*

—W.H. Auden

# Building a Native App with PhoneGap

Modern smartphones and tablets are capable of much more than browsing websites on the move. They have cameras, storage space, global positioning system (GPS) sensors, and more. These enhanced features have germinated a whole new industry of developing specialized applications—or apps—for mobile devices. The drawback from the developer's point of view is the proliferation of operating systems. You need to program in Objective-C for iOS, whereas Android apps are written in Java. BlackBerry and Windows Phone 7 use other operating systems.

**NOTES**

For an up-to-date list of the native features supported by PhoneGap, see www.phonegap.com/features.

PhoneGap is an open-source development tool that allows web developers to use familiar technologies—HTML, CSS, and JavaScript—and then convert them into native apps for the most widely available mobile operating systems. PhoneGap exposes access to a device's native features, such as a camera, GPS, and storage through a simple JavaScript application programming interface (API). If you can write JavaScript, you can start creating native apps right away.

Dreamweaver CS5.5 helps you get started developing native apps by incorporating support for PhoneGap. Although PhoneGap supports a wide range of mobile platforms, Dreamweaver currently supports only two:

▶ **Android.** Supported on Windows, Mac OS X 10.5, and Mac OS X 10.6

▶ **iOS.** Requires Mac OS X 10.6

This chapter describes how to set up Dreamweaver to work with PhoneGap. You'll build a simple travel notes app that stores the current location and displays it on a map. In addition to using parts of the PhoneGap API, the app introduces you to jQuery Mobile custom events. Most of this chapter is devoted to hand-coding JavaScript, jQuery, and SQL. All the code is explained in detail, but you might find this chapter a challenge without a basic knowledge of JavaScript.

You don't need an Android device or an iPhone, iPod touch, or iPad to follow along in this chapter. The Android and iOS software development kits (SDKs) include simulators that show how your app would work on a real device.

## Setting Up PhoneGap in Dreamweaver

To build native apps with PhoneGap, you need to install the SDK for each platform that you intend to target. If you already have the Android SDK installed, you simply need to tell Dreamweaver where to find it. Otherwise, you can have Dreamweaver install it for you.

To develop for iOS, you need to be running Mac OS X 10.6. Download and install the most recent versions of Xcode and the iOS SDK from the iOS Dev Center at http://developer.apple.com.

NOTES

Structured Query Language (SQL) is the most widely used language for communicating with databases. Although SQL is a formal standard, most database systems use their own dialect of SQL. The version adopted by mobile devices is SQLite (www.sqlite.org).

CLOSE-UP

**Developing for iOS**

Allow plenty of time for downloading and installing Xcode and the iOS SDK. The disk image is 4.6 GB, and the installation process can take an hour or longer. You need to register with Apple to download the SDK, but there is no need to pay the annual developer registration fee until you're ready to start deploying apps. The SDK includes simulators for the iPhone and iPad that allow you to launch and test your apps from within Dreamweaver.

Xcode and the iOS SDK cannot be installed on Windows. Dreamweaver's integration of the iOS SDK requires Mac OS X 10.6. Check with www.adobe.com/support for information about compatibility with later versions of OS X.

## Configuring Dreamweaver for Android and iOS

Apart from a slight difference in the dialog box, the setup process for working with your chosen SDK(s) is identical on Windows and Mac OS X.

1. Choose Site > Mobile Applications > Configure Application Framework to open the dialog box to tell Dreamweaver where to find the files it needs to convert web pages into native apps.

   In Windows, the only option in the dialog box is for the Android SDK (**Figure 7.1**).

   In the Mac version, the dialog box has options for Android and iOS (**Figure 7.2**).

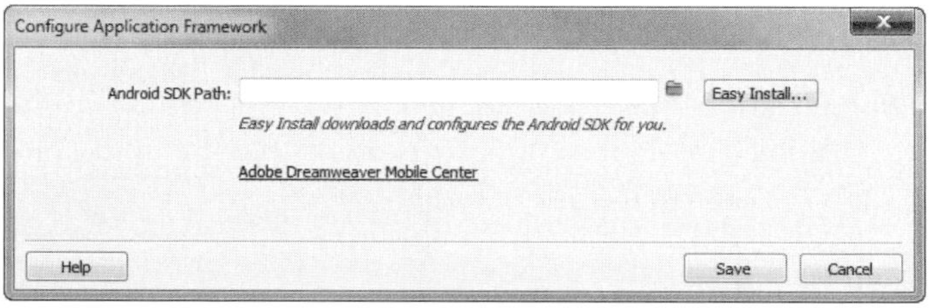

**Figure 7.1** The Windows version of Dreamweaver supports only Android.

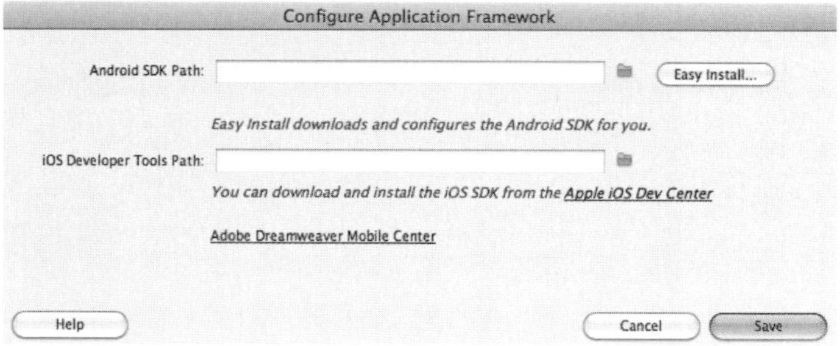

**Figure 7.2** You need the Mac version of Dreamweaver to develop for iOS.

2. If you don't have the Android SDK installed, skip to step 3.

   If you have already installed the Android SDK, click the folder icon next to the Android SDK Path text field, and choose the folder that contains the SDK. In the Windows version of Dreamweaver or Mac OS X 10.5, that's all you need to do. Just click Save and skip to the next section.

   If you're running Mac OS X 10.6 and have installed Xcode and the iOS SDK, skip to step 6.

3. If you don't have the Android SDK installed on your computer, click the Easy Install button. This opens your operating system's dialog box asking where you want to install the SDK (it's approximately 180 MB).

   You need to be connected to the Internet, because as soon as you click OK (Choose on a Mac), Dreamweaver starts downloading and installing the files (**Figure 7.3**).

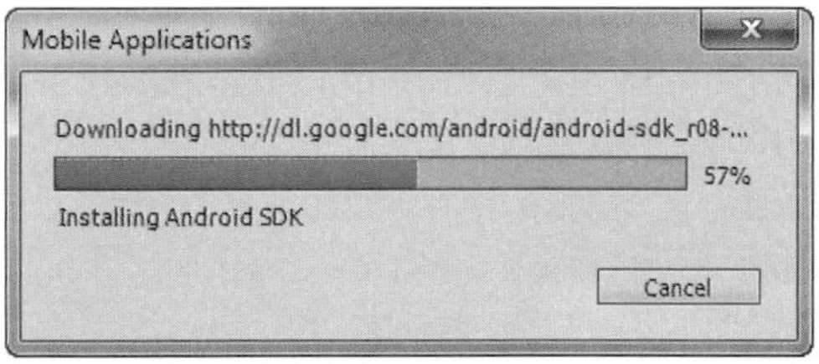

**Figure 7.3** Dreamweaver downloads the Android SDK directly from Google.

   If the Internet connection is dropped before the SDK has completed installing, just click Easy Install again.

4. Downloading and installing the Android SDK usually takes only a few minutes on a broadband connection. When the process is complete, Dreamweaver informs you that the SDK was installed successfully (**Figure 7.4**).

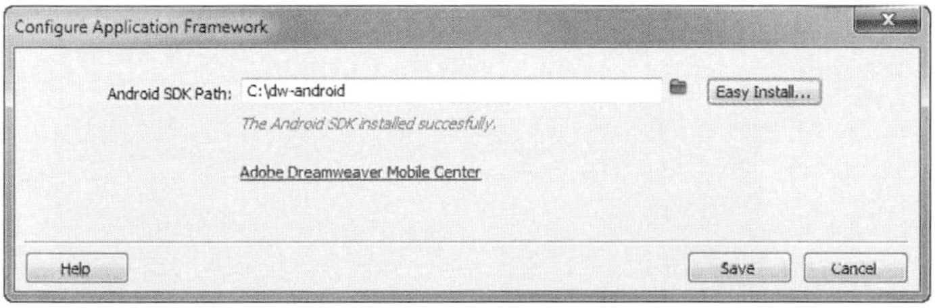

**Figure 7.4** Installing the Android SDK through Dreamweaver is much simpler than installing the individual components yourself.

   In the event that the installation fails, try clicking Easy Install again to overwrite the previous files. Alternatively, drag the folder to the Recycle Bin or Trash for a clean start. Also, make sure that you're logged in with administrative privileges and that the target folder is writeable.

5. Once the Android SDK has been successfully installed on Windows, click Save to close the Configure Application Framework dialog box.

6. On a Mac, if you have installed Xcode and the iOS SDK, enter the location of the iOS SDK in the iOS Developer Tools Path text field. The default location is /Developer (**Figure 7.5**). The path begins with a leading slash.

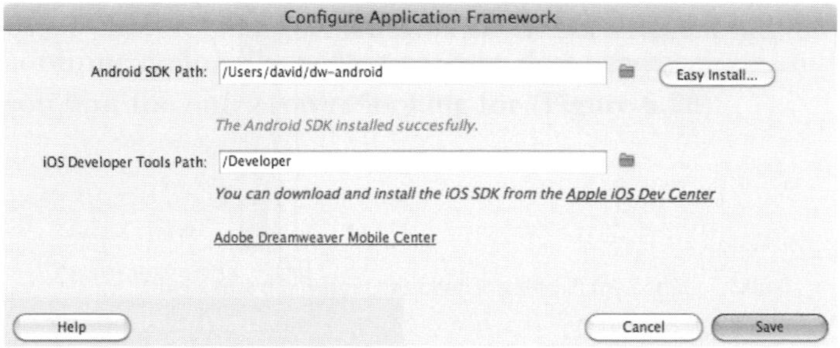

**Figure 7.5** Dreamweaver has been configured for Android and iOS on a Mac.

7. Click Save to close the Configure Application Framework dialog box.

### Setting Up a Dreamweaver Site for a Native App

Because PhoneGap packages your HTML, CSS, JavaScript, and images in a format suitable for installation in a mobile device, you need to create each app in a separate Dreamweaver site. You also need to specify the application settings.

The Mobile Starter pages in the New Document dialog box have an option for jQuery Mobile (PhoneGap) that creates a basic jQuery Mobile page with multiple page blocks. The only difference from the other Mobile Starter pages is that it includes a <script> tag in the <head> of the page that links to an external JavaScript file, phonegap.js. However, phonegap.js isn't copied to your site until you specify the application settings. Consequently, it's more convenient to start with a blank HTML page and add only the elements you actually need.

The following steps describe how to set up the site and specify the application settings for this chapter's case study, a simple app called Travel Notes.

1. Choose Site > New Site to open the Site Setup dialog box.

2. In the Site Name field, type **Travel Notes**.

3. In the Local Site Folder text field, create a new folder called **trnotes**.

4. Click Save to create the site in Dreamweaver.

5. Use Windows Explorer or the Finder to copy ic_launcher.png and splash.png from the ch07/begin folder. Paste them into the trnotes folder. These will be used as the app's launch icon (**Figure 7.6**) and startup screen (**Figure 7.7**).

6. Create a blank HTML page with an HTML5 DOCTYPE, and save it in the Travel Notes site root as **index.html**. You *must* use this name. Otherwise, PhoneGap won't know which page to load when the app launches.

7. Make sure the focus is in Design view, and click Page in the jQuery Mobile category in the Insert panel.

8. In the jQuery Mobile Files dialog box, select the Local radio button and click OK.

9. In the jQuery Mobile Page dialog box, type **home** in the ID field and select only the Header check box. Click OK to insert the jQuery Mobile page block.

10. Save index.html and click Copy when Dreamweaver prompts you to copy the dependent files to your site.

11. You now need to define the application settings. In the Travel Notes site, choose Site > Mobile Applications > Application Settings to open the Native Application Settings dialog box (**Figure 7.8**).

**Figure 7.6** The recommended bounding box for a square launch icon is 56 × 56 pixels, so it can't contain a lot of detail.

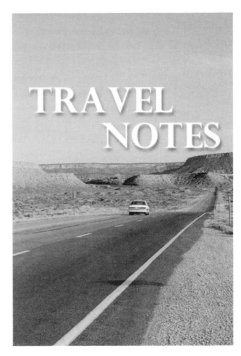

**Figure 7.7** The startup screen is displayed while PhoneGap launches.

I have followed the Android naming conventions for the launch icon and startup screen, but you can use any names you like for your own projects.

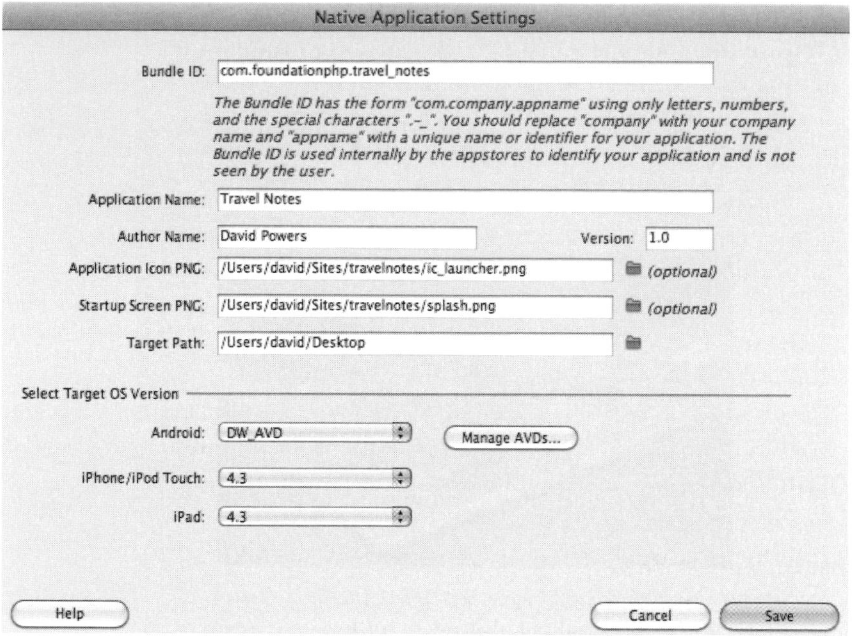

**Figure 7.8** You need to create a unique identity for each app and define its target operating system(s).

The main settings are the same in both Windows and Mac OS X. However, the Mac version also has options for iOS.

Here is a description of each setting:

▶ **Bundle ID.** This creates a unique ID for the app. When developing locally, the value is unimportant, but a unique value is required for distribution in an app store. By default, Dreamweaver sets the value to com.company.site_name. You should replace *com.company* with your own reverse domain name. For example, my website is foundationphp.com, so I've used com.foundationphp.travel_notes as the Bundle ID.

▶ **Application Name.** This is the name of the app as you want it to appear when installed in a mobile device. Dreamweaver automatically uses the same name as in your site definition.

- ▶ **Author Name.** This is the name of the person or company that creates the app.

- ▶ **Version.** By default, Dreamweaver sets this to 1.0. In the testing stage, you might want to use a lower number, such as 0.5.

- ▶ **Application Icon PNG.** Although this is marked as optional, it's a good idea to create an icon to distinguish your app from the thousands of others on the market. For the Travel Notes app, click the folder icon and select ic_launcher.png in the trnotes folder.

- ▶ **Startup Screen PNG.** It takes a few seconds for PhoneGap to load, so it's a good idea to create a 320 × 480 pixel startup screen. For the Travel Notes app, select splash.png in the trnotes folder. See the note in the margin if this field is missing.

- ▶ **Target Path.** This is where you want PhoneGap to build the app and store its related files. The default is on your Desktop.

- ▶ **Select Target OS Version.** On Windows, the only option is Android. By default, Dreamweaver sets the target version to DW_AVD. This is the Dreamweaver version of the Android Virtual Device (AVD), which simulates a mobile phone. The Manage AVDs button launches the Android SDK and AVD Manager, which you can use to download and install updates to the SDK, as well as AVDs for different versions of Android.

If you have installed the iOS SDK on Mac OS X, you can also select the versions of iOS that you want to target for the iPhone, iPod touch, and iPad. PhoneGap builds separate versions of the app for Android and iOS from your HTML, CSS, and JavaScript files.

12. Click Save to close the Native Application Settings dialog box. If you check the Files panel, you should now see that phonegap.js has been added to your site (**Figure 7.9**).

The Native Application Settings dialog box in the original release of Dreamweaver CS5.5 has a couple of rough edges that are expected to be eliminated in an update. When you select an image for the icon or startup screen, Dreamweaver displays a warning about document-relative paths, which you should ignore. Also, the Windows version doesn't have the option for the startup screen. Details of how to fix this problem are in "Specifying a startup screen in Windows" later in this chapter.

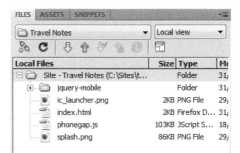

**Figure 7.9** The site now has the main files needed to develop the Travel Notes app.

**Launch Icons and Startup Screens**

Creating an icon and startup screen for an app is arguably just as important as the rest of the design and development process. The Android Developers Dev Guide has advice on what makes a good launch icon at http://developer.android.com/guide/practices/ui_guidelines/icon_design_launcher.html. You can also download a template pack in Photoshop format from http://developer.android.com/guide/practices/ui_guidelines/icon_design.html.

When developing in PhoneGap, a startup screen should be 320 × 480 pixels. It can be saved as a .png or .jpg file.

13. Although phonegap.js has been added to the site, you need to link it to index.html. In Code view, position the insertion point immediately before the closing </head> tag and click Script in the Common category in the Insert panel.

14. Type **phonegap.js** in the Source field and click OK. You're now ready to begin developing a native app.

### Specifying a startup screen in Windows

When PhoneGap was being integrated into Dreamweaver, only the iOS version of PhoneGap supported startup screens. As a result, the Windows version of Dreamweaver CS5.5 doesn't have an option to specify an image for a startup screen. However, if you're willing to make a minor edit to a Dreamweaver configuration file, you can enable the option.

If your version of the Native Application Settings dialog box looks like **Figure 7.10**, use the following instructions to reveal the Startup Screen PNG field.

**Figure 7.10** The Startup Screen PNG field is missing in the Windows version.

Editing configuration files always carries the risk of making changes that prevent Dreamweaver from working. However, the changes are so trivial that you should have no problem. If you have any doubts, back up the configuration folder first.

1. Close Dreamweaver CS5.5.

2. You need to edit a JavaScript file in the main Dreamweaver configuration folder. Notepad will do, but it's better if you have an editor that shows line numbers. To change a program file, being logged on as administrator is not sufficient. Locate the text editor in the Windows Start menu or use the editor's shortcut icon, right-click, and choose Run as Administrator.

3. In the text editor, choose File > Open, and navigate to C:\Program Files\Adobe\Adobe Dreamweaver CS5.5\ configuration\NativeAppFramework. On Windows 64-bit, the folder is in the same location in C:\Program Files (x86).

4. Select NativeAppSetup.js and open it. If you can't see it listed, set File Type to All Files (*.*).

5. Locate the section of code shown in **Figure 7.11**.

```
105        //The startup screen is only supported on iOS for now
106        if( !iOSSupported )
107            document.getElementById("startupScreenGroup").style.display = "none";
```

**Figure 7.11** These lines are responsible for hiding the startup screen field in Windows.

6. Comment out the code in lines 106–107 by typing // at the beginning of both lines, as shown in **Figure 7.12**.

```
105        //The startup screen is only supported on iOS for now
106        //if( !iOSSupported )
107        //   document.getElementById("startupScreenGroup").style.display = "none";
```

**Figure 7.12** Commenting out the two lines reenables the startup screen field.

7. Save NativeAppSetup.js and close your text editor.

8. Relaunch Dreamweaver CS5.5 and open the Travel Notes site.

**9.** Choose Site > Mobile Applications > Application Settings. You should now see the Startup Screen PNG field (**Figure 7.13**).

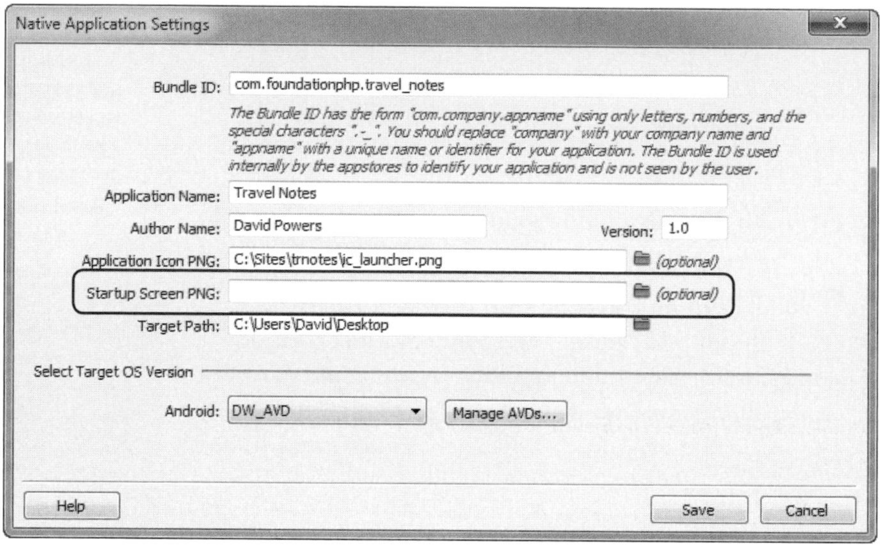

**Figure 7.13**  After editing the configuration file, you can specify a startup screen.

**10.** Select the startup screen for your app (splash.png in the case of the Travel Notes app) and click Save. You're now ready to begin developing the native app in the following case study.

## Case Study: A Travel Notes App

The PhoneGap API gives you access to the following native features of mobile devices:

- ▶ Accelerometer
- ▶ Camera
- ▶ Compass
- ▶ Contacts
- ▶ File (not on iOS)
- ▶ Geolocation
- ▶ Media (audio recording)
- ▶ Notification (sound)
- ▶ Notification (vibration)
- ▶ Storage

To demonstrate how to use some of these features, this case study builds a simple app that allows you to store brief travel notes about a place you're visiting. On a GPS-enabled device, it automatically detects and stores the current latitude and longitude (as long as the user gives consent). The stored coordinates are then used to display a map on demand.

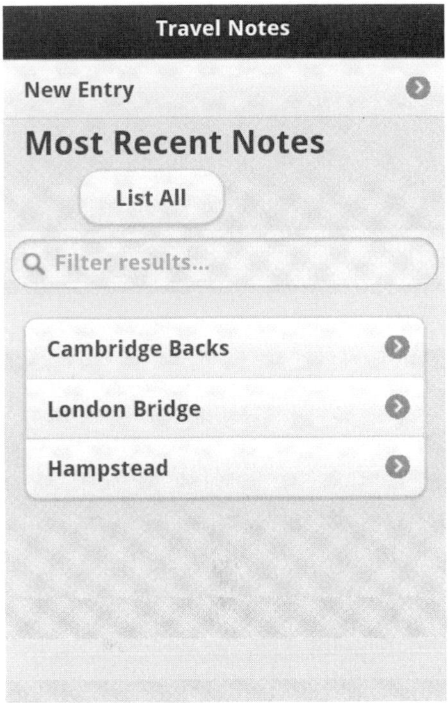

### Creating the App's HTML Structure

The Travel Notes app needs two forms: one for inserting new notes and the other for editing existing notes. It also needs to be able to display a searchable list of existing notes and link to a map. As soon as you start adding notes, a list of the most recent is displayed on the first page (**Figure 7.14**).

To build the app, you need five jQuery Mobile page blocks, as follows:

▶ **Home screen.** By default, this displays the 20 most recent notes but also has a button to retrieve all notes.

▶ **New entry.** This is a simple form that stores new notes.

▶ **Edit note.** This loads the contents of an existing note ready for updating.

▶ **Display note.** This displays an individual note and has Edit and Delete buttons. If GPS is enabled, it also links to a map of the location.

▶ **Display map.** This displays a map of the location.

The following steps describe how to build the HTML structure.

1. In index.html, change the page title and the `<h1>` heading to **Travel Notes**.

2. Delete the Content placeholder text, and with the insertion point still inside the `<div>`, click List View in the jQuery Mobile category in the Insert bar. Set the List Type to Unordered and Items to 1. Leave all the check boxes deselected, and click OK to insert the widget.

3. Change the placeholder text in the List View widget to New Entry, and type **#new** in the Link field in the Property inspector.

**Figure 7.14** The opening screen lets you create new notes and search existing ones.

**4.** Click <ul> in the Tag selector at the bottom of the Document window to select the List View widget, and press the right arrow key once to move the insertion point past the closing </ul> tag but still within the main content <div>.

**5.** The rest of the first screen needs to be hidden when there are no entries in the app's database. So, insert a <div> by choosing Insert > Layout Objects > Div Tag. In the Insert Div Tag dialog box, set Insert to "At insertion point" and type **entries** in the ID field. Click OK to insert the <div>.

**6.** Press Ctrl+2/Command+2 to convert the placeholder text into an <h2> heading, and change it to **Most Recent Notes**.

**7.** The rest of the code in the first page block needs to be the List All button and an empty List View widget. Although you can continue working in Design view, it's probably more efficient to switch to Code view and hand-code the remaining tags with the help of code hints. The finished code for the first page block looks like this:

```
<div data-role="page" id="home">
    <div data-role="header">
        <h1>Travel Notes</h1>
    </div>
    <div data-role="content">
        <ul data-role="listview">
            <li><a href="#new">New Entry
            ↪ </a></li>
        </ul>
        <div id="entries">
            <h2>Most Recent Notes</h2>
            <a href="#" data-role="button"
            ↪ data-inline="true" id="limit">
            ↪ List All</a>
            <ul id="recent" data-role=
            ↪ "listview" data-inset="true"
            ↪ data-filter="true">
            </ul>
        </div>
    </div>
</div>
```

The List All button is an <a> tag that has been assigned the data-role of button with data-inline set to true. The empty List View has data-inset set to true to inset it from the edges of the screen and data-filter set to true to add a search field.

Both elements have been given IDs to make it easy to attach event handlers with jQuery later.

8. Make sure the insertion point is outside the closing </div> tag of the first page block but still inside the <body>. Insert a new jQuery Mobile page, and set its ID to **new**. As before, the page block needs only a header.

9. Change the text in the <h1> heading to **New Note**.

10. Delete the Content placeholder text, and insert a form. Name the form **insert** and set the method to POST.

11. The form needs a jQuery Mobile Text Input widget, a Text Area widget, and a submit button. Name the Text Input widget **title**, the Text Area widget **details**, and the submit button **create**. Also, the opening <form> tag needs data-ajax set to false.

Using jQuery Mobile form widgets was covered in detail in Chapter 6, so I'll just show the completed code for the second page block.

```
<div data-role="page" id="new">
    <div data-role="header">
        <h1>New Note</h1>
    </div>
    <div data-role="content">
        <form action="" method="post"
        ↪ name="insert" id="insert" data-ajax=
        ↪ "false">
        <div data-role="fieldcontain">
            <label for="title">Title:</label>
            <input type="text" name="title"
            ↪ id="title" value=""  />
        </div>
        <div data-role="fieldcontain">
            <label for="details">Details:
            ↪ </label>
```

```
                                    <textarea cols="40" rows="8"
                                 ➥ name="details" id="details">
                                 ➥ </textarea>
                            </div>
                            <input name="create" type="submit"
                         ➥ id="create" value="Insert" />
                            </form>
                        </div>
                    </div>
```

**12.** Select the page block containing the new entry form and copy it to your clipboard. Move the insertion point outside the closing </div> tag, and paste the page block back into the page. You should now have two identical page blocks. However, Dreamweaver automatically detects the existing IDs in the code and appends 2 at the end of the duplicates. So, new becomes new2, title becomes title2, and so on.

**13.** The duplicate form is for updating existing notes, so the title2 and details2 IDs are OK, but you need to change the others to make the JavaScript code more understandable and easier to maintain. Edit the duplicate page block like this (the changes are highlighted):

```
<div data-role="page" id="editNote">
    <div data-role="header">
        <h1>Update Note</h1>
    </div>
    <div data-role="content">
        <form action="" method="post" name=
     ➥ "edit" id="edit" data-ajax="false">
            <div data-role="fieldcontain">
                <label for="title2">Title:
             ➥ </label>
                <input type="text" name=
             ➥ "title2" id="title2"
             ➥ value=""  />
            </div>
            <div data-role="fieldcontain">
                <label for="details2">Details:
             ➥ </label>
```

```
        <textarea cols="40" rows="8"
        ➥name="details2" id=
        ➥ "details2"></textarea>
      </div>
      <input name="update" type="submit"
      ➥ id="update" value="Update" />
   </form>
 </div>
</div>
```

**14.** Make sure the insertion point is outside the closing </div> tag of the page block you have just edited, and insert another jQuery Mobile page block. Set its ID to **display**.

**15.** Change the text in the <h1> heading to **Display Note**, and delete the Content placeholder text in Design view.

**16.** With the insertion point still between the content <div> tags, right-click, and choose Insert HTML from the context menu. This displays a mini panel that lets you insert an HTML tag at the current location (**Figure 7.15**).

Type **art** to select the code hint for article, and press Enter/Return twice to insert an empty pair of <article> tags. This element will be used to display the contents of the selected travel note.

**Figure 7.15** Choose Insert HTML from the context menu in Design view to add HTML5 semantic tags to a page.

**17.** You need to add a button to display the map. Unfortunately, Dreamweaver's handling of HTML5 semantic tags in Design view is still rather unpolished, so it's best to add the button and a <footer> element in Code view like this:

```
<article></article>
<p><a href="#" id="showmap" data-role=
➥ "button">Show Map</a></p>
<footer></footer>
```

The <footer> element will be used to display the date the note was originally entered and, if appropriate, updated.

**18.** Create a blank new line after the closing </footer> tag in Code view, and click Button in the jQuery Mobile category in the Insert panel. In the dialog box, use the following settings:

- ▶ **Buttons.** 2
- ▶ **Button Type.** Link
- ▶ **Position.** Group
- ▶ **Layout.** Horizontal

This inserts the code for a grouped pair of buttons. Edit the code to change the button labels and add IDs like this:

```
<div data-role="controlgroup" data-type=
➥ "horizontal"><a href="#" data-role="button"
➥ id="editItem">Edit Note</a>
➥ <a href="#" data-role="button" id="delete">
➥ Delete Note</a></div>
```

**19.** Make sure the insertion point is outside the closing </div> tag of the page block you just created, and insert a new jQuery Mobile page block. Set the ID of the new page block to **map**.

**20.** Change the text in the <h1> heading to **Display Map**, and delete the Content placeholder text.

**21.** The HTML structure is now complete, but you need to add a <style> block in the <head> of the page to display the <article> and <footer> tags as block-level elements. Add the following code to the <head> of index. html:

```
<style>
article, footer {
    display: block;
}
</style>
```

22. Activate Live view. The List All button is too far below the Most Recent Notes heading and sits directly on top of the search box (**Figure 7.16**).

23. Add the following definitions to the <style> block that you created in step 21:

```
#home h2 {
    margin-bottom: 5px;
}
#limit {
    margin: 0 auto 20px 40px;
}
```

Refresh Live view by clicking anywhere inside or by pressing F5. The button is now evenly positioned between the heading and search box (**Figure 7.17**).

You can compare your code with index_struct.html in ch07/complete.

### Programming the App

Although the HTML structure consists of five page blocks, you can access only two of them at the moment: the initial screen and the new entry form. To bring the app to life, you need to develop the programming logic that creates the database, populates it with data, and displays the location map. The HTML page has access to three JavaScript libraries:

▶ **jQuery Core.** This simplifies the selection of page elements, reducing the complexity of code needed to attach event handlers and manipulate the Document Object Model (DOM) to display and remove content on the fly.

▶ **jQuery Mobile.** This exposes extra events that are specific to mobile applications, for example, allowing you to trigger page transitions or rebuilding content dynamically.

▶ **PhoneGap.** This gives you access to native features, such as database storage and geolocation.

**Figure 7.16** The List All button is badly positioned.

**Figure 7.17** That looks better!

Each library has its own methods and properties, but they all work together seamlessly. And because they're all written in JavaScript, they all share the same syntax. All are well documented:

▶ **jQuery Core.** http://docs.jquery.com

▶ **jQuery Mobile.** http://jquerymobile.com

▶ **PhoneGap.** http://docs.phonegap.com

### Planning the app's functionality

The Travel Notes app needs to do the following:

▶ Create a database on the mobile device.

▶ Retrieve a list of existing records.

▶ Get the user's current location.

▶ Store new records, including the current location.

▶ Update and delete existing records.

▶ Display a map of a specific location.

The functions that implement these features also need to be bound as event handlers to the relevant buttons in the HTML structure. For ease of maintenance, all the JavaScript coding is stored in an external file.

### Combining your own JavaScript with jQuery Mobile

When jQuery Mobile starts executing, it triggers it triggers an event called `mobileinit`, which lets you set custom properties and override default values. Because the event is triggered immediately, a `mobileinit` event handler must be defined before the jQuery Mobile script is loaded. So, the recommended order of scripts is as follows:

1. jQuery Core

2. Custom script

3. jQuery Mobile

Create a file for the custom script and attach it to index. html as follows:

1. Choose File > New and select Blank Page from the list on the left of the New Document dialog box.

2. Select JavaScript as the Page Type, and click Create.

3. Create a folder called **js** in the Travel Notes site root, and save the file as **trnotes.js** in the new folder.

4. Open index.html in Code view, and position the insertion point immediately before the `<script>` tag that attaches the jQuery Mobile file.

5. Click Script in the Common category in the Insert panel, and then click the folder icon next to the Source field.

6. Navigate to the js folder, select trnotes.js, and click OK (Choose on a Mac).

7. Click OK to close the Script dialog box.

   The new `<script>` tag should have been added between those that attach the jQuery and jQuery Mobile files like this:

   ```
   <script src="jquery.mobile/jquery-1.5.2.min
   ➥ .js" type="text/javascript"></script>
   <script type="text/javascript" src="js/
   ➥ trnotes.js"></script>
   <script src="jquery.mobile/jquery.mobile-1
   ➥ .0a4.min.js" type-"text/javascript">
   ➥ </script>
   ```

8. To keep the files organized, select phonegap.js in the Files panel and drag it into the js folder. When Dreamweaver asks if you want to update the links, click Update.

   The phonegap.js `<script>` tag should have been updated like this:

   ```
   <script type="text/javascript" src="js/
   ➥ phonegap.js"></script>
   ```

### Storing data with the Web SQL Database API

The Web SQL Database API is a World Wide Web Consortium (W3C) specification (www.w3.org/TR/webdatabase) that defines how web pages can store and retrieve data from a database. It has been adopted by WebKit browsers, such as Safari and Google Chrome. It's also supported by Android, iOS, BlackBerry 6, and Palm. However, in the complex and sometimes political atmosphere of web standards development, the W3C's Web Applications Working Group has stopped work on the specification and is now devoting its efforts to the Indexed Database API (www.w3.org/TR/IndexedDB).

The Web SQL Database API has been abandoned because of a dispute over which database to use. All implementations of the API use SQLite. The W3C wants the API to be database-neutral. Although that's a noble ambition, there are no implementations of the W3C's favored solution, whereas the Web SQL Database API is in active use.

Normally, I hesitate to recommend using a specification that's no longer under active development. However, I think it's safe to use the Web SQL Database API in the closed environment of a native app. But it's unsuitable for use in a website because Firefox and Internet Explorer (IE) don't support it.

Using the Web SQL Database API is fairly simple. You first need to connect to a database with the openDatabase() method, which expects the following arguments:

▶ **Database name.** This shouldn't contain spaces, hyphens, or special characters.

▶ **Version number.** Only one version can be open at a time.

▶ **Display name.** This is a text description of the database. It can contain spaces and special characters.

▶ **Maximum size.** This specifies in bytes the maximum amount of storage space allocated to the database.

If the database doesn't already exist, it's automatically created the first time you call openDatabase(). Opening the database returns a JavaScript object, which you need to store in a variable like this:

```
var db = openDatabase('trnotes', '1.0', 'Travel
➥ Notes', 2*1024*1024);
```

This creates or opens version 1.0 of a database called trnotes, which has a maximum size of 2 MB, and stores a reference to it as db.

To insert, update, delete, or select data, you call the transaction() method on the database object. The basic syntax looks like this:

```
db.transaction(function(t) {
    t.executeSql(SQL, arguments, success, fail);
}
```

The arguments passed to the executeSql() method are as follows:

▶ A SQL query with question marks as placeholders for variables

▶ An array of variables that contain the values represented by the placeholders (optional)

▶ A callback function to be executed if the transaction succeeds (optional)

▶ A callback function to be executed if the transaction fails (optional)

Using question marks as placeholders for variables in the SQL query is designed to prevent SQL injection and to preserve the integrity of your database.

CLOSE-UP

**SQL Injection**

SQL injection is a common type of attack that attempts to inject spurious data into a database query. Depending on the nature of the attack, it can insert malicious scripts into your data, gain unauthorized access to protected areas, reveal sensitive information, or completely wipe your database. It exploits scripts that fail to handle quotation marks and other special characters correctly. The Web SQL Database API protects against SQL injection by automatically formatting the values that replace the question mark placeholders.

### Setting up the app's database

The Travel Notes app interacts with the database all the time. So, the script uses the `mobileinit` event to establish a connection to the database on startup, and it stores the database object as a custom property of the jQuery Mobile `$.mobile` object.

1.  Add the following code to trnote.js:

    ```
    $(document).bind("mobileinit", function(){
        $.mobile.notesdb = openDatabase('trnotes',
        ➥ '1.0', 'Travel Notes', 2*1024*1024);
    }
    ```

    This binds a `mobileinit` event handler to the document. All code inside the event handler is executed as soon as jQuery Mobile starts.

    The Web SQL API's `openDatabase()` method opens (or creates) version 1.0 of a database called `trnotes` and sets its maximum storage limit at 2 MB (1 MB = $1024 \times 1024$ bytes). The database object is stored as the `notesdb` property of `$.mobile`, giving access to it through the rest of the script.

2.  The first time you open the database, you need to define its structure. The database needs a table to store the following information:

    ▶ An ID to identify each record (primary key)

    ▶ Title

    ▶ Details

    ▶ Latitude

    ▶ Longitude

    ▶ Date created

    ▶ Date updated

Amend the code in the `mobileinit` event handler to execute a SQL query to build the table like this:

```
$(document).bind("mobileinit", function(){
    $.mobile.notesdb = openDatabase('trnotes',
    ➥ '1.0', 'Travel Notes', 2*1024*1024);
    $.mobile.notesdb.transaction(function(t) {
        t.executeSql('CREATE TABLE IF NOT
        ➥ EXISTS notes (id INTEGER NOT NULL
        ➥ PRIMARY KEY AUTOINCREMENT,
        ➥ title TEXT NOT NULL, details TEXT
        ➥ NOT NULL, entered TEXT NOT NULL,
        ➥ updated TEXT, latitude REAL,
        ➥ longitude REAL);');
    });
```

The SQL query creates a table called `notes` and defines the data type for each column. The table needs to be created only once, so the query uses the command `CREATE TABLE IF NOT EXISTS`. The `id` column is designated as the table's primary key and is set to `AUTOINCREMENT`, which automatically increments the number by 1 each time. SQLite stores dates as `TEXT`. The `latitude` and `longitude` columns use the `REAL` data type, which stores the values as floating point numbers.

In this case, only one argument is passed to the `executeSql()` method. There are no placeholders in the SQL query, so the second argument is not needed. Using callback functions for success and failure has little value here, because the query will succeed only once—when the table is created. Thereafter, it will always fail. You can use a browser's debugging tools to check whether your code works.

3. Save trnotes.js and index.html. With index.html the active document, choose File > Preview in Browser, and then choose either Safari or Google Chrome. The page should look the same as it did when you tested it earlier in Live view (see Figure 7.17 in "Creating the App's HTML Structure").

**Primary Key**

A primary key is a unique value that identifies a record in a database. It plays a vital role in selecting specific records, as well as updating and deleting them. Although any unique value can be used as a primary key, it's common to use an automatically incremented number. In more complex databases, primary keys are used to link records in different tables.

**NOTES**

Windows users, if you don't have Safari or Chrome listed in the Preview in Browser submenu, choose Edit Browser List to open the Preview in Browser category in the Preferences panel. Click the plus icon next to Browsers, and add your browser of choice. Safari is in Program Files, but Google Chrome is located in your user account's AppData\Local or Application Data folder, which is normally a hidden folder.

4. In Safari, open the Web Inspector by pressing Ctrl+Alt+I/Option+Command+I. Select Storage and expand Databases. You should see the `trnotes` database and the `notes` table listed (**Figure 7.18**).

**Figure 7.18** Confirmation in the Safari Web Inspector that the database and table have been created.

In Chrome, open the Developer Tools by pressing Ctrl+Shift+I/Option+Command+I. Select Resources and expand Databases. You should see the `trnotes` database and the `notes` table listed (**Figure 7.19**).

**Figure 7.19** The Chrome Developer Tools provide the same information in a slightly different location.

If the database and table weren't created, select Console in the Safari Web Inspector or Chrome Developer Tools to see if any JavaScript errors are listed. Also, check the SQL code carefully. Because it's in a JavaScript file, it mustn't be broken across several lines.

You can check your code with trnotes_create.js in ch07/complete.

### Getting the current location and inserting data

When the user taps on the New Entry button, the app needs to get the current latitude and longitude to store along with the user input. The PhoneGap `geolocation` object provides access to the device's GPS sensor, and the getCurrentPosition() method does exactly what you would expect. The method expects up to three arguments: a callback to be executed on success, a callback to be executed on failure, and an options object.

The jQuery Mobile framework provides a pageshow event that is triggered after a page block is displayed. So, we'll use the new page block's pageshow event to trigger the acquisition of the GPS data.

The following instructions also show how to dynamically load a page using the $.mobile.changePage() method.

See the PhoneGap documentation at http://docs.phonegap.com for full details of the geolocation object and examples of its use.

1. Add the following code to trnotes.js:

```
$(function() {
    $('#new').live('pageshow', getLocation);
    $('#insert').live('submit', insertEntry);
});
```

This document-ready handler binds a function called getLocation()to the new page block's pageshow event and a function called insertEntry() to the submit event of the insert form. You'll define both functions in a moment.

Other event handlers will be added to the document-ready event handler as you continue to build this script. They'll be added at the same time as the functions are defined to avoid generating errors by calling undefined functions.

2. You need access to the latitude and longitude values in several places. Rather than creating global variables for both, create an object to store commonly used values. Add the following code immediately after the preceding block:

```
var trNotes = {
    lat: null,
    lng: null,
    limit: 20
};
```

This initializes an object called trNotes with three properties: lat, lng, and limit. The first two properties are for the latitude and longitude. The third property sets the default number of records to be retrieved from the database.

**3.** Add the definition for the getLocation() function:

```
function getLocation() {
    navigator.geolocation.getCurrentPosition(
        locSuccess,
        locFail,
        {enableHighAccuracy: true}
    );
}
```

The PhoneGap geolocation object is accessed through the JavaScript navigator object. The first two arguments to getCurrentPosition() call two new functions, locSuccess() and locFail(), which you'll define next. The third argument is an object that sets the enableHighAccuracy property to true. This tells the app to get the best possible results from the GPS sensor.

**4.** The code for the locSuccess() function looks like this:

```
function locSuccess(position) {
    trNotes.lat = position.coords.latitude;
    trNotes.lng = position.coords.longitude;
}
```

If the getCurrentPosition() method succeeds, it returns an object containing the data from the GPS sensor, which is automatically passed as the first argument to the success callback. The coords property of this object contains the latitude and longitude, which are stored as the lat and lng properties of the trNotes object that you created in step 2.

**5.** The locFail() function looks like this:

```
function locFail(error) {
    var msg = 'Cannot determine location.';
    if (error.code == error.PERMISSION_DENIED)
    {
        msg += ' Geolocation is disabled.';
    }
    try {
        navigator.notification.alert(
        ➥ msg, null, 'Geolocation');
```

```
    } catch (e) {
        alert(msg);
    }
};
```

If the getCurrentPosition() method fails, it returns an object containing details of the error, which is automatically passed as the first argument to the failure callback. If the code property of the error object is PERMISSION_DENIED, it indicates that the user or the system refused access to the GPS sensor, so this information is added to the message stored in msg.

The try/catch blocks attempt to display the message using the PhoneGap notification object, which uses the mobile device's native alert panel. The first argument passed to the alert() method is the text of the message. The second is a callback function to be executed when the user dismisses the alert. In this case, it has been set to null because no callback is needed. The third argument is used as the title of the panel. You can also pass a fourth argument to set the text of the button (the default is "OK").

Desktop browsers don't support PhoneGap, so the catch block displays the default browser alert.

6. Define the insertEntry() function by adding the following code at the bottom of trnotes.js:

```
function insertEntry(e) {
    var title = $('#title').val(),
        details = $('#details').val();
    $.mobile.notesdb.transaction(function(t) {
        t.executeSql('INSERT into notes (title,
        ↪ details, entered, latitude,
        ↪ longitude) VALUES
        ↪ (?,?,date("now"),?,?);',
            [title, details, trNotes.lat,
            ↪ trNotes.lng],
            function() {
                $.mobile.changePage('#page',
                ↪ 'slide', false, true);
                $('#title').val('');
```

```
                              $('#details').val('');
                    },
                    null
              );
         });
         e.preventDefault();
    };
```

The function begins by storing the values entered in the `title` and `details` fields of the form. These values are passed to the SQL query together with the latitude and longitude stored in `trNotes.lat` and `trNotes.lng`.

Let's take a quick look at how the values are passed into the query. To make it easier to understand, the SQL query is formatted with line breaks:

```
INSERT into notes
(title, details, entered, latitude, longitude)
VALUES (?,?,date("now"),?,?);
```

The comma-separated list in the first set of parentheses specifies the names of the columns into which the data is to be inserted. The second set of parentheses specifies the values for each column in the same order as the first list. With the exception of `entered`, each value is a question mark placeholder. The value for `entered` is `date("now")`, which is SQLite's way of inserting the current date.

The values represented by the placeholders are in the following argument, which is a JavaScript array:

```
[title, details, trNotes.lat, trNotes.lng]
```

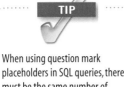

**TIP**

When using question mark placeholders in SQL queries, there must be the same number of elements in the array of values as placeholders—and they must be in the same order.

In other words, the value held in the `title` variable is inserted in the `title` column, the value held in the `details` variable is inserted in the `details` column, and the values in `trNotes.lat` and `trNotes.lng` are inserted in the `latitude` and `longitude` columns, respectively.

Following the array of variables is the callback function that's executed if the executeSql() method succeeds. Viewed in isolation, it looks like this:

```
function() {
    $.mobile.changePage('#home', 'slide',
    ↪ false, true);
    $('#title').val('');
    $('#details').val('');
}
```

The key feature here is $.mobile.changePage(), which dynamically loads a new jQuery Mobile page block. It takes four arguments, as follows:

▶ The destination page block or URL.

The type of page transition, using one of the values in "Controlling page transitions" in Chapter 6.

Whether the transition should be in reverse (the default is false).

▶ Whether to update the URL (the default is true).

Because the last two arguments use the default values, they could be omitted, but I have included them to show their meaning.

The last two lines of the callback function reset the values of the title and details fields to empty strings to prevent the form from loading the same values the next time.

The failure callback is set to null. This has been done for simplicity. In a commercial app, you should use $.mobile.changePage() to redirect the user to a page block that describes the reason for the error.

The final line of the insertEntry() function calls the jQuery preventDefault() method on the event object. This is the same as calling return false and prevents the submit event handler from reloading the form.

7. Save trnotes.js and reload index.html in the browser. Test the code so far by clicking the New Entry button. Depending on your setup, you might be prompted to allow the browser to disclose your location. Even if you

do so, you might see an alert that the location couldn't be determined. If so, dismiss the alert. Testing geolocation on a desktop or laptop is unreliable. What's important is seeing the messages.

8. Enter some text in the `title` and `details` fields, and click the Insert button. You should be taken back to the initial screen.

9. The new entry isn't listed on the initial screen because that part of the script hasn't been created yet. However, you can check that the script is working by refreshing the Databases display in the Safari Web Inspector or Chrome Developer Tools (**Figure 7.20**).

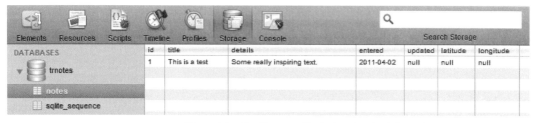

**Figure 7.20**  The first record is displayed in the Safari Web Inspector.

Safari displays columns without values as null, whereas Chrome leaves them blank. This is unimportant. Also note that the date is formatted as YYYY-MM-DD in the database. You'll learn later how to customize the format when displaying the value in the app.

You can check your code against trnotes_insert.js in ch07/complete.

### Displaying a list of existing records

Now that you have at least one record in the database, you need to add the code to display a list of travel notes on the first screen. The list is displayed each time the first page block loads, so you can use another jQuery Mobile event, `pagebeforeshow`, to trigger the function before the transition takes place.

The code needs to perform the following tasks:

▶ Retrieve a list of records in the database.

▶ If records are found, populate the `recent` List View widget in the initial screen.

▶ Store each record's primary key in the button that loads it into the `display` page block.

- ▶ Bind a click event handler to each button to pass the primary key to a function that retrieves the selected record and loads its details in the display and editNote page blocks.

- ▶ Display the entries <div> in the initial screen.

- ▶ If no records are found, hide the entries <div> in the initial screen.

The following steps describe the code in detail and show you how to handle the result of a SQL query.

1. Amend the document-ready event handler at the top of trnotes.js to bind a new function called getTitles() to the pagebeforeshow event of the home page block like this:

```
$(function() {
    $('#home').live('pagebeforeshow',
    ↪ getTitles);
    $('#new').live('pageshow', getLocation);
    $('#insert').live('submit', insertEntry);
});
```

I've added it as the first item because it needs to run immediately when the app is first launched. Using the pagebeforeshow event also means that the getTitles() function is executed each time you return to the first screen.

2. Add the code for the getTitles() function. It's not really important where you locate it in trnotes.js. However, your code is easier to maintain if you organize functions in the order they're used. In the download files, I have put it after the definition of the trNotes object and before the getLocation() function. The code looks like this:

```
function getTitles() {
    var list = $('#recent'),
        items = [];
    $.mobile.notesdb.transaction(function(t) {
        t.executeSql('SELECT id, title FROM
        ↪ notes ORDER BY id DESC LIMIT ?',
```

**TIP**

The constraints of the printed page result in many lines being broken up, so you might find it easier to study the code for the getTitles() function in trnotes_titles.js in ch07/complete.

```
                    [trNotes.limit],
                    function(t, result) {
                        var i,
                            len = result.rows.length,
                            row;
                        if (len > 0 ) {
                            for (i = 0; i < len; i += 1) {
                                row = result.rows.item(i);
                                items.push('<li><a href="
                                ➥ #display" data-trnote="'
                                ➥  + row.id + '">' + row.
                                ➥ title + '</a></li>');
                            }
                            list.html(items.join());
                            list.listview('refresh');
                            $('a', list).live('click',
                            ➥ function(e) {
                                getItem(($(this).attr(
                                ➥ 'data-trnote')));
                            });
                            $('#entries').show();
                        } else {
                            $('#entries').hide();
                        }
                    })
                });
            }
```

The function begins by creating two variables: `list` holds a reference to the empty unordered list in the home page block, and `items` is an empty array that will be used to populate the list with the results of the SQL query.

The `SELECT` query retrieves the `id` and `title` columns from the `notes` table in descending (reverse) order, so the most recent appears first. The query uses a `LIMIT` clause to restrict the number of results. The number is represented by a question mark placeholder, and the specified value (`trNotes.limit`) is passed to the query as a single-element array in the second argument to `executeSql()`.

NOTES

Even when there's only one place-holder in a SQL query, the second argument to `executeSql()` still needs to be an array.

The rest of the code is an anonymous callback function that handles the result. When a SQL query is successfully executed, two objects are automatically passed to the callback: the first is the transaction object, and the second is an object containing the results of the query. It's the second object, which I have called `result`, that you're interested in.

The `result` object has a `rows` property, which contains an array of the records that the `SELECT` query retrieved from the database. By storing the length of the array in `len`, the function determines if any records were found. If `len` is greater than zero, a loop iterates through each record, building an array of list items for the empty unordered list. The code that builds each item looks like this:

```
'<li><a href="#display" data-trnote="' +
↪ row.id + '">' + row.title + '</a></li>'
```

This builds an HTML `<a>` tag nested in an `<li>` tag. The link points to the `display` page block, and it contains a custom data attribute that I have called `data-trnote`, which stores the ID of the current record. Each record in the result is extracted to a temporary variable called `row`. To get the value stored in each column, you append the column name after a period. So, `row.id` gets the value from the `id` column, and `row.title` gets the value from the `title` column. Storing the record's ID or primary key like this ensures that you select the correct record from the database when the user taps a link. When the JavaScript variables are substituted by their values, the resulting string looks similar to this:

```
'<li><a href="#display" data-trnote="1">
↪ This is a test</a></li>'
```

After the loop, the `items` array is converted to a single string using the standard JavaScript `join()` method and is passed to the jQuery `html()` method, populating the previously empty unordered list. Because the list has been updated, you need to call `listview('refresh')`, which tells jQuery Mobile to rebuild the List View widget.

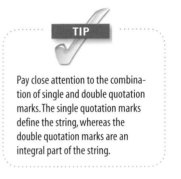

**TIP**

Pay close attention to the combination of single and double quotation marks. The single quotation marks define the string, whereas the double quotation marks are an integral part of the string.

The next section of code binds a click event handler to each link in the List View widget like this:

```
$('a', list).live('click', function(e) {
    getItem($(this).attr('data-trnote'));
});
```

The jQuery selector uses `list` as a second argument, limiting the target elements to the `recent` List View widget. The event-handler function calls a function called `getItem()` and passes it `$(this).attr('data-trnote')` as an argument. `$(this)` refers to the event target—in other words, the `<a>` link—and the `attr()` method retrieves the value of `data-trnote`. In effect, this passes the primary key of the selected item as an argument to `getItem()`.

After the List View widget has been built, the jQuery `show()` method displays the `entries` `<div>`, which contains the List All button, the search field, and the List View widget.

The code that builds and displays the List View widget is wrapped in a conditional statement, so it's executed only if there are any results from the `SELECT` query. If there are no results, the `else` clause uses the jQuery `hide()` method to conceal the `entries` `<div>`.

3. Save trnotes.js and reload index.html in your browser. You should see the title of your first record listed in the initial screen.

4. Click New Entry and insert one or two more items. When you click Insert, you should be taken back to the initial screen where each item is displayed, with the most recent one first (**Figure 7.21**).

You can check your code against trnotes_titles.js in ch07/complete.

### Displaying an individual record's details

The `getItem()` function has to do the following:

▶ Retrieve the selected item's details from the database.

▶ Display the item's details in the `display` page block.

**Figure 7.21** New items are added at the top of the List View widget.

▶ Control the button to display a map of the specified location.

▶ Bind event handlers to the Edit Note and Delete Note buttons.

▶ Populate the form in the editNote page block, so the item is ready for updating.

Here's the full listing:

```
function getItem(id) {
    $.mobile.notesdb.transaction(function(t) {
        t.executeSql('SELECT * FROM notes
        ➥ WHERE id = ?',
        [id],
        function(t, result) {
            var row = result.rows.item(0),
                entered = convertToMDY(
                ➥ row.entered),
                updated = row.updated;
            $('#display h1').text(row.title);
            $('#display article').text(
            ➥ row.details);
            if (row.latitude == null) {
                $('#showmap').parent('p').hide();
            } else {
                $('#showmap').parent('p').show();
                $('#showmap').unbind('click');
                $('#showmap').click(displayMap);
            }
            $('#display footer').html('<p>
            ➥ Created: ' + entered + '</p>');
            if (updated != null) {
                updated = convertToMDY(updated);
                $('#display footer').append('<p>
                ➥ Updated: ' + updated + '</p>');
            }
            $('#delete, #update').attr(
            ➥ 'data-trnote', id);
            $('#title2').val(row.title);
            $('#details2').val(row.details);
        })
    });
}
```

The getItem() function takes as its argument the ID of the selected item and uses it in the WHERE clause of the SELECT query to retrieve the item's details from the database. The callback function that handles the result of the query assigns the result to row and then uses it to populate the display page block. The value of the entered column is passed to a utility function called convertToMDY(), which converts it to an American date format.

The value of the title column replaces the text in the <h1> heading, and the value of details populates the <article> element.

If the value of latitude is null, there's no map to show, so the paragraph that contains the Show Map button is hidden. Otherwise, the paragraph is displayed and a function called displayMap() is bound to the button as a click event handler. However, to prevent multiple click events from being bound to the Show Map button each time the getItem() function runs, the unbind() method first removes any previous event handler.

The reformatted date is displayed in the <footer> element, and if updated is not null, it's reformatted and appended to the HTML in the <footer>.

Finally, the item's primary key is stored as data-trnote in the Delete and Update buttons, and the title and details fields of the update form are prepopulated with the relevant values. Even if the user doesn't intend to update the item, prepopulating the update form avoids the need to query the database again.

Because getItem() calls two functions that haven't yet been created, you can't test it yet.

1. Add the getItem() function definition to trnotes.js.

2. Add the following definition for the convertToMDY() function:

```
function convertToMDY(date) {
    var d = date.split('-');
    return d[1] + '/' + d[2] + '/' + d[0];
}
```

This uses basic JavaScript to split the date, which SQLite stores in the YYYY-MM-DD format, into an array using the hyphens as a separator. So, the first element of the array contains the year, the second contains the month, and the third contains the date. The array elements are returned reordered with slashes in between as MM/DD/YYYY.

3. You'll define the `displayMap()` function later, but you need to create a dummy function to prevent the script from generating an error. Add this to trnotes.js:

```
function displayMap() {
}
```

4. Save trnotes.js and refresh index.html in your browser. Click one of the items in the list in the initial screen. A new screen should load and display the details of the item you selected (**Figure 7.22**).

If your network connection permits geolocation data to be accessed, you should also see the Show Map button (**Figure 7.23**).

The Show Map, Edit Note, and Delete Note buttons don't do anything yet.

You can check your code with trnotes_item.js in ch07/complete.

### Updating and deleting items

The functions for updating and deleting items follow the same pattern as the other functions that you already created, so you can add them to the script at the same time. In addition to defining the functions, you also need to bind them as event handlers to the relevant buttons, as described in the following steps.

1. Amend the document-ready event handler at the top of trnotes.js to bind the new functions to the Edit Note, Delete Note, and Update buttons:

```
$(function() {
    $('#home').live('pagebeforeshow',
    → getTitles);
```

**TIP**

To convert the date to the European DD/MM/YYYY format, just swap the positions of d[1] and d[2] in the last line of the convertToMDY() function.

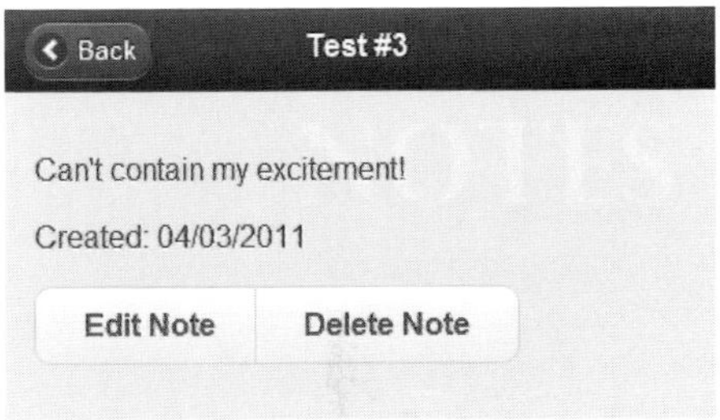

**Figure 7.22** The date is reformatted American style when the selected item's details are shown.

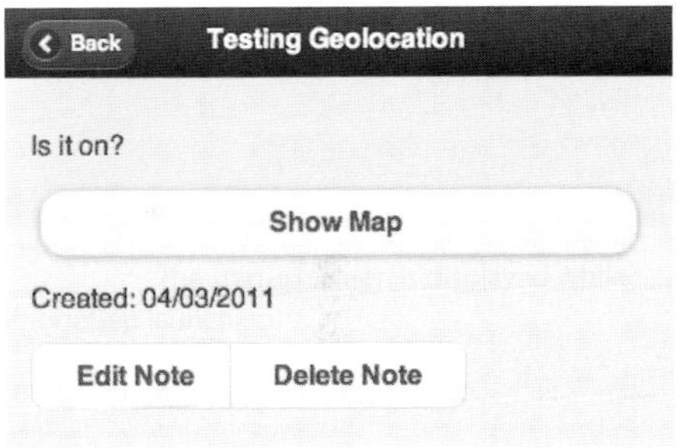

**Figure 7.23** The Show Map button is displayed only if the latitude has been detected.

```
$('#new').live('pageshow', getLocation);
$('#insert').live('submit', insertEntry);
$('#editItem').live('click', editItem);
$('#delete').live('click', deleteItem);
$('#update').live('click', updateItem);
});
```

2. Add the function definitions related to the three buttons. The code looks like this:

```
function editItem() {
    $.mobile.changePage('#editNote',
    ➥ 'slideup', false, true);
}


function deleteItem(e) {
    var id = $(this).attr('data-trnote');
    $.mobile.notesdb.transaction(function(t) {
        t.executeSql('DELETE FROM notes WHERE
        ➥ id = ?',
        [id],
        $.mobile.changePage('#home', 'slide',
        ➥ false, true),
        null);
    });
    e.preventDefault();
}


function updateItem(e) {
    var title = $('#title2').val(),
        details = $('#details2').val(),
        id = $(this).attr('data-trnote');
    $.mobile.notesdb.transaction(function(t) {
        t.executeSql('UPDATE notes SET title =
        ➥ ?, details = ?, updated = date("now")
        ➥ WHERE id = ?',
        [title, details, id],
        $.mobile.changePage('#home', 'flip',
        ➥ false, true),
        null);
    });
    e.preventDefault();
}
```

The editItem() function simply calls the jQuery Mobile $.mobile.changePage() function to load the editNote page block. To indicate the screen's different purpose, the transition is set to slideup. The form fields were populated earlier by the getItem() function, so editItem() doesn't need to do anything else.

The deleteItem() and updateItem() functions obtain the record's primary key from the data-trnote attribute stored on the relevant button, execute the SQL query, and reload the initial screen.

3. Save trnotes.js and reload index.html in your browser. Test the amended script by selecting an item and updating it. If you edit the title, the revised version should be displayed immediately when you return to the initial screen (**Figure 7.24**).

4. Select the same item. This time when it's displayed, you should also see when it was updated (**Figure 7.25**).

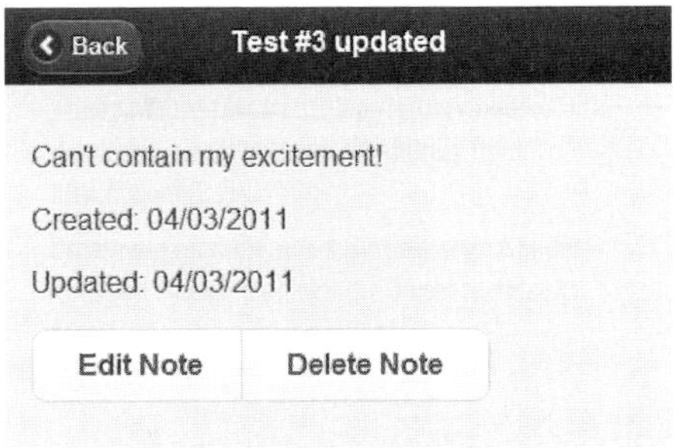

5. Add the following rules to the <style> block in the <head> of index.html:

```
footer p {
    text-align:right;
    font-style:italic;
    font-size:90%;
    margin: 5px inherit;
}
#entries {
    display: none;
}
```

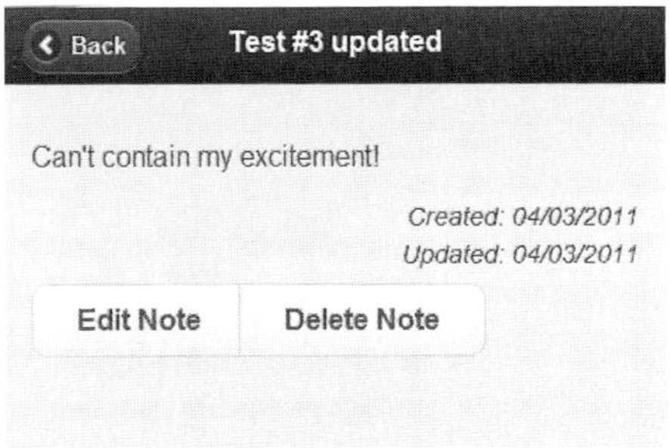

6. Save index.html and reload it in your browser. Although the second style rule you just added sets the display property of the entries <div> to none, the List All button, search field, and List View widget of recent travel notes are still visible. That's because the getTitles() function displays the <div> when there are records in the database.

7. Click one of the items to view its details. The dates are now aligned right and in a smaller italic font (**Figure 7.26**).

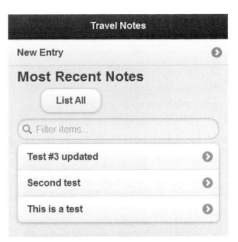

**Figure 7.24** The updated title is displayed immediately.

**Figure 7.25** The dates need to be styled differently from the rest of the text.

**Figure 7.26** The dates now look less overpowering.

8. Test the Delete button. When the initial screen reloads, the item that you deleted is no longer listed.

9. Delete the remaining items. After you delete the last one, the List All button and search field are no longer displayed.

10. Add a new entry. The List All button, search field, and List View widget all reappear.

11. The List All button doesn't do anything yet. So, let's fix that. Add the following line to the document-ready event handler at the top of trnotes.js:

```
$(function() {
    $('#home').live('pagebeforeshow',
    ↪ getTitles);
    $('#new').live('pageshow', getLocation);
    $('#insert').live('submit', insertEntry);
    $('#editItem').live('click', editItem);
    $('#delete').live('click', deleteItem);
    $('#update').live('click', updateItem);
    $('#limit').live('click', swapList);
});
```

12. Add the swapList() function definition at the bottom of the script:

```
function swapList() {
    var btn = $('#limit');
    if (btn.text() == 'List All') {
        btn.text('List Most Recent');
        $('#entries h2').text('All Notes');
        trNotes.limit = -1;
    } else {
        btn.text('List All');
        $('#entries h2').text('Most Recent
        ↪ Notes');
        trNotes.limit = 20;
    }
    getTitles();
}
```

The List All button has the ID limit, so this stores a reference to it as btn. The conditional statement then uses the text() method to check the value of the text in the button and toggle it to List Most Recent. At the same time, the <h2> heading in the entries <div> is also changed.

If the button displays List All before it's clicked, you want the SELECT query in the getTitles() function to retrieve all results. SQLite ignores the LIMIT clause if a negative number is supplied, so trNotes.limit is set to -1. When you click List Most Recent, the limit is changed back to 20.

Finally, the function calls getTitles() to refresh the List View widget.

**13.** Save trnotes.js and index.html, and reload index.html in your browser. Click the List All button. The text changes, but the button collapses (**Figure 7.27**).

**14.** To find out why this happens, you need to inspect the dynamically generated HTML code. You can't use Dreamweaver's Live Code in this case, because Live view doesn't support some of the features used in this script. However, Safari's Web Inspector and Chrome's Developer Tools come to the rescue.

Reload index.html in your browser so the List All button is restored to its normal size and shape. Right-click the text in the List All button, and choose Inspect Element from the context menu (it's the same in both browsers), as shown in **Figure 7.28**.

This launches the Web Inspector or Developer Tools panel with the element highlighted. As **Figure 7.29** shows, the List All text is dynamically wrapped in two <span> tags. The text is in a <span>, which has the class ui-btn-text.

**Figure 7.27** The button loses its style as soon as the text is replaced.

**Figure 7.28** Use Inspect Element in Safari or Chrome to see the generated HTML code.

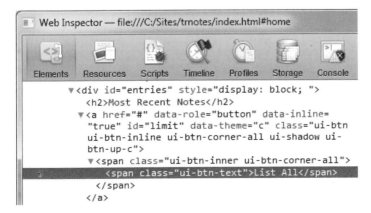

**Figure 7.29** Inspecting the generated code reveals how the button text is styled.

**TIP**

You might need to expand some of the collapsed elements in the Web Inspector or Developer Tools panel to see the button text.

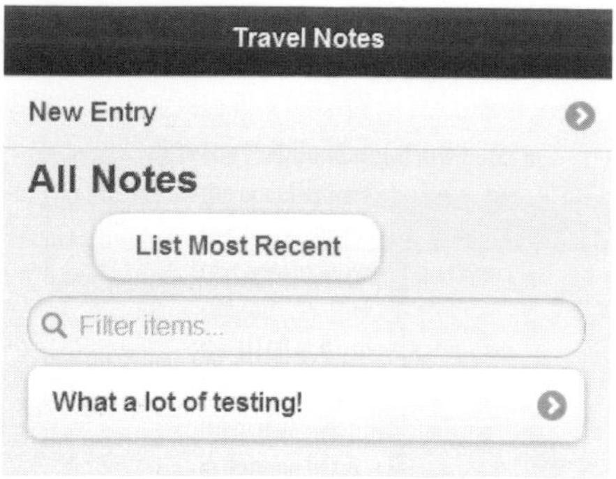

Figure 7.30 The button no longer collapses when the text changes.

Figure 7.31 Android gives users a choice of how to load the map.

**15.** Edit the selector in the first line inside the `swapList()` function definition to add the `ui-btn-text` class like this:

```
function swapList() {
    var btn = $('#limit .ui-btn-text');
```

**16.** Save trnotes.js and reload index.html. This time, when you click the List All button, it retains its styling (**Figure 7.30**).

**17.** To test whether the List All button retrieves the correct amount of records, change both instances of `trNotes`. `limit: 20` in the script to `trNotes: 1`. As long as you have more than one record, only one will be displayed normally. But they should all be displayed when you click List All.

Change both instances back to `20` after you have finished testing.

You can check your code against trnotes_update.js and index_update.html in ch07/complete.

### Displaying the map

The final section of the script displays a map of the location if geolocation is enabled. The ideal approach would be to launch the mobile device's Maps application, giving you access to all its interactive features. However, PhoneGap can't do that—at least not at the time of this writing.

As a compromise, I used `window.location` to load Google Maps directly into the app. On Android, this prompts the user to choose whether to complete the action through the device's browser or by launching the Maps application (**Figure 7.31**).

As a result, the map is loaded in a separate application, allowing the user to interact with it. Clicking the Android Back button returns to the Travel Notes app.

On iOS, calling `window.location` loads the map directly into the app. That's great until you realize that iOS devices don't have a Back button, so there's no way to exit the map. To get round this problem, I loaded a static map as an image in the map page block. It's not interactive, but at least you can continue using the Travel Notes app after viewing the map by clicking the Back button generated by jQuery Mobile.

The script uses the PhoneGap device object to detect which operating system the app is running on.

The following steps describe how the script works.

1. The displayMap() function needs access to some of the information retrieved from the database by getItem(). To pass data to an event handler in jQuery, you need to create an object that's attached to the Event instance. Amend the getItem() function by adding the highlighted code:

```
function getItem(id) {
    $.mobile.notesdb.transaction(function(t) {
        t.executeSql('SELECT * FROM notes
        ➥ WHERE id = ?',
        [id],
        function(t, result) {
            var row = result.rows.item(0),
                entered = convertToMDY(
                ➥ row.entered),
                updated = row.updated,
                opts = {};
            $('#display h1').text(row.title);
            $('#display article').text(
            ➥ row.details);
            if (row.latitude == null) {
                $('#showmap').parent('p').
                ➥ hide();
            } else {
                $('#showmap').parent('p').
                ➥ show();
                opts.title = row.title;
                opts.lat = row.latitude;
                opts.lng = row.longitude;
                $('#showmap').unbind('click');
                $('#showmap').click(opts,
                ➥displayMap);
            }
```

```
                            $('#display footer').html('<p>
                         ⇥ Created: ' + entered + '</p>');
                            if (updated != null) {
                                updated = convertToMDY(
                             ⇥ updated);
                                $('#display footer').append(
                             ⇥ '<p>Updated: ' + updated +
                             ⇥ '</p>');
                            }
                            $('#delete, #update').attr(
                         ⇥ 'data-trnote', id);
                            $('#title2').val(row.title);
                            $('#details2').val(row.details);
                    })
                });
        }
```

The first line of new code assigns an empty pair of curly braces to opts, initializing it as an empty object.

The next three lines of new code assign the title, latitude, and longitude values from the database as properties of the opts object.

Finally, the opts data object is passed to the click() method like this:

```
$('#showmap').click(opts, displayMap);
```

This ensures that the opts properties are passed to the displayMap() function when the Show Map button is clicked.

2. You now need to add the code to the displayMap() function. The complete function looks like this:

```
function displayMap(e) {
    var title = e.data.title,
        latlng = e.data.lat + ',' + e.data.lng;
    if (typeof device !='undefined' &&
 ⇥ device.platform.toLowerCase() ==
 ⇥ 'android') {
        window.location = 'http://maps.google.
         ⇥ com/maps?z=16&q=' +
         ⇥ encodeURIComponent(title) + '@'
         ⇥ + latlng;
```

```
    } else {
        $('#map h1').text(title);
        $('#map div[data-role=content]').html(
        ➝ '<img src="http://maps.google.com/
        ➝ maps/api/staticmap?center=' + latlng
        ➝ + ' &zoom=16&size=320x420&markers='
        ➝  + latlng + '&sensor=false">');
        $.mobile.changePage('#map', 'fade',
        ➝ false, true);
    }
}
```

When you pass a data object to an event handler, its properties are assigned to the event's data property. The event is passed to displayMap() as e, so displayMap() receives the value of opts.title as e.data.title, opts.lat as e.data.lat, and opts.lng as e.data.lng.

The displayMap() function begins by storing the item's title as title and by combining its latitude and longitude as a comma-separated value in latlng.

The rest of the function consists of a conditional statement that determines how to display the map depending on the platform. The condition uses the platform property of PhoneGap's device object to detect if the app is running on Android. Because the object isn't supported by all devices, you need to test for its existence like this:

```
if (typeof device !='undefined' . . .)
```

The rest of the condition uses toLowerCase() to convert the value of device.platform to lowercase and compare it with "android." If the app is running on Android, the script calls window.location and points it to Google Maps. The else clause loads a Google static map as an image into the map page block and then calls $.mobile.changePage() to load the map page block. In both cases, the latitude and longitude are incorporated in the URL to display the map of the selected location.

NOTES

For details of the Google Maps and Google Static Maps APIs, see http://code.google.com/apis/maps/index.html.

**Figure 7.32** The map needs to be moved up and to the left.

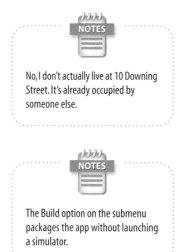

NOTES

No, I don't actually live at 10 Downing Street. It's already occupied by someone else.

NOTES

The Build option on the submenu packages the app without launching a simulator.

3.  To test the script, you need to use a computer that can access geolocation information. Save the files and reload index.html in your browser. Then access an item and click the Show Map button. This loads the map page block because desktop browsers don't support the PhoneGap `device` object. As **Figure 7.32** shows, there's an unsightly gap on the top and left of the map.

4.  Add the following rule to the `<style>` block in the `<head>` of index.html:

```
#map div[data-role=content] {
    padding:0;
}
```

This eliminates the 15-pixel padding surrounding the content `<div>` in the map page block and moves the map into the correct position.

That completes the code for the Travel Notes app. You can compare your code with index.html and trnotes.js in ch07/complete.

### Building and Testing the Native App

After you have created the HTML, CSS, and JavaScript for an app, it needs to be packaged in a format that the target platforms understand. As long as you set up the Native Application Settings as described in "Setting up a Dreamweaver Site for a Native App" earlier in this chapter, you're just a couple of clicks away.

The following steps describe how to test the Travel Notes app.

1.  Choose Site > Mobile Applications > Build and Emulate.

    On Windows and Mac OS X 10.5, you have only one option: Android.

    If you installed Xcode and the iOS SDK on Mac OS X 10.6, you have the choice of iPhone, iPad, and Android.

2.  Select the target device from the submenu. Dreamweaver displays a progress bar that keeps you informed of what's happening.

    If you selected Android, be prepared to wait a couple of minutes. The Android emulator takes a long time to start up. The iOS simulator is much quicker off the mark.

3. When PhoneGap has finished building the native app, Dreamweaver installs it in the appropriate simulator and displays a message telling you where the files have been created. Dismiss the message, and switch to the simulator.

4. If the Android emulator displays the screen shown in **Figure 7.33**, use your mouse to drag the green padlock icon to the right.

**Figure 7.33** The Android emulator often needs to be unlocked in the same way as a real device.

The Android and iOS SDKs both include software for you to simulate running your apps on a mobile device. Android calls its program an emulator, whereas iOS uses the term simulator. They both do the same thing.

5. After unlocking the screen in the Android emulator, the Travel Notes splash screen should display as soon as the app loads (**Figure 7.34**).

**Figure 7.34** The splash screen provides visual interest while the app is being initialized.

**6.** The simulators don't support touch gestures, but you get an immediate feel for how the app behaves. For example, if your network connection permits access to geolocation information, you'll see a native dialog box rather than one generated by a browser (**Figure 7.35**).

**7.** Click the New Entry button and put the focus in the Title field. The simulator displays the native keypad (**Figure 7.36**).

The simulator stores data, so you can also test inserting, updating, and deleting entries.

**Figure 7.35** Using a simulator lets you see the app in a more realistic environment.

**Figure 7.36** The simulator shows the type of keypad displayed when a form field has focus.

### Removing apps from a simulator

If you need to rebuild an app, running Build and Emulate automatically replaces an existing version. However, if you make significant changes to an app and it ceases to work as expected, you should uninstall it from the simulator.

You remove an app from a simulator in the same way as on a real device. To remove an app from the Android emulator, follow these steps.

1. Click the Home icon on the right of the emulator panel.

2. Click the Launcher icon (**Figure 7.37**) at the bottom of the screen.

3. Click the Settings icon. Then click Applications followed by Manage Applications to display a list of apps installed in the emulator.

4. Click the name of the app that you want to uninstall.

5. Click Uninstall and confirm that you want to uninstall the app.

To remove an app from the iOS simulator:

1. Click the Home button at the bottom of the simulator.

2. Drag the simulator screen horizontally until you can see the app's launch icon.

3. Position your mouse pointer over the icon and hold down the mouse button until the icon begins shaking.

4. Click the icon's Close button (**Figure 7.38**) and confirm that you want to uninstall the app.

5. Click the Home button to stop the other icons from shaking.

**Figure 7.37** Use the Launcher icon to access the Android emulator's settings and other apps.

**Figure 7.38**
Click the Close button to remove the app from the iOS simulator.

## Going Further

The case study in this chapter provides only a brief insight into developing native apps with PhoneGap, showing how to store and update data, accessing the GPS sensor, displaying native alerts, and detecting the device's platform. In addition to the core PhoneGap API, there are plug-ins that extend access to other native features. The integration of PhoneGap in Dreamweaver CS5.5 simplifies the mechanics of installing the Android SDK and of building apps ready for launch in a simulator. However, developing an app requires a solid understanding of JavaScript and the PhoneGap API.

If you plan to deploy your app in the Android or Apple markets, you need to remove debugging code and sign the app with a digital certificate. The procedure is different for each operating system. Check the Android Developers website at http://developer.android.com or the iOS Dev Center at http://developer.apple.com for the most up-to-date information.

Adobe describes the mobile development features in Dreamweaver CS5.5 as the first part of a multirelease effort, so there should be plenty to look forward to as the mobile scene develops.

# Index